KS3
Success

English

Complete Coursebook

Age 11-14

Steve Eddy

Contents

Contents

Contents

After completing this chapter you should know:
- how and when to skim, scan and read closely
- how to infer meaning from a text
- how to read critically
- how to compare two texts
- how to approach pre-20th-century texts.

1.1 Skimming, scanning and close reading

Skimming

Skimming is reading a text quickly for an overview. This can be useful when you need a rough idea of what a text is about – for example, to decide whether it is worth reading in detail.

Even if you know you are going to read a text in detail, it is still helpful to skim it first. This is especially true of **informative writing**, though it could also be useful to skim a novel extract in an exam before reading it in detail.

How to skim

When we read, our eyes do not glide steadily along a line: we take in a few words at a time, as if taking snapshots. Watch someone's eyes as they read and you will see this. To skim, practise just taking one or two 'snapshots' of each line.

Pay attention to headings, **paragraph** openings and names. In non-fiction, a heading should tell you what the section is about. Paragraphs often start with a **topic sentence** introducing the paragraph.

Practice

Skim the following text. Then shut the book and make notes on what key points you remember.

India, it is often said, is not a country, but a continent. Stretching from the frozen summits of the Himalayas to the tropical greenery of Kerala, its expansive borders encompass an incomparable range of landscapes, cultures and people. Walk the streets of any Indian city and you'll rub shoulders with representatives of several of the world's great faiths, a multitude of castes and outcastes, fair-skinned, turbaned Punjabis and dark-skinned Tamils. You'll also encounter temple rituals that have been performed since the time of the Egyptian Pharaohs, onion-domed mosques erected centuries before the Taj Mahal was ever dreamt of, and quirky echoes of the British Raj on virtually every corner.

That so much of India's past remains <u>discernible</u> today is all the more astonishing given the pace of change since Independence in 1947. Spurred by the free-market reforms of the early 1990s, the economic revolution started by Rajiv Gandhi has transformed the country with new consumer goods, technologies and ways of life. Today the land where the Buddha lived and taught, and whose religious festivals are as old as the rivers that sustain them, is the second-largest producer of computer software in the world, with its own satellites and nuclear weapons.

> **discernible** visible

Scanning

Scanning means searching for specific information. Words with capital letters stand out, as do numbers in numeral form, such as dates. If scanning a longer information text, look for headings.

To scan a text, look down it as if skimming, but keep in mind the type of information that you are looking for.

Practice

Scan the text about India above for the following information:

1. When did India become independent?
2. Who started India's 'economic revolution'?
3. What two ethnic groups are mentioned?
4. What signs are there of India's rapid modernisation?

Close reading

Close reading is reading in detail, as you would read a passage in an exam. It involves reading every word, but also paying attention to grammar and punctuation. Notice the **signposting** or **linking words** and phrases, such as:

however	moreover
despite this	as a result
but	although
on the other hand	

> Your close reading will improve if you understand the grammar of compound and subordinated sentences. See Topics 5.3 and 5.4.

Practice

Read the next paragraph of the *Rough Guide* text on India closely, then answer the questions.

However, the presence in even the most far-flung market towns of internet cafés and Japanese hatchbacks has thrown into sharp relief the problems that have <u>bedevilled</u> India since long before it became the world's largest <u>secular</u> democracy. Poverty remains a harsh fact of life for around a quarter of India's inhabitants; no other nation on earth has slum settlements on the scale of those in Delhi, Mumbai and Kolkata (Calcutta), nor so many malnourished children, uneducated women and homes without access to clean water and waste disposal.

bedevilled plagued, troubled

secular non-religious

1. What is the paragraph's main subject?
2. What type of settlements are mentioned?
3. What problems relating to children, women and homes are mentioned?

'Skim' your room by looking around and noting what main items it contains. Note them down. Then scan it for three things beginning with 'd'.

1. What is skimming?
2. What two types of information are easiest to spot when scanning?
3. What types of word are useful to note when close reading?

Progress Check

🎧 **2**

1.2 Inferring meaning

Inferring meaning is 'reading between the lines': working out what a text implies, or suggests, beyond its obvious meaning. This skill can be applied to fiction or non-fiction.

Examples

- Her champagne and caviar days had long since passed. (She was no longer rich.)
- Over 100,000 teenagers are ensnared by tobacco every year. (Smoking is a 'snare', a life-threatening trap into which teenagers fall.)
- If a grizzly bear chases you, your best defence is prayer. (You have little chance of escape.)
- Nobody ever went broke underestimating the intelligence of the American public. (H. L. Mencken) (Most Americans are stupid.)

In the patriotic **poem** below, Jessie Pope encourages young men to fight in World War I. What does she imply the war will be like? From what you know about the war, was she right?

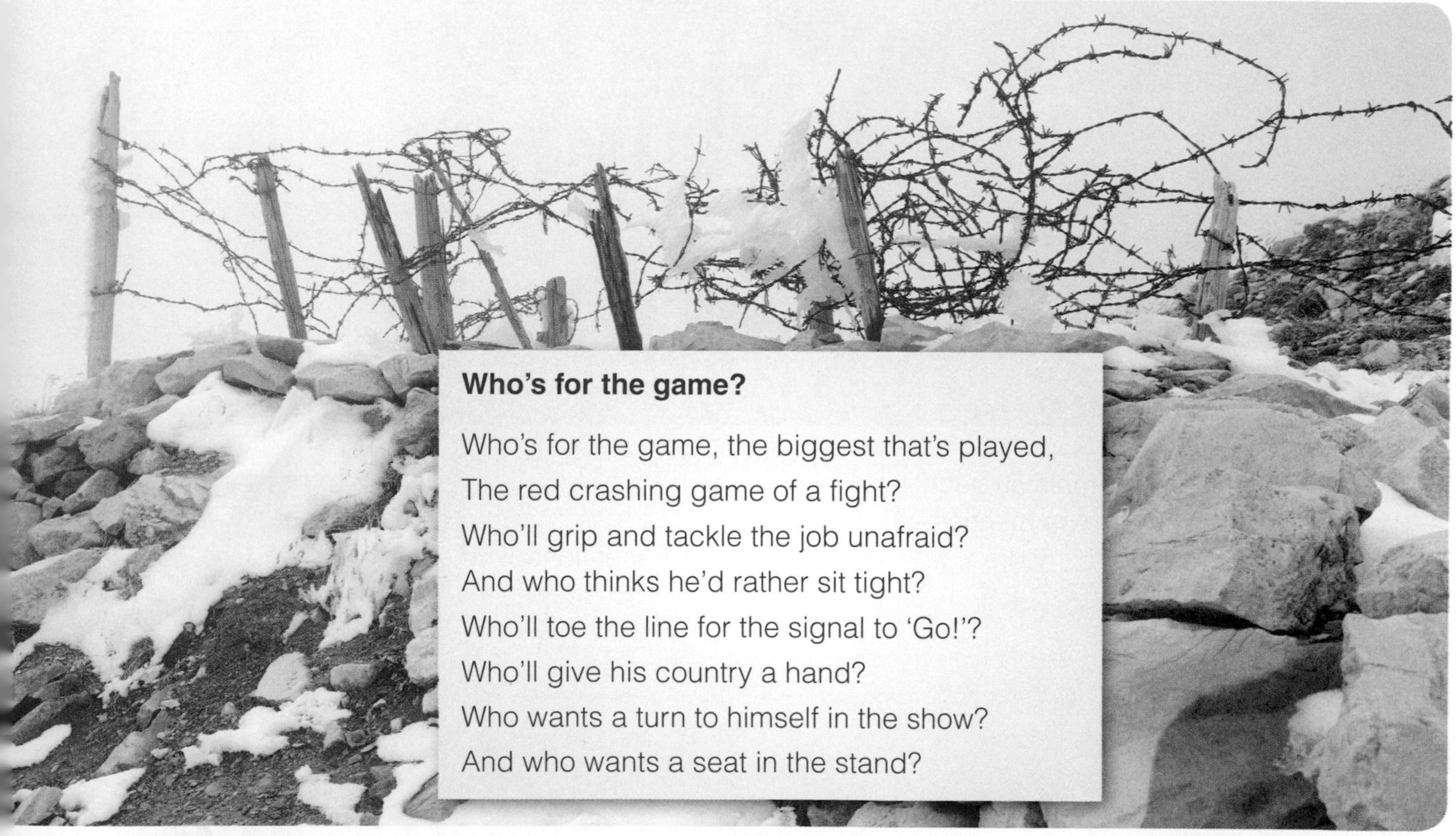

Who's for the game?

Who's for the game, the biggest that's played,
The red crashing game of a fight?
Who'll grip and tackle the job unafraid?
And who thinks he'd rather sit tight?
Who'll toe the line for the signal to 'Go!'?
Who'll give his country a hand?
Who wants a turn to himself in the show?
And who wants a seat in the stand?

Irony

There is a special kind of implied meaning in **irony**. Ironic texts suggest a meaning by saying the opposite of what they really mean. Read an example of this opposite. Jonathan Swift was an Irishman who was bitterly critical of English exploitation and neglect of the starving Irish. Knowing this, what meaning can you infer in this text? What did Swift really mean?

I have been assured by a very knowing American of my acquaintance in London, that a young healthy child well nursed, is, at a year old, a most delicious nourishing and wholesome food, whether stewed, roasted, baked, or boiled; and I make no doubt that it will equally serve in a fricassée, or a ragout....A child will make two dishes at an entertainment for friends, and when the family dines alone, the fore or hind quarter will make a reasonable dish, and seasoned with a little pepper or salt, will be very good boiled on the fourth day, especially in winter.

Jonathan Swift, *A Modest Proposal*

 Watch TV advertisements, looking out for implied meaning. For example, a new car might be said to be 'not for the faint-hearted', meaning that it is really fast!

1. What does *infer* mean?
2. What does *imply* mean?
3. Can meaning be implied by a single word choice?

Progress Check

1.3 Reading critically

 3

To read a text critically is to read it in order to appreciate it and assess its value. The first step towards **critical reading** is to understand it, and to consider the author's intention. For example, if the author wanted to write a comedy, is it funny?

Criteria

The **criteria** (measures of success) that you apply should depend on the type of text. For example, information writing should be clear and easy to follow. For a novel or story, you might ask yourself:

- Does it make me want to read on?
- Does the author use vivid language to bring the text to life?
- Are characters and their thoughts and actions believable?
- Does the author use a range of **sentence** types and lengths for effect – such as short sentences for dramatic tension?
- Does the author sometimes *imply* meaning rather than making everything obvious?

With non-fiction, you should also consider whether the text is suitable for its purpose, audience and context. See Topics 2.1 and 2.2.

Run on the spot till your heart beats faster and you are a little out of breath. Notice how this feels and use it to describe someone fleeing from danger. Use vivid language.

Have a go

In this extract from an adventure novel for teenagers, Matt is being chased by some monstrous dogs. The writer wants to create tension and excitement. Does he succeed? If so, then how?

The first of the creatures had already halved the distance between itself and Matt,[1] yet it didn't seem to be moving fast. It hovered in the air between each bound, barely touching the grass before jumping up again. There was something hideous about the way it ran. A panther or leopard closing in for the kill[2] has a certain majesty. But the dog was deformed, lopsided, ghastly. The flesh on one of its flanks had rotted and a glistening ribcage jutted out.[3] As if to avoid the stench of the wound, the animal had turned away, its head hanging close to its front paws. Strings of saliva trailed from its mouth. And every time its feet hit the ground, its whole body quivered, threatening to collapse in on itself.

Matt reached the fence and clawed at it with his hands, crashing his fingers against the wire.[4] He thought he had run in a straight line, following the way he had come, but he seemed to have got it wrong. He couldn't find the gap. He looked behind him. Two more bounds and the dogs would reach him. There was no doubt that they would tear him apart.[5]

Anthony Horowitz, *Raven's Gate*

Here are some different ways in which Horowitz could have expressed the highlighted phrases. Bearing in mind his aim, which do you think are better, and why?

1. was already catching up.

2. hunting its prey.

3. its skeletal frame was protruding.

4. hitting the fence with his fingers.

5. The dogs were now getting very close and they would definitely catch him.

Progress Check

1. Why is the author's intention important if you are evaluating a text?
2. What are 'criteria'?
3. Should an author always make the meaning obvious?

1.4 Reading to compare texts 🎧 4

Text **comparison** is a useful skill that you may also need in English exams. Some characteristics to look for are:

- the **content** – what it is about
- the **voice** – how the author addresses the reader
- **tone** – for example, angry, serious, light-hearted
- the kinds of sentences used
- word choices
- imagery.

Read the two extracts and see what they have in common, and how they differ.

Extract 1: Edith Bone, *Seven Years Solitary*

Edith Bone, a British subject, was falsely imprisoned by the Hungarian Communist authorities in 1949 on suspicion of spying. Throughout her imprisonment she defied her captors whenever possible.

I decided to refrain from absolutely everything except lying on my bed and sleeping. This I carried out quite thoroughly. I did not eat, I did not answer when I was spoken to, I did not move when the sergeant brought in a broom in the morning and I did not do any of the other chores either. I found that for some mysterious reason my behaviour alarmed my guards, and on the third or fourth day of this performance I had a visit. A man came in with one of the secret police officers, whom I had already seen at headquarters. His rank was lieutenant-colonel, and he was the man who had told me that I would be hanged. The other man was a civilian. He was big and fat; his fat being of an unhealthy kind that hung loosely on him; he had a very red face, pale flaxen frizzy hair, a flat bridgeless nose and very thick lips. Altogether a most repulsive-looking creature. He was wearing a red tie. That denoted that he was a member of the Party. Party members in civvies used to wear red ties. He came to my bedside and yelled at me. 'Why don't you eat?'

Extract 2: Brian Keenan, *An Evil Cradling*

Brian Keenan was kidnapped in Beirut in 1985 and held hostage for four and a half years. He was determined not to cooperate with his captors.

Hunger-strike is a powerful weapon in the Irish psyche. It overcomes fear in its deepest sense. It removes and makes negligible the threat of punishment. It powerfully commits back into the hunger striker's own hands the full sanction of his own life and of his own will….

One way or the other I was committed to confrontation. But the days of hunger, or rather of indifference to hunger, had steeled my purpose. I remember as I refused to eat each meal feeling myself grow stronger.

A fierce kind of pride met a fierce determination of will as the food heaped in the corner. My resolve was banked equally high and my purpose became more strongly fixed. Within the hour, the door of my cell was opened and in came the kidnapper who had been in the car when I was taken. He read the note quietly to himself, pointed to some words he was unsure of and I explained them at length. He looked around the cell. I lifted the plastic and pointed to the food. He appeared very anxious and upset by this. There was no anger. His voice was pleading when he asked 'Why you don't eat?'

Comparing the extracts

You might find it helpful to use a table like the one below to compare texts.

	Edith Bone	**Brian Keenan**
Content	Describes her protest strike, including not eating, and how the Party member yelled at her.	Describes his motives, his feelings as his strike progressed, and the manner of the man asking why he does not eat.
Language	**Repetition** of 'I did not' emphasises determined resistance. Describes her own behaviour in a slightly **formal**, detached way: 'refrain'; 'behaviour'; 'performance'.	Repeated sentences beginning with 'It…' forcefully states what hunger-striking does; also repetition of 'fierce'. Uses **abstract nouns** to describe his attitude: 'confrontation'; 'indifference'; 'purpose'; 'determination'; 'resolve'. He uses some imagery: 'steeled', 'banked'.
Tone	Slightly amused, detached.	Serious, quietly passionate.
How the captor is described	Party member described in some physical detail, then as 'a most repulsive-looking creature' (like an animal; she feels superior to him).	'anxious and upset…no anger… pleading'. Describes the man quite sympathetically: does not make him seem ugly or unreasonable.

Identifying aspects to compare will make the task manageable. Then, when you write your comparison, you should write about each aspect in turn, for each text. In the example below, useful comparison phrases are emboldened.

Write out the example passage comparing the two texts. Add your own evidence and detail where missing text is indicated (…).

Edith Bone describes her protest strike, what she refuses to do, and how the authorities react. Brian Keenan **focuses more** on the power of hunger-striking, and on his own attitude of defiance, using a number of abstract nouns **to convey this**…**Both writers use** repetition to convey a sense of their determination. **For example**…**However**…Edith Bone's tone is slightly detached…**whereas** Keenan seems quietly passionate…**They both describe** the man who wants them to eat, **but**…

Progress Check

1. What is the author's 'voice'?
2. What are 'angry', 'serious', and 'light-hearted' examples of?
3. How should your comparison be structured?

1.5 Understanding pre-20th-century texts

🎧 5

You may find the language of older texts challenging. But remember that people in past times cared about the same things as us, even if society was different in some ways.

Words, phrases and sentences

You may have to look up some words in a dictionary, and some expressions may no longer be in common use. However, you will often be able to work out roughly what they mean from their **context**. In addition, some words have just changed their meaning slightly. One of the techniques you may find in older texts is **personification**, in which something abstract, such as time, life, love or war is described as if it were a person, a god or an animal; another is **simile**, which compares two things using *like*, *as* or *than*.

Read the extract on the next page, from *A Christmas Carol*, by Charles Dickens, describing Scrooge. The notes show you what kind of thing to look out for.

> Older texts contain more subordinated sentences. If you follow the punctuation, you should be able to understand these sentences. See Topics 5.4 and 6.4.

A
CHRISTMAS CAROL
IN PROSE
BEING
A Ghost Story of Christmas
BY
CHARLES DICKENS
ILLUSTRATED BY
JOHN LEECH

LONDON
HAZELL, WATSON & VINEY, LTD.

1. Old word meaning 'as well'

2. Chests (modern meaning has narrowed)

3. We would say 'struck three' (though few clocks strike now)

4. Simile ending a long subordinated sentence; *ruddy* is red, *palpable* is an old word for 'touchable': the air is thick with polluted fog

5. Means 'of the narrowest kind'; we would just say 'very narrow'

6. *Mere* means 'only' or 'just'; they looked like ghosts – could barely be seen

7. Old-fashioned expression, using personification for Nature. *Hard* by means 'near'. The fanciful idea is that Mother Nature lives nearby and is creating steam by brewing beer!

8. Place where financial accounts are done

9. So he could

10. Old word: top it up (with more coal)

11. Scrooge threatens to fire the clerk for wanting more coal; the indirect way this is expressed is a euphemism

Look online and read the opening paragraphs of *A Christmas Carol* leading up to the extract passage. Try to work out the meaning of the more difficult words and sentences.

It was cold, bleak, biting weather: foggy <u>withal</u>:[1] and he could hear the people in the court outside, go wheezing up and down, beating their hands upon their <u>breasts</u>,[2] and stamping their feet upon the pavement stones to warm them. The city clocks had only just <u>gone three</u>,[3] but it was quite dark already – it had not been light all day – and candles were flaring in the windows of the neighbouring offices, <u>like ruddy smears upon the palpable brown air</u>.[4] The fog came pouring in at every chink and keyhole, and was so dense without, that although the court <u>was of the narrowest</u>,[5] the houses opposite <u>were mere phantoms</u>.[6] To see the dingy cloud come drooping down, obscuring everything, <u>one might have thought that Nature lived hard by, and was brewing on a large scale</u>.[7]

The door of Scrooge's <u>counting-house</u>[8] was open <u>that he might</u>[9] keep his eye upon his clerk, who in a dismal little cell beyond, a sort of tank, was copying letters. Scrooge had a very small fire, but the clerk's fire was so very much smaller that it looked like one coal. But he couldn't <u>replenish</u>[10] it, for Scrooge kept the coal-box in his own room; and so surely as the clerk came in with the shovel, the master <u>predicted that it would be necessary for them to part</u>.[11]

Progress Check

1. In what general way are sentences in older texts different from those in modern ones?
2. Why are some words in older texts misleading?
3. How is it often possible to work out the meanings of words?

1.6 Appreciating Shakespeare

There are two main differences between Shakespeare's times, 400 years ago, and now:
- how people lived and thought
- the use of English.

Shakespeare's times

Shakespeare's **plots** and **imagery** are influenced by what life was like in his times. There are several areas in which things were different.

Class divisions

Britain was very class-conscious and **class divisions** were quite rigid. At the top of the social ladder was the king or queen, believed to rule by God's will. Then came the **nobles**, a wealthy, educated minority. Ordinary people – **commoners** – were considered inferior. Shakespeare was a commoner, but almost all his main characters are nobles.

Women

Women had to obey their fathers, then their husbands. They had little power, no right to own property (unless widowed), and no career opportunities. The one exception was Queen Elizabeth!

Beliefs

Everyone went to church, and almost everyone believed in God, and in heaven and hell. There was also widespread belief in magic, witchcraft and ghosts. People married in church; no one divorced.

Health

Disease was widespread, especially the Black Death (plague), which could wipe out whole villages. Women often died in childbirth; children often died young.

Travel

People travelled on foot, on horseback, in horse-drawn carts or in boats and sailing ships. Shipwrecks were common.

Entertainment

People made their own entertainment or went to plays. In London the theatre was popular with all social classes.

Shakespeare's language

Verse

Commoners in Shakespeare's plays normally speak in prose, but most of the speeches delivered by nobles are in **blank verse**. *Blank* means unrhymed, and the verse used is **iambic pentameter**.

Iambic refers to the **rhythm**. Rhythm in speech or writing is created by patterns of stressed (emphasised) and unstressed **syllables**. If we did not stress some syllables, we would sound like robots! Here is a line of blank verse showing which syllables are stressed when speaking it naturally:

> If <u>mu</u>sic <u>be</u> the <u>food</u> of <u>love</u>, play <u>on</u>

Speak this aloud, tapping out the rhythm. This rhythm, with pairs of unstressed and stressed syllables, is called *iambic*. How many stressed syllables are there in the line? Answer: there are five. It is called *pentameter* because *pent* (as in *pentangle*) means five.

Shakespeare does, however, vary his blank verse for effect. For example, when his character Macbeth is depressed and imagines the future plodding on tediously till the end of time, he says:

> *Tomorrow, and tomorrow, and tomorrow*
> *Creeps in this petty pace from day to day.*

It is impossible to speak this naturally with the normal iambic rhythm. Try it! It drags, reflecting the meaning. The extra syllable in the first line adds to this. Count the syllables for yourself.

Shakespeare does also sometimes use **rhyming couplets** – pairs of rhyming lines, especially at the end of a scene.

Reading and understanding Shakespeare's language

Here are some tips:

- Get up, **move around**, and speak it **aloud**, using **body language**.
- **Take your time**, and think about the meaning.
- Read according to **punctuation**, not line by line – if there is no punctuation at the end of a line, do not pause there.
- Look up difficult words, but don't feel you have to understand every word – focus on how characters **feel** and **why** they say what they do.
- Be aware that some words have **shifted in meaning** (e.g. *rude* meant 'rough' or 'basic').
- Notice the meaning and emotional effect of **imagery**.
- Notice **sound effects** – such as alliteration (e.g. Your el**d**est **d**aughters have for**d**one themselves,/ And **d**esperately are **d**ead).

Read these two speeches from Capulet, Juliet's father, in *Romeo and Juliet*. In the first, he sympathetically compares her to a ship that risks being wrecked. But what is his mood in the second, when Juliet has refused to marry the husband of his choice? And how are the things listed above under 'Shakespeare's times' reflected?

> How now! A <u>conduit</u>, girl? What, still in tears?
> Evermore showering? In one little body
> <u>Thou counterfeit'st a bark</u>, a sea, a wind;
> For still thy eyes, which I may call the sea,
> Do ebb and flow with tears; the bark thy body is,
> Sailing in this salt flood; the winds, thy sighs;
> Who, raging with thy tears, and they with them,
> Without a sudden calm, will overset
> Thy tempest-tossed body. How now, wife!
> Have you deliver'd to her <u>our decree</u>?

conduit water pipe

Thou counterfeit'st a bark You pretend to be (You are like) a ship

our decree my ruling (that she should marry Paris)

> Hang thee, young baggage! Disobedient wretch!
> I tell thee what: get thee to church o' Thursday,
> Or never after look me in the face:
> Speak not, reply not, do not answer me;
> <u>My fingers itch</u>. Wife, we scarce thought us blest
> That God had lent us but this only child;
> But now I see this one is one too much,
> And that we have a curse in having her:
> Out on her, <u>hilding</u>!

My fingers itch I'd like to hit her

hilding worthless wretch

Speak each of Capulet's speeches in turn, using an appropriate tone and body language.

1. Why is blank verse called 'blank'?
2. How many pairs of syllables are there in a normal line of iambic pentameter?
3. What signs of Shakespeare's times are there in the two speeches above?

Progress Check

Worked questions

1. **Read the following text and answer the questions. Support your answers with evidence from the text.**

> Mary Ann Dwight, 'Adelsberg Grotto', *Chambers' Edinburgh Journal* (155), 19 December 1846
>
> Of all the forms into which this cavern dew had hardened, by far the most beautiful was that named 'the banner', and which was indeed exactly like a flag of spotless white, hanging in light folds, each one of which was exquisitely formed, and completed by a border of yellowish hue. It was strange thus to find the minute perfection which characterizes all the works of nature displaying itself in these hidden realms of darkness. We are accustomed to perceive it in the admirable workmanship of every tiny leaf or fragile blossom on the earth; but here, where no eye was ever to behold them, the very colouring of each one of these little stalactites was correct and beautiful, as though touched by an artist's most delicate pencil. When the guide struck on any of the pillars with a small stick, it emitted a strange metallic sound, that was remarkably melodious, and added to the singular effect produced by the various murmurs already floating through those dismal chambers. These were caused principally by the currents of air rushing through the numberless passages, and also by the peculiar manner in which the interminable echoes told upon each other from arch to arch and rock to rock. The perpetual dropping of water throughout the whole vault produced by itself a hollow, ceaseless reverberation, that I know not why, caused a shuddering sensation; indeed it was no easy matter to avoid fancying that this terrific cavern was inhabited by unearthly beings

a) What would you say is Mary Ann Dwight's purpose in this text? *(2 marks)*
She wants to describe her experience of visiting the cave vividly so that people who have never been in a cave can imagine it. It is full of descriptive phrases, <u>such as</u> 'hanging in light folds...yellowish hue'.

b) What does Dwight carefully explain? *(2 marks)*
She uses simile to explain the murmuring sounds as coming from a <u>combination</u> of rushing air currents and echoes rebounding between the arches and rocks of the cave.

c) What imagery does she use to bring the description to life? *(3 marks)*
She describes 'the banner' as being 'exactly like a flag of spotless white', <u>emphasising its purity</u>.[1] The stalactites are equally delicate, 'as though touched by an artist's most delicate pencil', highlighting their fine detail and subtle colouring, and <u>her sense of their having been deliberately created</u>.[2]

Useful phrase for introducing examples

Gives both parts of the answer

1. Explains quote

2. Infers meaning

d) How does Dwight appeal to our senses? *(4 marks)*

Much of the **description** *is very visual, showing shape and colour, as in the 'light folds, each one of which was exquisitely formed, and completed by a border of yellowish hue'. She also mentions the 'strange metallic sound, that was remarkably melodious' from hitting one of the formations. <u>This gives a sense of the sound and comments on her response to it</u>.[1] The phrase 'various murmurs... floating' through the cave also gives a sense of the sound, <u>and suggests human voices with the word 'murmurs'</u>.[2]*

1. Explains double effect

2. Infers meaning from word choice

e) How does Dwight use personification, what is the effect, and how does this reflect the age of the text? *(4 marks)*

She <u>refers to</u>[1] 'all the works of nature' and 'admirable workmanship', both of which suggest that nature is a workman or work-woman who has designed natural forms. This makes us more likely to appreciate the delicate natural formations. The phrase 'hidden realms of darkness' <u>implies</u>[2] that there is a ruler of this underworld, perhaps like Hades in Greek mythology, because a 'realm' is a kingdom. <u>This suggests that anyone entering the cave is at the mercy of this power</u>.[3] This gives the cave an exciting air of mystery and danger. <u>Personification was more commonly used in Dwight's day</u>,[4] and the idea of nature, or God, having created the cave formations also reflects her time.

1. Good phrase for introducing embedded quotation

2. Useful word for introducing inference

3. Explains impact fully

4. Background knowledge

f) How does the author's language express her feelings? *(5 marks)*

<u>Her overwhelming impression is of beauty</u>.[1] This is expressed when she describes a formation as 'by far the most beautiful', implying that there were many beautiful formations. Elsewhere she describes them as 'exquisitely formed', 'correct and beautiful', and as showing 'minute perfection'. <u>These phrases suggest that</u>[2] their beauty was delicate and somehow exactly right, <u>in turn implying</u>[3] that they were deliberately formed by nature. <u>However, a second feeling she has</u>[4] is of a 'a shuddering sensation', which seems to refer to her own physical reaction to the sounds, as if they make her a little frightened. This sense of fear is added to by her 'fancying that this terrific cavern was inhabited by unearthly beings'. <u>Her choice of the word 'terrific'</u>[5] probably suggests a hint of terror, not just the modern sense of 'wonderful'. Her use of 'dismal' and 'vault', which could refer to a burial place, adds to this sense.

1. Sums up first part of answer before giving evidence and explaining

2. Explains what they imply

3. Introduces another level of meaning

4. Introduces second part of answer

5. Focuses on one word

Practice questions

1. **Read the passage and answer the questions.**

> **Diary entry by John Evelyn, 3 September 1666, on the Great Fire of London**
>
> The fire having continued all this night (if I may call that night which was light as day for 10 miles around, after a dreadful manner) when conspiring with a fierce eastern wind in a very dry season, I went on foot to the same place, and saw the whole south part of the city burning from Cheapside to the Thames, and all along Cornhill, Tower Street, Fenchurch Street, Gracious Street, and so along to Barnyards Castle, and was now taking hold of St Paul's Church, to which the scaffolds contributed exceedingly. The conflagration was so universal, and the people so astonished, that, from the beginning, I know not by what despondency, or fate, they hardly stirred to quench it; so that there was nothing heard, or seen, but crying out and lamentation, running about like distracted creatures, without at all attempting to save even their goods; such a strange consternation there was upon them, so it burned both in breadth and length, the churches, public halls, Exchange, hospitals, monuments, and ornaments; leaping, after a prodigious way, from house to house, and street to street, at great distances one from the other. For the heat, with a long set of warm and fine weather, had even ignited the air, and prepared the materials to conceive the fire, which devoured after an incredible manner, houses, furniture, and everything.

a) Why does Evelyn hesitate to use the word 'night'? *(1 mark)*

b) What two conditions help the fire to start and spread? *(2 marks)*

c) Put into your own words 'The conflagration was so universal'. *(1 mark)*

d) Referring to the text, explain people's reaction to the fire, and what surprises Evelyn about it. *(2 marks)*

e) How does Evelyn give us a sense of the extent of the blaze in the first sentence? *(1 mark)*

f) Evelyn describes the fire 'leaping, after [in] a prodigious way'. What do you think 'prodigious' means here? (Consider the context if you do not know the word.) *(1 mark)*

g) Which word in the final sentence makes the fire sound like an animal? *(1 mark)*

2. **Read the passage from Shakespeare's *Macbeth* and answer the questions.**

Macbeth, about to fight a battle that he knows he will probably lose, hears that his wife is dead.

> She should have died hereafter;
> There would have been a time for such a
>   word.
> Tomorrow, and tomorrow, and tomorrow,
> Creeps in this petty pace from day to day
> To the last syllable of recorded time,
> And all our yesterdays have lighted fools
>
> The way to dusty death. Out, out, brief
>   candle!
> Life's but a walking shadow, a poor player
> That struts and frets his hour upon the stage
> And then is heard no more: it is a tale
> Told by an idiot, full of sound and fury,
> Signifying nothing

a) What is Macbeth's mood and what is the main message of his speech? *(2 marks)*

b) In what way (or ways) do you think the opening two lines could be interpreted? *(2 marks)*

c) How does the rhythm of the third line match the meaning? *(2 marks)*

d) How does Shakespeare use personification here? *(2 marks)*

e) Explain the impact of the imagery in the final six lines. *(4 marks)*

2.1 How purpose and context influence style 🎧 7

Purpose

When authors start to write a text, they think about what they want it to achieve. For example:
* Is the aim to *instruct* readers in how to make an apple crumble?
* Will the text try to *persuade* them to adopt a family of polar bears?
* Will it *advise* them on what smartphone to buy?
* Will it *warn* them about the risks of using social media like Facebook?
* Will it *review* a film, to help readers decide whether to see it themselves?
* Will it fascinate and entertain them by *describing* a canoe trip in the Amazon jungle?

All of these purposes will affect what content the author includes, and how they use language. For example, a World Wildlife Fund writer trying to persuade you to make a donation to help protect polar bears might tell you that global warming is melting the Arctic ice and making it difficult for the bears to survive: this is the **content**.

They will also choose language that makes polar bears seem beautiful and worth saving, but which also makes you feel sorry for them, like this:

> *The young cub will face a long, gruelling swim in treacherous ocean currents to reach the island. His anxious mother will do her best to keep him afloat, but the melting ice means that there will be few resting places.*

The writer's language choice is what creates the **style** of the text.

Context

Context means where the text will appear and what form it will take. This is also sometimes called **text type**. For example, the text of a leaflet will have to make its main points in a limited space; it will have to be entertaining enough to make people read on; it may be helped by pictures.

You see examples of writing contexts all through the day, from when you read the back of a cornflakes packet at breakfast, to when you read the plot summary of a TV programme and decide whether to watch it. To increase your understanding of how context affects content and style, try to notice the differences between texts. How is the language on your cereal packet different from the language on the swimming pool notice telling you not to dive-bomb other swimmers, or in your school history book?

See if you can match up these different contexts, or types of text, with the factors that will influence their content and style:

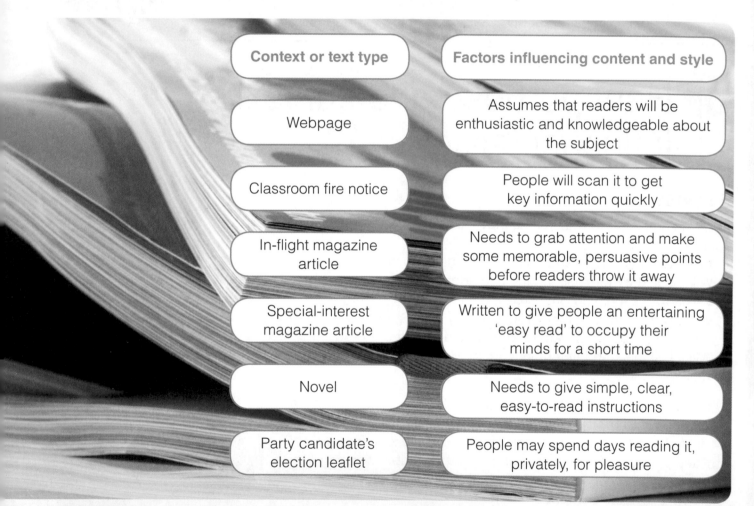

Context or text type	Factors influencing content and style
Webpage	Assumes that readers will be enthusiastic and knowledgeable about the subject
Classroom fire notice	People will scan it to get key information quickly
In-flight magazine article	Needs to grab attention and make some memorable, persuasive points before readers throw it away
Special-interest magazine article	Written to give people an entertaining 'easy read' to occupy their minds for a short time
Novel	Needs to give simple, clear, easy-to-read instructions
Party candidate's election leaflet	People may spend days reading it, privately, for pleasure

Progress Check

1. Name three possible writing purposes.
2. A leaflet, a webpage, a novel and a contract are all examples of what?
3. How do you think this coursebook's purpose has influenced its style?

2.2 Identifying the audience 8

How audiences differ

Authors adjust their content and style to suit their **audience**. Depending on context, they may need to ask themselves several questions:

- How much will readers already know?
- What will they want to know, or find interesting?
- Will most be in a particular age group?
- Will they understand complex ideas and language?
- Will the readership be local, nationwide, or even worldwide?
- Are they more likely to be male or female?

For example:
- **Content** – a football club webpage will assume that readers know the rules of the game.
- **Style** – the language in a school magazine article for parents will be more formal than one aimed at students.

Specialist audiences

Look at the shelves in any newsagent and you will find magazines aimed at people who have particular hobbies or interests – from tropical fish to tractors. Their content and language reflects what readers will already know – including specialist terms, and what they will find interesting.

Magazine articles may also be written for a local readership, focusing on local issues and assuming that readers have local knowledge.

Some specialist audiences are temporary. Who is likely to read a National Health leaflet called 'All About Chickenpox'? What will they need to know? Which of the following are likely to be features of this leaflet's content and style?

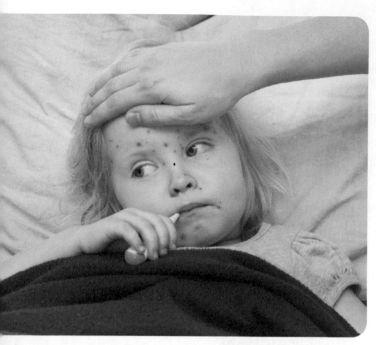

- Pictures showing symptoms.
- Chickenpox jokes.
- A reassuring tone.
- Horror stories about extreme chickenpox cases.
- Clear advice.
- Factual description of symptoms.
- Exciting, dramatic language and vivid description.

Readers' age

> Non-standard English may use non-standard grammar such as 'ain't', as well as slang and dialect words and phrases. See Topic 2.3.

Many texts have a target age group – for example, teenagers. Writing aimed at younger readers is usually less formal than writing aimed at older readers, so it is likely to use more **colloquial** phrases and **non-standard English**.

How would this cover appeal to its target audience?

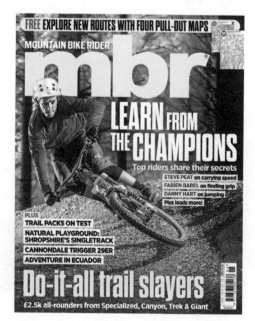

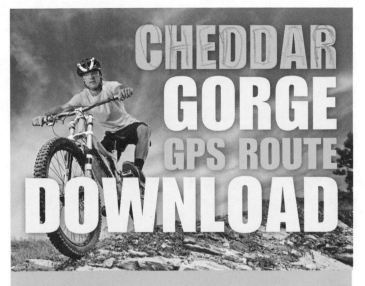

CHEDDAR GORGE GPS ROUTE DOWNLOAD

This one's a route of three halves, and that's despite it being quite modest in length. There's a whole load of variety in these <u>15 miles: speed, singletrack, trees, open moor, horrible technical climbs, amazing views, dirt, stone, roots, whoops, woes, scrumpy and cheese.</u>[1]

For the <u>cruisers and carvers</u>[2] there's the open moorland of Black Down, which as well as having lots of <u>cutesy flora and fauna and wild ponies and stuff</u>[3] also has a great speedy descent that will have your eyes watering and <u>your grinning teeth covered in midges.</u>[4] The moorland gives way to the woodland playground of Rowberrow Warren. Our route passes quite simply through the forest, but there are plenty of fun singletrack detours to be had if you're confident of being able to get back on track.

After a cruise back over Black Down and some pleasant <u>tarmac bashing,</u>[5] it's time to finish with the last dash down the Cheddar Gorge trail. First, though, comes the small matter of getting up to the top of the descent. Did someone say 'hike-a-bike'? Anyway, it's over pretty quick, thankfully.

1. Key information presented informally, ending in Cheddar joke

2. Biker types: jokey labels that bikers will understand

3. Informal language implies that flowers and wildlife are only of passing interest to 'real' bikers

4. Assumes readers will love it!

5. Informal term for road-riding: bikers will understand

Find two magazines, leaflets, adverts or other texts. Flick through them and read one or two paragraphs in each. Write a brief description of the target audience for each, and how they differ. Alternatively, use online magazine websites.

1. What two main features of a text will be influenced by target audience?
2. How will content and style be reflected in a text aimed at a specialist audience?
3. What type of target audience is likely to appreciate relatively informal language?

Progress Check

🎧 **9** **2.3** What is register?

Formality

Context is where readers will encounter a text, such as in a leaflet or a webpage. See Topic 2.1.

Register refers to the type of language used in a particular **context**, especially its level of **formality**. You are likely to speak more formally in a 'serious' situation, such as a job interview, than in a relaxed, casual situation, such as a chat with a friend. In writing you would use more formal language in a job application than in a Facebook status update.

Subject matter

Written language is usually more formal than spoken, but some texts are more formal than others. This is partly because serious **subject matter** requires more formal language. For example, here is a newspaper report on a factory closing down:

> It was announced yesterday that the Hillingham Azco petrochemical plant was to close owing to ongoing financial difficulties. It is expected to result in over a thousand job losses. The plant, which opened in 2001, has had a history of setbacks.

A newspaper report on tigers giving birth might be less formal:

> London Zoo staff are today celebrating the birth of twin tiger cubs. Proud mum Rani gave birth to the cuddly kittens at midnight, but devoted keeper Brian Davies waited up (who wouldn't!) and captured the first official footage of the happy event on his i-Phone.

Typical features of formal and informal texts

Study the table below. Then read the two passages and find all the formal and informal features you can in each. Which is more formal?

Formal	Informal
Standard English grammar and **vocabulary**	**Slang** and colloquial (popular) expressions; non-standard grammar (e.g. 'ain't'); more like speech
Longer sentences, some sub-clauses	Shorter sentences, dashes, asides
Abstract language, e.g. 'financial difficulties', 'closure'	More direct, simple language
Impersonal language	Humour; playful language, e.g. 'cuddly kittens'
Sophisticated vocabulary	**Contractions** (e.g. 'wouldn't')
Longer paragraphs	Shorter paragraphs

Christy Brown describes hearing classical music for the first time

It was slow, majestic, noble, and to my ears it sounded almost intolerably lovely. It seemed to sink down and touch a chord deep inside me that made my whole soul quiver with a kind of ecstasy. I sat, staring into a world that the music had wrought for me, until the last beautiful strains had faded away. Then I sat silently for a long time, only gradually finding my way back to the ordinary world of every day.

Listen to a short piece of music. Then write a paragraph describing it in a formal register, and another describing it informally. Annotate features in each description that make it formal or informal.

Shout *magazine review (Kendrick sings while tapping a rhythm which involves a plastic cup)*

Well, well, well. We remember seeing Anna Kendrick doing this cups thing on a TV show months ago. It was pretty cool. We also liked it in the movie *Pitch Perfect*. And now it's kind of gone viral (57 million views on YouTube and counting) and is being released as a single! We should also mention that despite being an actress by profession, the gorgeous Anna has now signed a record deal! We can't wait to hear more from her!

1. How can subject matter affect register?
2. How does written language tend to differ in register from spoken language?
3. What sort of register uses more non-standard English?

Progress Check

10   2.4   What is tone?

If someone speaks to you in a tone which is, for example, angry, friendly or reassuring, you will probably be able to identify it quite easily. Their choice of words will create the tone, but it will be backed up by their tone of voice and body language. The tone of a text is similar, but it depends entirely on the writer's language choices.

Tone in a text is a product of several factors:
* the mood created by the language
* the writer's apparent attitude towards the subject
* the writer's attitude towards the reader.

A thriller might use a tense, urgent tone to create excitement. A political journalist might write about social injustice in an angry, judgemental tone, using words like 'appalling' and 'shocking'. A teenage magazine article about celebrities might be written in a humorous, gossipy tone. It would also probably express a friendly, familiar attitude towards readers:

Hey all you Keanu Reeves fans – you'll never guess what he's been up to now!

How does language create tone?

The writer chooses to use particular words and sentence structures. These choices create tone. For example, what is the tone of each of these descriptions of a TV talent show?
* A dazzling array of rising stars.
* An inspiring testimony to the power of human endeavour.
* A sad little procession of whining wannabes.
* A mildly amusing way to pass the time before the pizza arrives.
* A shameful media exploitation of young people's dreams.
* If you're like me, a cracking night in on the telly!

One way to begin to comment on these is to look at how positive or negative the writer's attitude is.

> Tone is closely related to register. A friendly tone will tend to be informal; a more detached tone will be more formal. See Topic 2.3.

> Imagine you are the producer of the TV talent show. Write the phrases on separate pieces of paper. Clear a space to put them on, and move them around so that the one you would most like a reviewer to say about your show is at the top, and the one you would least like them to say is at the bottom. Move the others to appropriate places in between.

How individual words create tone

The most obvious way in which a text expresses attitude is through **adjectives**. In each of the phrases above, there is an adjective, or **adjectival phrase** (like 'sad little' and 'mildly amusing') expressing attitude and creating tone. Find the key adjectives. What tone do they create?

Other types of word choice also create tone. For example, the first example uses a **noun phrase**, 'rising stars'. This helps to create a positive, enthusiastic tone. It assumes that the contestants will all become celebrities. In the 'shameful media exploitation' example, the writer could have replaced 'exploitation' with 'use', but 'exploitation' is much stronger. It creates a critical, even angry tone.

Tone in fiction

In fiction, **verbs** can be particularly powerful in creating tone. For example:

> The battered truck **lurched** round the corner and **shuddered** to a halt outside the Embassy. A dozen soldiers **spilled** out and **surged** up the steps into the building. Moments later they burst out, **propelling** frightened embassy staff before them at gunpoint.

Here the verbs create a sense of dynamic movement. The tone is active and energetic.

Progress Check

1. Tone is the same as register: true or false?
2. What type or class of words most obviously expresses an author's attitude?
3. What type or class words is especially vivid in creating tone in fiction?

11 2.5 Commenting on language

Tips for commenting on language

Be aware of:
* purpose, **target audience** and context
* register and tone and how they are expressed
* the writer's word choices
* the types of sentence and punctuation used.

Above all, remember that the writer has *chosen* all the words and types of sentence, and that these choices create the meaning. You may find it helpful to ask yourself, 'What other word, phrase or type of sentence could the writer have used?' and 'How would this have a different impact?'

First analyse, then comment

Read the text closely and work out how its purpose, target audience and context have influenced its content and style. This will be particularly relevant with non-fiction. Read the text below and study the annotations.

1. Clearly states global problem; dramatic one-word sentence, 'Fast'

2. Threatening phrase sums up problem

3. Conjunction signposts explanation

4. Negative adjective

5. Adjective suggests destruction

6. List emphasises range of species

7. Involves 'us'

8. Repetition links our wellbeing to the ice cap

9. Simple 'call to action'

The Arctic ice we all depend on is disappearing. Fast.[1]

In the last 30 years, we've lost as much as three-quarters of the floating sea ice cover at the top of the world. The volume of that sea ice measured by satellites in the summer, when it reaches its smallest, has shrunk so fast that scientists say it's now in a 'death spiral'.[2]

For over 800,000 years, ice has been a permanent feature of the Arctic ocean. It's melting because[3] of our use of dirty[4] fossil fuel energy, and in the near future it could be ice free for the first time since humans walked the Earth. This would be not only devastating[5] for the people, polar bears, narwhals, walruses and other species[6] that live there – but for the rest of us too.[7]

The ice at the top of the world reflects much of the sun's heat back into space and keeps our whole planet cool, stabilising the weather systems that we depend on to grow our food. Protecting the ice means protecting us all.[8]

To save the Arctic, we have to act today. Sign now[9]

Greenpeace webpage

Using Point, Evidence, Explanation (PEE)

To comment on a text, you need to make a point, provide evidence, and explain your point. You may find it helpful to use the **PEE** technique. It works like this:

P The webpage is aimed at people who have some sense of responsibility for the earth.[1]

E This is why it uses the inclusive pronouns 'we', 'our' and 'us' in phrases like 'we all depend', 'our use' and 'the rest of us'.[2]

E These imply that we are all responsible for global warming, and that we can all work together to stop it.[3]

Varying PEE

Improve the quality of your comments by varying your use of PEE: there is no need to stick to the same order all the time, or to make each element a different sentence. For example:

The negative phrases 'death spiral', 'dirty' and 'devastating', with their dead-sounding **alliteration**, create a sense of the deadly threat of global warming.

Notice how this sentence uses another sophisticated technique: **embedded quotations**. In other words, the phrases quoted as evidence run on as part of the sentence. Where do the main point, evidence and explanation come in the sentence?

---

1. Point about target audience

2. Evidence, using a phrase to link it to the opening sentence ('This is why')

3. Explanation of what the language 'implies'

To 'imply' is to suggest something without stating it more obviously. If you work out what is implied, you are *inferring* the meaning. See Topic 1.2.

Write three PEE sentences about how the webpage uses statistics (how fast we are losing the ice; how long it has been there). Cut them out and move them into a different order. Rewrite them as one or two sentences in this new order, making whatever changes are necessary for sense.

---

1. Why are word choices important?
2. What does PEE stand for?
3. You should always use PEE in the same order: true or false?
4. What adjective describes quotations run on within a sentence?

Progress Check

12 🎧 2.6 Reading texts which inform or explain

Texts whose main purpose is to inform or explain (**explanatory writing**) need to present information in a clear way that the target reader will understand – like the text you are reading right now.

News features

One type of information text is a news feature. Here is an online newspaper article:

Serial burglar jailed after police tracked him through iPad app

A man has been jailed following a string of burglaries after a Find My iPhone app was used by police to help finally capture him.

Ion-Liviu Radita, 36, stole an iPad during one of 11 break-ins committed during a three-week crime spree in Kent from 3 May.

But unknown to him, the Apple device had installed an app which enabled police to track it down to one of several properties in Ilford, Essex.

Outside one of the homes was a red Nissan Primera which detectives were able to prove was used to travel to Kent at the exact time of the burglaries.

A raid on Radita's home then uncovered a gems box with about 100 pieces of jewellery inside. Police said laptops and other electronic devices were also taken during the break-ins.

Radita, a Romanian, was convicted of conspiracy to commit burglary by a jury at Maidstone crown court this week and was jailed for seven years.

The Guardian, 25 October 2013

> **Work out where the five listed types of information are presented. Make a table listing them. Add notes on each from the text.**

News features usually give the following key information:
- *What* has happened
- *Who* was involved
- *Where* it happened
- *When* it happened
- *How* it happened (explanation)

Sometimes they also explain *why* something happened. In this case, this might involve an account of why Mr Radita needed the money.

Ways of presenting information

Texts can use a number of techniques to present information. For example:

- Giving precise facts and figures in a logical order

> (On Sonya Thomas, 7-stone eating champion) To give some idea of this woman's unlikely ability, consider just some of the records she currently holds: 8.2lbs of chilli-and-cheese-covered French fries in ten minutes, 8.3lbs of Vienna Sausages in ten minutes, 552 oysters in ten minutes, 5.95lbs of meatballs in 12 minutes, 162 chicken wings in 12 minutes…
>
> Andrew Buncombe, *Independent*, 17 June 2006

- Using an anecdote (short true story) to reveal character

> By the time he was two, Ian had already emerged as an uncompromising competitor. 'We had organised a short race among Navy children,' his mother recalls. 'Ian wasn't much of a sprinter in those days but this time he got out in front. Near the finishing line he turned and knocked down the other children, one by one, and finished the race by himself.'
>
> Dudley Doust, *Sunday Times* Magazine, on cricketer Ian Botham

Including more detail

Some texts include more detail: for example, revealing what an experience was like:

> I was aware that my legs were surrounded by water, but my top half was almost dry. I seemed to be trapped in something slimy. There was a terrible, sulphurous smell, like rotten eggs, and a tremendous pressure against my chest. My arms were trapped but I managed to free one hand and felt around – my palm passed through the wiry bristles of the hippo's snout. It was only then that I realised I was underwater, trapped up to my waist in his mouth.
>
> Paul Templer, as told to Chris Broughton, *The Guardian*, 4 May 2013

The details appealing to our senses of touch and smell bring this to life.

1. What five types of information are always included in news features?
2. What extra type of information is only sometimes included in a news feature?
3. Why might an information text appeal to the senses?

Progress Check

2.7 # Reading persuasive texts

Techniques of persuasion

Persuasive writing is used in advertising, charity appeals, election flyers, news editorials and company webpages. It uses several techniques:

- **logical argument**
- **emotive language** – to get an emotional response
- **rhetorical devices**, such as alliteration and imagery.

Logical argument

An author may rely on giving reasons in an order that makes sense, using linking words like these:

however	moreover
despite this	because
in addition	on the other hand

These are also known as **discourse markers**, and as 'signposting words' because they indicate what sort of idea will be coming next, which could be part of the main argument, or a **counter-argument**.

Here is an example of logical argument:

1. Gives main reason, backed up by statistic

The biggest reason for lowering the speed limit to 20mph in built-up areas is that it would save lives. First, it would reduce the number of accidents. Even more important, a pedestrian hit by a car at 30mph is seven times more likely to die than one hit at 20 mph.[1]

2. Gives counter-argument and dismisses it, with explanation

Some motorists claim that a 20mph limit would double their journey times. However, research shows that the average urban car journey would take only 40 seconds longer, because traffic and junctions make it impossible to cruise at a steady 30mph.[2]

3. Lists other reasons in logical order

This small increase in journey time is offset by many benefits apart from saving lives. Fuel consumption would decrease, reducing pollution and global warming. More children would walk to school, and more adults would cycle to work, thus reducing motor traffic and encouraging fitness. Moreover, towns and cities would become quieter, pleasanter places for residents and pedestrians.[3]

This is a well-structured argument. Look for the linking words and phrases, such as 'Even more important'. See if you can work out how they prepare the reader for the next step.

Emotive language and rhetoric

Emotive language aims to produce an emotional response. For example, the argument on page 34 could have included negative emotive language:

> *Our towns have become death-traps, where innocent lives are lost daily to speeding steel monsters.*

Rhetoric is the use of language techniques for impact. For example, the sentence above uses metaphor, presenting cars as monsters. Another rhetorical technique is the **triad (triple)** – listing things in threes.

See how this webpage uses positive emotive language to promote an experience as exciting fun.

What nouns add to the positive message?

The classic and original Go Ape Tree Top Adventure experience

We'll brief you for safety before you fly down a huge zip wire or leap off Tarzan Swings and enjoy our high ropes obstacles in some of Britain's most breathtaking[1] scenery.

Days out at Go Ape are about living life more adventurously, having fun on our high ropes with friends and family and getting in touch with your inner Tarzan (he's in there, we promise).[2]

The Go Ape experience involves fun and adventure across up to six sites. Each site features our award winning high ropes, awesome crossings, tunnels, bridges and an epic wind-in-your-face zip wire to finish.[3]

1. Positive adjective

2. Triad (triple) of good things, with humour

3. List, with positive emotive adjectives

Go and stand for five minutes at a safe distance from a busy road, or go and sit in a quiet park or garden. Or study the two pictures below. Then write an emotive argument against building a road through local parkland or countryside.

Progress Check

1. What sort of argument relies on reasoning?
2. What kind of language aims for an emotional response?
3. What is rhetoric?
4. What is a triad?

🎧 14 2.8 Reading texts which advise or warn

Types of advice text

There are many forms of **advice writing**, such as:
- safety leaflets
- legal advice leaflets
- health advice
- agony aunt or uncle columns.

> Other types of writing may also contain elements of advice. For example, reviews may advise you on whether or not to read a novel, see a play, or buy a product. See Topic 2.9.

Characteristics of good advice writing

Here is some text from a leaflet on caving safety.

Caving safety

Caving is a great sport, offering physical challenge and fantastic underground scenery. But if you're new to it, be aware that it has risks, which you can minimise by taking precautions:

- Go with experienced caving club members, and never alone.
- Wear the right clothes. A caving wet suit (thicker than a surfing one) will keep you warm in a wet cave; a quick-drying 'furry suit' with a waterproof oversuit is adequate for drier caves.
- Carry the right equipment. Never wander down a cave with a candle and a woolly hat! Wear a caving helmet with a well-charged caving lamp, and carry emergency lighting.
- Stick together. You may be tempted to try some solo exploration, but you could get lost.
- If you start to feel exhausted, tell your companions so that you can all turn back.
- On ladder pitches, use a lifeline, attached to a karabiner on a harness and belay belt.
- Never enter a flood-prone cave in unsettled weather.
- Never dive a sump (underwater passage) unless you are certain that it is short enough to pass in a few seconds.
- Always tell a reliable person where you're going and when they should dial 999 and ask for Cave Rescue if you don't turn up or phone.

Look for these characteristics if you are assessing and commenting on advice writing:

* awareness of what the target audience needs
* an appropriate tone (for example, sympathetic but firm for an agony column)
* direct address to reader ('You may feel that…')
* awareness of variables (e.g. 'If the casualty is conscious…')
* clear structure and language
* **imperative** verbs (e.g. 'tell') saying what to do and not do, with explanation if necessary.

Imagine that the images on this page are going to be used in advice leaflets. Decide what advice the people pictured could need. Choose one, and write a bullet point list in an appropriate tone.

1. Advice texts should say 'It is advisable to' rather than 'You should'. True or false?
2. What kind of verb tells you to do or not do something?
3. What is an appropriate tone for an agony column?

Progress Check

🎧 15 **2.9** # Reading reviews

Types of review

Reviews could be for:

- novels
- concerts
- play performances
- art exhibitions
- films
- CDs
- products.

The content and language of a review

The content of a review will vary according to what is being reviewed. For example, a review of a novel will normally summarise the plot but without revealing the ending – especially if the novel is one that aims to keep readers in suspense. It will also discuss how effectively the author has created believable and engaging characters, as well as the novel's themes and style.

A film review is also likely to include plot and characterisation but will also discuss the acting and the camera work. A music review like the one above focuses on a live event, so it will probably attempt to give the reader a strong sense of what it was like to be there. A special challenge in music reviews is to convey in words what the music was like. Elisa Bray, for example, describes Katy B's voice as 'soaring effortlessly'.

The language of a review will also reflect the subject but it will also relate to what the reviewer expects readers to know. Elisa Bray uses phrases like 'R&B vocals' and 'dubstep and garage arrangements' because she knows that most people reading this review will understand and appreciate them. They may enjoy feeling that they are 'in the know', understanding these terms while others may not.

A famous New York theatre reviewer, Clive Barnes, once said, 'A critic [reviewer] is someone who rides in after the battle and shoots the wounded'. His opinion was so highly regarded that if he gave a Broadway play a bad review, it could flop and be taken off in a week.

Types of review reader

People read reviews for different reasons:
- They are thinking of going to a play, reading a book, etc.
- They have already seen it, read it, been to it, and want to compare their experience with someone else's.
- They are interested in the writer, artist, band, etc.
- They missed a performance and wonder *what* they missed.
- They just want to be entertained.

This means that the review has to provide:

- key information (what, where, when, who)
- evaluation – the reviewer's opinion
- entertainment value.

See how the review extract (below) of Katy B does the following:

- tells readers what it was like to be at the concert
- gives background information
- evaluates the performance
- is entertaining in itself.

From 'Katy B, Roundhouse, London', Elisa Bray, _Independent_, 25 July 2011

Cute as a button, with a mane of bright red hair, she is keen to strike a level with her fans. 'This one's about being in a club and looking at the person next to you and you know nothing about them, but you feel you have so much in common,' she says, introducing 'Perfect Stranger'. A club frequenter since she was 16, it's this experience that she draws from in her observational lyrics.

Performing her songs – her effortless R&B vocals turning dubstep and garage arrangements into pop gems – to a crowd of young revellers could not be more natural. Live, her singing is even more impressive; no amount of pogoing and on-the-spot running affects her singing. Things take off with 'Broken Record', her voice soaring effortlessly. Her live band throw everything into the show, too, the two-man brass section of trumpet and saxophone bolstering the two-step jazz and Latin vibes.

A review combines information with evaluation. See Topics 2.6 and 8.10.

Listen to a music track that you like. Imagine that you are hearing it at a performance. (Move to the music if it helps!) Write a section of a review of the performance, providing some information and some evaluation. Write in the present tense, as in the Katy B review.

1. Review readers have always seen, read or heard the thing reviewed. True or false?
2. What three things should a review provide?
3. A book review should _not_ just summarise the plot. True or false?

Progress Check

🎧 16 2.10 Reading descriptive writing

Where you will find descriptive writing

- Novels
- Travel writing
- Holiday brochures
- Magazine articles

What descriptive writing does

Descriptive writing attempts to bring something to life by choosing details well and using vivid language. It can be about a place, a person or a thing, but it may also reveal the writer's feelings through the choice of language.

Features of descriptive writing

Some of the features of descriptive writing are:
- well-chosen details
- appealing to the senses
- vivid adjectives
- imagery.

In Extract A, Laurie Lee is going to school for the first time – with a potato for his lunch. How does the description show what it was like for him?

1. Simile, with alliteration

2. Sense appeal

3. Representative details suggest strangeness

4. Noun choice suggests roughness

5. Threatening details

6. Adjective conveys his fear

7. List of what they did to him

Extract A: Laurie Lee, *Cider with Rosie*

I arrived at the school just three feet tall and fatly wrapped in my scarves. The playground <u>roared like a rodeo</u>,[1] and the potato <u>burned</u>[2] through my thigh. <u>Old boots, ragged stockings, torn trousers and skirts</u>,[3] went skating and skidding around me. The <u>rabble</u>[4] closed in; I was encircled; grit flew in my face like shrapnel. Tall girls with frizzled hair, and huge boys with <u>sharp elbows</u>,[5] began to prod me with <u>hideous</u>[6] interest. They <u>plucked at my scarves, spun me round like a top, screwed my nose, and stole my potato</u>.[7]

In Extract B, Gerald Durrell describes his boyhood meeting with 'the rose-beetle man'. Try to picture the man and imagine the buzzing beetles. How does Durrell use vivid details and language, including imagery?

Extract B: Gerald Durrell, *My Family and Other Animals*

The pockets of [his coat] bulged, the contents almost spilling out: combs, balloons, little highly coloured pictures of the saints, olive-wood carvings of snakes, camels, dogs and horses, cheap mirrors, a riot of handkerchiefs, and long twisted rolls of bread decorated with seeds.

His trousers, patched like his coat, drooped over a pair of scarlet *charouhias*, leather shoes with upturned toes decorated with a large black-and-white pompon. This extraordinary character carried on his back bamboo cages full of  pigeons and young chickens, several mysterious sacks, and a large bunch of fresh green leeks. With one hand he held his pipe to his mouth, and in the other a number of lengths of cotton, to each of which was tied an almond-size rose-beetle, glittering golden green in the sun, all of them flying round his hat with desperate, deep buzzings, trying to escape from the thread tied firmly round their waists. Occasionally, tired of circling round and round without success, one of the beetles would settle for a moment on his hat, before launching itself off once more on its endless merry-go-round.

When you have read about the rose-beetle man, shut the book and see what details you can remember. Make notes on them. Then go back and find the details. What made them vivid enough for you to recall?

Writing your own descriptions will increase your appreciation of other descriptive writing. See Topics 8.4 and 8.5.

Progress Check

1. Should a description include every possible detail?
2. What is meant by 'sense appeal'?
3. Which extract gives a stronger sense of how the author felt at the time, and how?
4. From the details, how do you think the rose-beetle man makes a living?

Worked questions

Read the extract and answer the questions fully. Remember to refer to evidence in the text.

Lone yachtswoman Ellen MacArthur describes passing an iceberg as she takes part in a sailing race

I took pictures and a video of it, in complete and utter awe at the beauty of this massive block. I could see families of birds on top of it as we grew closer, and clearly see and hear the waves breaking around its base as on a rocky shore in a storm. The wind was up to 30 knots by now, a rise of 5, which was pushing us closer and closer to the side of the berg, and though we made it safely round we passed at well within a mile. As we rounded its most northern point I was stunned to see two enormous ice caves, perfectly arch-like in shape and sinking away to darkness deep within the berg itself. Each was large enough to sail *Kingfisher* into – a trip, though, from which there would be no coming back for sure. Its sides were tinted with an aqua-blue colour, and it looked so white against the inky-grey sea and darkening sky. There was an aura around this berg, a feeling of complete and utter isolation. I knew that it was highly unlikely that human eyes had even seen it before.

1. **How does MacArthur make us aware of the challenge of what she is doing?** *(3 marks)*

   She says that the wind is strong and rising ('up to 30 knots') and that it is pushing her boat 'closer and closer' to the iceberg. The repetition of 'closer' helps us to imagine the pace at which this threat is growing.[1] Her use of 'though we made it safely' implies[2] that she and her boat might not have got through, and that therefore there was danger involved.

1. Focuses on the impact of one phrase
2. Infers meaning, using 'implies' correctly

2. **How does the passage remind us that MacArthur is sailing past the iceberg and not viewing it in some other way?** *(3 marks)*

The phrase 'grew closer' <u>shows that her approach is gradual and constant</u>.[1] Giving the wind speed in a technical format ('30 knots ... a rise of 5') emphasises the attention to wind speed and accurate measurement that is necessary in sailing. The need for large safety margins in sailing is shown by the phrase <u>'well within a mile'</u>[2] being used to indicate a relatively short distance – almost too close for comfort.

1. Correct inference

2. Good use of embedded quote, with correct understanding of its meaning

3. **How does MacArthur use language to help us to imagine the iceberg and sea around it?** *(5 marks)*

She provides the detail of the families of birds on the iceberg, and helps us to picture the waves breaking <u>'as on a rocky shore in a storm', as if the iceberg is the size of an island</u>.[1] She gives us a further sense of its bulk when she describes the ice caves<u>: if even these ice caves are 'enormous', the whole iceberg must be huge</u>.[2] An even more vivid impression of the caves' size is given by her <u>statement that</u>[3] it would be possible to sail her boat into them.

She describes the shape of the caves as 'arch-like', suggesting cathedral architecture, <u>as if they were created by an invisible hand</u>.[4] The phrase 'sinking away to darkness deep within' creates a sense of mystery, but <u>the alliteration of 'darkness deep' creates a hint of menace</u>,[5] as does the use of the word 'sinking', since that is the last thing she wants her boat to be doing.

Another feature of her description is the use of colour: the iceberg's sides are 'tinted aqua-blue' but the extreme whiteness of the iceberg overall contrasts with the 'inky-grey sea and darkening sky'.

1. Uses embedded quote and infers meaning

2. Colon to signal an explanation

3. Paraphrases extract without quoting

4. Personal response based on evidence

5. Correct literary terms, embedded quote, explanation of effect

4. **Explain how MacArthur feels about this experience, and how we know** *(6 marks)*

We know from the first that MacArthur does not see the iceberg just as an obstacle to be avoided: <u>she is in 'complete and utter awe' at its beauty</u>.[1] She is also 'stunned' to see the size and beauty of the ice caves, the word suggesting that she is deeply affected. This is backed up by the rather <u>fanciful</u>[2] idea of *Kingfisher* sailing into one of the caves, never to return, as if descending into the underworld. This combines her sense of awe with her awareness of the danger.

MacArthur has <u>an almost religious feeling</u>[3] for the iceberg, sensing its 'complete and utter isolation' as if in awe of something so far removed from normal human life.

It is as if she feels somehow privileged to be, probably, the first person to see the iceberg: 'it was highly unlikely that human eyes had ever seen it before'. <u>Her use of the phrase 'human eyes'</u>,[4] rather than just 'anyone', emphasises the remoteness of the place and how special it is for her to be here.

1. Colon signalling explanation of point

2. Comments by choice of adjective

3. Effective personal interpretation

4. Focus on significance of one phrase

Practice questions

1. Study the page from the Royal National Lifeboat Association's leaflet 'In the surf: your guide to surfsport safety'.

SURFING GREAT BRITAIN

Surfing GB is the national governing body for surfing and bodyboarding. For further information, accredited training centres and recognised schools visit **www.surfinggb.com** or email **info@surfinggb.com**.

EQUIPMENT

As well as the basic safety equipment, you'll need the following kit to get started:

Board – when selecting a board you need to consider your height, weight and ability. When starting out, a soft foam board is ideal as it is thick and wide, making it easier to float, paddle and catch waves.
Leash – always wear one around the ankle of your back foot so you don't lose your board if you fall off!
Wax – apply this to the deck of your board to give you grip.
Fins – these are vital when bodyboarding to help you catch waves and swim against strong currents.

RNLI Lifeboats

Then write answers to the following questions.

a) Comment on how the content and style – including register and tone – are
reflected in the following: *(6 marks)*
  - the main purpose of the page, and any secondary purpose
  - the target audience
  - context – the fact that this is a leaflet.

b) Comment on how all the visual aspects of the page (images, type, headings)
fit the content and style of the text. *(4 marks)*

2. Read the extract below, from Bill Bryson's *A Walk in the Woods*. It is from an early
chapter, in which the author is planning to go hiking in the American woods. Answer
the questions that follow.

Imagine, if you will, lying in the dark alone in a little tent, nothing but a few microns
of trembling nylon between you and the chill night air, listening to a 400-pound
bear moving around your campsite. Imagine its quiet grunts and mysterious
snufflings, the clatter of upended cookware and sounds of moist gnawings, the pad
of its feet and the heaviness of its breath, the singing brush of its haunch along
your tent side. Imagine the hot flood of adrenalin, that unwelcome tingling in the
back of your arms, at the sudden rough bump of its snout against the foot of your
tent, the alarming wild wobble of your frail shell as it roots through the backpack
that you left casually propped by the entrance – with, you suddenly recall, a
Snickers bar in the pouch. Bears adore Snickers bars, you've heard.

And then the dull thought – oh, God – that perhaps you brought the Snickers bar in
here with you, that it's somewhere in here, down by your feet or underneath you or…
here it is. Another bump of grunting head against the tent, this time near your
shoulders. More crazy wobble. Then silence, a very long silence, and – wait, shhhhh…
yes! – the unutterable relief of realizing that the bear has withdrawn to the other side of
the camp or shambled back into the woods. I tell you right now. I couldn't stand it.

a) Explain what you think is Bryson's purpose in this extract. Back up your explanation
with evidence from the text. *(2 marks)*

b) Describe Bryson's attitude towards bears, and why you think he asks us to imagine
them in such vivid detail. *(4 marks)*

c) Explain what you think are the register and tone of this piece of writing, and how
the language used creates them. For example, here are some phrases you could
consider: *(8 marks)*
  - nothing but a few microns of trembling nylon
  - mysterious snufflings
  - that unwelcome tingling
  - alarming wild wobble
  - Bears adore Snickers bars, you've heard
  - wait, shhhhh…yes!
  - I tell you right now. I couldn't stand it.

Learning Summary

After completing this chapter you should understand:
- how setting helps to create atmosphere
- characterisation and themes in novels and plays
- plot and structure
- how to comment on texts and compare them
- dialogue in novels and plays.

🎧 17 **3.1** Setting and atmosphere

What is setting?

Setting is:
- where the action of at least part of a novel, story or play takes place
- the time of day
- the weather.

An author describes these things to bring the story to life for the reader, but also to create a suitable atmosphere for the unfolding events.

A menacing crime scene might take place in an old warehouse with dangerous, creaking old machinery. A tender, intimate meeting between lovers might take place in the privacy of a walled rose garden on a sunny summer afternoon.

What sort of action or atmosphere would you associate with the scenes here?

What is atmosphere?

Atmosphere is the mood created by the way a setting is described, and the details included. Read the extract below, from a ghost story, *The Woman in Black*. The narrator, solicitor Arthur Kipps, plans to stay overnight at remote Eel Marsh House, cut off from the mainland at high tide, so that he can work on the will of the deceased owner, Mrs Drablow. He goes for a walk on the small island on which the house is set, in the direction of an old graveyard. See how details and language create atmosphere.

Go for a walk and make brief notes on what you see. Then describe them as a setting, choosing details and language to create a particular atmosphere. This could be, for example, pleasantly relaxed, exciting, tense or ghostly.

Ahead, where the walls ended in a heap of dust and rubble, lay the grey water of the estuary. As I stood, wondering, <u>the last light went from the sun, and the wind rose in a gust, and rustled through the grass</u>.[1] Above my head, that <u>unpleasant, snake-necked bird</u>[2] came gliding back towards the ruins, and I saw that its beak was hooked around a fish that writhed and struggled helplessly. I watched the creature alight and, as I did so, it disturbed some of the stones, which toppled and fell out of sight somewhere.

Suddenly conscious of <u>the cold and the extreme bleakness and eeriness</u>[3] of the spot and of the <u>gathering dusk of the November afternoon</u>,[4] and not wanting my spirits to become so depressed that I might begin to be affected by all sorts of <u>morbid fancies</u>,[5] I was about to leave, and walk briskly back to the house, where I intended to switch on a good many lights and even light a small fire if it were possible, before beginning my preliminary work on Mrs Drablow's papers. But, as I turned away, I glanced once again round the burial ground and <u>then I saw again the woman with the wasted face</u>,[6] who had been at Mrs Drablow's funeral.

1. Dusk and wind are unsettling ('gust' and 'rustle' make a whispering sound)

2. Bird described menacingly ('snake')

3. Comfortless – cold, bleak and sinister

4. Light fading; dreary time of year

5. Imagined anxieties about death and the dead

6. He thought he was alone: shocked to see woman with ghostly thin face, in the graveyard

Here, all the circumstances of setting, including time of year, time of day, and weather, combine to 'spook' the narrator. The author chooses details and language to create the atmosphere. For example, how might the bird have been described very differently in a nature documentary?

1. What are the three features of setting?
2. How does setting relate to plot?
3. How could a writer create different atmospheres from description of the same setting?

Progress Check

18 **3.2** Characterisation and themes

How is character portrayed?

Characterisation is how authors reveal what characters are like. They do this in several ways:

- what they *do*
- what they *say*
- what they *think*
- how *others* speak about or respond to them
- direct commentary.

Authors occasionally use **direct commentary**, simply telling us about a character:

Emily was a difficult woman to please, and she demanded absolute loyalty of her friends.

However, it is usually more interesting to find out about characters from their actions, speech and thoughts than to be told about them in this direct way.

What are themes?

Themes are the main ideas that an author explores, such as:

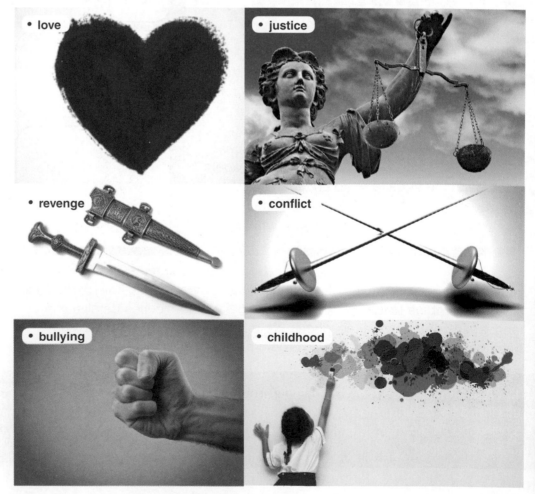

- love
- justice
- revenge
- conflict
- bullying
- childhood

These are closely connected to the characters and what they do. See what themes you think the author of the extract here might explore, based on the extract.

Bernard Ashley, *Little Soldier*

Kaninda became a boy soldier in Africa after his family were killed by a rival tribe, the Yusulu. Now at school in London, he is introduced to another boy from his country.

'This is Kaninda Bulumba. And this is Faustin N'gensi.'

The boy had just <u>the split second</u>[1] to lift his face to Kaninda's before he was thrown back over the low chair by the sudden crack of Kaninda's <u>frenzied</u>[2] attack, a fierce chop with the hard edge of the hand to his throat and a lunge at the windpipe with <u>guerrilla</u>[3] fingers.

'Kill Yusulu!' [4] Kaninda shouted, backing his head for a butt to the nose before he broke the neck. *'Kill Yusulu!'*

But Miss Mascall was on him, shouting, trying to pull him off, and before he could kill Faustin N'gensi, Kaninda was hauled off and held in a fierce lock by a big tank of a teacher.

'Oi! What's he done to you?'

Others came running, and for all his training in hand-to-hand, Kaninda <u>couldn't break free</u>[5] from so many of them. <u>He went rigid, still, saved himself for the next</u> chance.[6] Faustin N'gensi, being helped up, mouthed a plea for protection from this mad boy.

'He's Kibu! I'm Yusulu.'

'So? You're all Thames Reach Comprehensive while you're here, sonny.' The big London teacher who was holding Kaninda in a painful lock gave him a jerk to emphasise the fact.

1. Kaninda is fast

2. He's almost crazed

3. Refers to his training

4. Single-pointed desire for revenge

5. Keeps struggling

6. Self-disciplined: stops, already planning next attempt

Draw a mind map, spidergram or other visual representation of the themes in any novel that you have recently read.

What is your impression of Kaninda? What do we learn about his victim, and about the teacher who restrains Kaninda?

1. Authors can describe a character directly, but in what ways is it usually more interesting to find out about them?
2. What are the most obvious themes that could emerge from the *Little Soldier* extract?
3. What do we learn about Kaninda's background that has shaped his character?

Progress Check

3.3 How dialogue reveals character

What is dialogue?

Dialogue refers to what characters say, how they say it, and how this is reported. It can also be thought of as including any small actions in between what they say:

'Here's what I think of him,' she said, *spitting into the dust at their feet*.

The actual words that characters say always appear in speech marks. It is not always necessary for the author to give the name of the speaker, at least when there are only two speakers, because a new paragraph is begun to show a change of speaker.

What does dialogue do?

Dialogue does several things. It:
- brings the story to life
- reveals what characters are like
- reveals relationships between characters – such as who is more powerful
- expresses ideas that the author is exploring
- moves the story on.

Read the following extract from *Holes*, by Louis Sachar, and see how it does these things. Stanley has just arrived at a labour camp for delinquent boys in the middle of the desert. Mr Sir is the camp warder.

What impression do you get of Stanley and Mr Sir in this extract? What is their relationship, and how is it revealed?

Reported speech

Reported speech (also known as 'indirect speech') is dialogue that is paraphrased within the main text without the exact words being quoted, as follows:

She asked me if I had seen a tall bearded man in a sheepskin jacket. I thought for a moment, then told her that no one of that description had passed by while I had been standing there. She thanked me briefly and hurried on.

Actual dialogue is usually more interesting to read than reported speech. Reported speech is useful if an author needs to sum up a dialogue in a few words, especially if the facts are more important than the exact words used. You do not need to begin a new paragraph or use speech marks for reported speech.

> Sit where you can listen to some real-life dialogue. Make brief notes on it. Record it if you can do this with the speakers' permission. Then try to write it down, using correct punctuation. How does it suggest character? How might you have to change it for a story?

'Take a good look around you,' Mr Sir said. 'What do you see?'

Stanley looked out across the vast wasteland. The air seemed thick with heat and dirt. 'Not much,' he said, then <u>hastily</u>[1] added, 'Mr Sir.'

<u>Mr Sir laughed</u>.[2] 'You see any guard towers?'

'No.'

'How about an electric fence?'

'No, Mr Sir.'

'There's no fence at all, is there?'

'No, Mr Sir.'

'You want to run away?' Mr Sir asked him.

Stanley looked back at him, unsure what he meant.

'If you want to run away, go ahead, start running. I'm not going to stop you.'

<u>Stanley didn't know what kind of game Mr Sir was playing</u>.[3]

'I see you're looking at my gun. Don't worry. I'm not going to shoot you.' He tapped his holster. 'This is for yellow-spotted lizards. <u>I wouldn't waste a bullet on you.</u>'[4]

'I'm not going to run away,' Stanley said.

'Good thinking,' said Mr Sir. 'Nobody runs away from here. We don't need a fence. Know why? Because we've got the only water for a hundred miles. You want to run away? <u>You'll be buzzard food in three days</u>.'[5]

Stanley could see some kids dressed in orange and carrying shovels dragging themselves toward the tents.

'You thirsty?' asked Mr Sir.

'Yes, Mr Sir,' Stanley said <u>gratefully</u>.[6]

'<u>Well, you better get used to it. You're going to be thirsty for the next eighteen months.</u>'[7]

1. Why this adverb?

2. Enjoys this

3. Stanley's thought – shows he is baffled

4. What is his attitude to Stanley?

5. Would he care?

6. Adverb shows how he speaks: he is the new boy – not yet tough

7. Enjoys disappointing Stanley

1. What key punctuation is used with dialogue?
2. Why is it not always necessary to name the speaker?
3. What two key functions of characterisation does dialogue perform?
4. What two adverbs reveal Stanley's character in the extract?

Progress Check

3.4 Plot and structure

The plot of a novel, story or play is its story, or **narrative**. The **structure** is the shape that the plot takes. This will normally relate to a problem or **conflict** faced by one or more of the characters, and how they deal with it. Usually the author will encourage us to care most about one character, known as the hero/heroine or **protagonist**. If they have a particular enemy, this is the **antagonist**.

Some types of plot conflict

* Between individuals

* Individual versus authority

* Individual/group versus external forces

* Individual versus self

Making us want to read on

The novelist has to make us want to read on. They do this by keeping us in **suspense** and gradually increasing the **tension**. Will the problem be resolved, and if so, how? The protagonist will usually face a main **crisis**, but there may be smaller crises leading up to this.

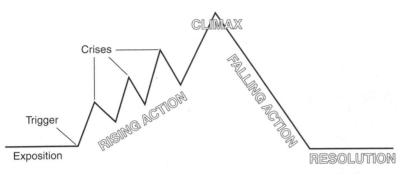

Term	Explanation
Exposition	Introduction: setting and characters
Trigger/initiating incident	Problem or conflict sets the rest of the story in motion
Rising action	Events gradually intensify ('hot up'), with crises leading to a main crisis
Climax	Moment of greatest danger and suspense (may also be main crisis)
Falling action	Conflict approaches resolution, though there could be a moment of final suspense
Conclusion/resolution	Events come to a close, with sense of completion (happy or tragic)

How does this model fit the stories you know?

This structure model will make more sense to you if you see how well it fits one or two novels or plays that you know. Bear in mind that there are variations within it. For example, in Bernard Ashley's *Little Soldier* (see Topic 3.2) the **trigger** or **initiating incident** is the protagonist's family being killed in a clan war in Africa. However, the novel is set in London, after he has been sent there as a refugee. We learn about the trigger event in flashbacks and in the protagonist's thoughts.

Choose six objects in your room and see if you can devise a simple plot in which each object fits into one stage of the structure. Make yourself the protagonist if you wish.

1. What essential factor drives a plot?
2. What is a protagonist?
3. What is the term for a moment of particular danger or suspense?
4. When would you expect tension to relax?

Progress Check

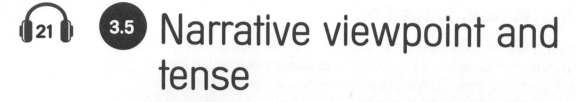

3.5 Narrative viewpoint and tense

Narrative viewpoint is the point of view from which a story is told. There are three main viewpoints:

- First person

'I was worried. I wondered if I should lie.'

- Third person, from character's viewpoint

'She was worried. Should she lie?'

- Third person, all-knowing author

'Izzie was worried. She wondered whether she should lie.'

First person can make the story seem very real, with the narrator springing to life. However, the narrator can only describe events that he or she actually witnesses or hears about.

Writing in the **third person** as an all-knowing ('omniscient') author, who can comment on every aspect of the plot and 'see inside' every character's head, gives the author power, but it may be more difficult for us to identify with the characters.

Many authors choose the compromise of writing in the *third person but from one character's viewpoint*. See how Catherine Forde does this in the following extract.

Catherine Forde, _Fat Boy Swim_

Jimmy finds himself alone with Ellie at school. He is used to being mocked or avoided because he is overweight. Ellie gets bullied because she is short-sighted. 'Busty' is their domestic science teacher.

Ellie groaned again. 'I've never followed a recipe.'

'Me neither.'

Jimmy sifted flour into a bowl, raising his sieve really high so that flour particles fell like the lightest snowflakes.

'Busty's got the amounts wrong anyway. If I use all the butter she says these'll never puff up right.'

'You've done this before?'

Ellie was so close she practically bumped the sieve from Jimmy's hand. The length of her arm touched his own, but she didn't pull it away like anyone else would do. Her touch made Jimmy shivery then hot inside, like he'd gulped from a mug of cocoa on a cold, cold day.

'I'm no help here,' Ellie groaned again, watching Jimmy cut butter into tiny squares and drop them into boiling water. 'I was looking forward to music, not domestic science.'

'Me too,' said Jimmy, swallowing the urge to ask her if she liked the same singers and bands as he did. That would have been pushing his luck way further than it had gone already. Just keep her by your side like this a wee bit longer, he cautioned himself. 'Whip this cream,' he told Ellie, 'I'll do the rest.'

We find out about the characters from what they do – and what Ellie does _not_ do. What do you think is the one thing that Jimmy is really good at, and how do we know? The viewpoint also gives us an insight into Jimmy's thoughts and feelings. How is he affected by Ellie? What advice does he mentally give himself, and why?

Past or present tense

Novels and stories are usually written in the past **tense**, as in: 'Ellie groaned again.' However, they can also be in the present tense:

> _Izzie looks around her. Seeing that she is alone, she reaches out…_

The present tense can seem strange at first, but it can also make the action seem as if it is actually happening now. Which do you prefer?

Plays are not written in any tense, because they consist only of dialogue. However, **stage directions** are always in the present tense:

> IZZIE (_suddenly noticing Jed_) Oh – you made me jump! I'm just here to buy a present.

> Whatever tense a novel is in, you should always write about it in the present tense. This is because you are discussing what happens in the story, not what happened in real life or history. See Topic 3.7.

> Find three or four novels. Read enough of each one to work out what the viewpoint and tense are. Then draw a diagram based on the one on page 54, substituting lines from your actual novels to represent their viewpoint and tense.

1. What person and tense is 'I said…'?
2. What person and tense is 'James opens the letter…'?
3. What is the viewpoint in 'He needed to phone her – now! But what was the number?'
4. What is the limitation of writing in the first person?

Progress Check

3.6 Style and imagery

The **style** of a text means how the author has chosen words and formed sentences. For example, it could be very simple:

Danny ran to the park. He did not want to be late for the fireworks.

Or it could be complex, using fanciful language, with more unusual vocabulary.

Danny sprinted to the park as if all the hounds of hell were snapping at his heels, because he dreaded arriving too late to see what promised to be an astounding display of pyrotechnics.

Most authors will vary their style to some extent – for example, using short, simple sentences to create a sense of tension, and perhaps longer ones with more unusual word choices to describe a scene.

Imagery

Imagery refers to the use of **similes** and **metaphors** to create word pictures. In both cases, they compare one thing with something that is similar in at least one way.

Similes

A simile does this using *like*, *as* or *than*. It makes us see a thing, or a character, or something the character does, more vividly by making a **comparison:**

*As the sense of his recent victory faded, he came down to earth **like** a parachutist falling from sunlit heights through rain clouds, to land in a muddy ditch.*

Another type of simile uses *as* or *than*:

Hard and sharp **as** flint, from which no steel had ever struck out generous fire; secret, and self-contained, and solitary **as** an oyster....

No wind that blew was bitterer **than** he, no falling snow was more intent upon its purpose, no pelting rain less open to entreaty.

Charles Dickens describing Scrooge in *A Christmas Carol*

Metaphors

A metaphor also creates a vivid picture by comparing two things, but it is more compressed: it does not use *like*, *as* or *than*. Instead, it speaks as if the subject actually *is* the thing to which it is compared:

Small flames stirred at the bole of a tree and crawled[1] away through leaves and brushwood, dividing and increasing. One patch touched a tree trunk and scrambled up like a bright squirrel.[2] The smoke increased, sifted, rolled outwards. The squirrel leapt[3] on the wings of the wind[4] and clung to another standing tree, eating[5] downwards. Beneath the dark canopy of leaves and smoke the fire laid hold on the forest and began to gnaw.[5]

William Golding, *Lord of the Flies*

1. Verb choice – like an animal

2. Simile

3. Becomes a metaphor

4. Metaphor, as if the wind is a bird

5. Behaving like a squirrel

Style in a first-person narrative

The style of a first-person narrative must reflect the character and style of speech of the narrator. The narrator of this extract is an uneducated but imaginative teenage girl in a poor family. See how the style reflects this. Also see if you can find the two metaphors, and try to picture what they suggest. Note that this novel, unusually, is laid out like a poem.

Go to a tap and run some water into a pan, or run a bath or a shower. Write a paragraph describing the water. Use a simile, or a metaphor, or both.

Daddy
put a pail of kerosene
next to the stove
and Ma,
fixing breakfast,
thinking the pail was
filled with water,
lifted it,
to make Daddy's coffee,
poured it,
but instead of making coffee,
Ma made a rope of fire.
It rose up from the stove
to the pail
and the kerosene burst
into flames.

Ma ran across the kitchen,
out the porch door,
screaming for Daddy.
I tore after her,
then,
thinking of the burning pail
left behind in the bone-dry kitchen,
I flew back and grabbed it,
throwing it out the door.
I didn't know.
I didn't know Ma was coming back.
The flaming oil
splashed
onto her apron,
and Ma,
suddenly Ma,
was a column of fire.

Karen Hesse, *Out of the Dust*

1. Which type of image uses 'like', 'as' or 'than'?
2. How is a metaphor different from a simile?
3. What should the style of a first-person narrative reflect?

Progress Check

3.7 Using evidence to comment on a text

When you are asked to comment on a novel, story or play, you will usually be asked to focus on the characters, the style and imagery, and any themes that are suggested by a passage. Sometimes you might be asked to comment on an extract and how it fits into the whole text.

As when writing about non-fiction, it is useful to use the **PEE** technique:

- make a **Point**
- give **Evidence**, perhaps in the form of a quote
- **Explain** how your evidence proves your point.

However, your commentary will be more effective if you do not always use the same order.

Read the following extract once, then again taking special note of the emboldened sections.

Link, a homeless teenager, is sitting in a café. He has been let down by a friend, or thinks he has, and so he has decided to become a self-sufficient loner – until Gail walks in.

The New Me. That's what I was thinking. I don't need anyone. Solo and coping, right? Right.

I nursed the coffee. It was warm in here and raw outside so **it paid to stay put**. I was halfway down the mug **when she walked in**.

She was dossing, I could see that, but she was the best looking dosser I'd ever seen. I noticed her hair first. Chestnut, spilling from under her green knitted cap **like fire**. Her eyes were terrific, too – dark and wide and shining **like she'd just had twelve hours' kip**. She had on a battered waxed jacket, torn muddy jeans and broken-down trainers, but she **soared** above her scruffiness – her looks and bearing sort of cancelled it out.

She didn't look at anybody as she crossed the caff, but everybody looked at her. I couldn't tear my eyes away. She got a Coke and turned, looking for somewhere to sit. Her eyes – those fantastic eyes – met mine for a second and I smiled. **No chance, I told myself**.

Robert Swindells, *Stone Cold*

How to comment

Supposing you are asked, 'What do we learn about Link in this passage?'
You could answer using PEE:

Point

The opening paragraph seems unconvincing, as if Link is trying to persuade himself that he can cope alone.

Evidence

The capitals for 'New Me', the simple statement 'I don't need anyone', and the way he seems to be talking to himself in 'Solo and coping, right?'...

Explanation

...all suggest that as he looks back he is mocking himself for even trying to believe that.

Point and Evidence

When he answers his own question with 'Right', he could even be speaking ironically, bitterly commenting on how wrong he was.

Explanation

This suggests that he has quite a lot of self-awareness, or at least that he has developed this by the time he is narrating the story.

You could also comment on:
- 'it paid to stay put', showing that he has nowhere to go and is trying to keep warm
- his use of 'street' slang, such as 'dossing' and 'kip', showing he is streetwise
- how quickly he seems to be falling for Gail; how he describes her eyes and hair; the phrase 'I couldn't tear my eyes away'
- his poetic appreciation of her looks, shown by the simile 'like fire' and the metaphor 'soared'.

A helpful piece of advice is:

Say a lot about a little.

This means be selective and focus closely on the phrases you select, as in the second PEE example above focusing on one word ('Right') and showing an awareness of different possible interpretations.

Remember: always try to comment on the actual words used, not just the ideas that they convey or what happens.

When writing about a novel, story or play, you will not normally need to comment on the purpose, audience or context as you would when writing about non-fiction. However, the PEE technique is useful for both. See Topic 2.5.

Choose one of the highlighted phrases in the *Stone Cold* extract. Write down different possible interpretations of what it shows about the character, on pieces of paper. Then move them around in order of which you think is most likely.

Progress Check

1. Character is one aspect of a passage that you could focus on; name another one.
2. There is always a correct interpretation of every phrase and detail in a novel. True or false?
3. What form is the evidence in a PEE statement most likely to take?
4. What does 'Say a lot about a little' mean?

3.8 Comparing texts

One way to highlight the characteristics of a text is to compare it with another one, especially if they have obvious similarities. This could be done at the level of the whole text, or in more detail, comparing two short passages.

Comparing whole texts

Write 'both', 'however', 'whereas', 'of the two', 'because', 'in addition' and 'ultimately' on separate pieces of paper. Turn these over so that you cannot see them. Then take three at random and try to use them in a short comparison of two novels or other texts.

If you were comparing two novels, you might focus on the plot, main characters and themes. One way to begin is to make a table like the one below.

	Bernard Ashley, *Little Soldier*	Beverley Naidoo, *The Other Side of Truth*
Plot	Kaninda, former boy soldier in Africa, comes to London as refugee. Wants to get back to fight for his clan, to avenge the killing of his family. Gets involved in gang warfare in London, and with foster family's daughter, Laura, who is guilt-stricken because of her part in a hit-and-run car accident.	Sade (*Shad-deh*) and brother Femi are sent from Nigeria to London for their safety when their mother is murdered for political reasons. Their uncle fails to meet them and they are fostered. At school, Sade is bullied into stealing. Her father flees to Britain but faces deportation and death. Sade prevents this by going to a newscaster and publicising the story.
Characters	Kaninda misses his family but is driven by his determination to get back to fighting his war of personal revenge. He is secretive and resourceful, biding his time, only reluctantly becoming involved in gang warfare. Laura rebels against a strongly Christian mother, but is guilt-stricken and seeks a way out.	Sade is resourceful and is forced to be secretive because she is afraid of endangering her father. She feels guilty when pressurised into shoplifting. She is brave, determined and loyal, making herself seek out a newscaster to save her father. She has to cope with Femi becoming remote and uncooperative.
Themes	Political and tribal conflict, guilt, family, loyalty	Political conflict and corruption, guilt, family, authority

The language of comparison

The language of comparison is similar whether you are comparing whole texts or passages. See how similarities and differences are underlined below.

Both novels[1] are stories of personal tragedy set against a backdrop of wider-scale conflict – tribal war in the case of *Little Soldier* and political corruption in *The Other Side of Truth*. Both main characters are Africans who come to London reluctantly and who miss their families and face difficulties on their arrival. However,[2] Kaninda is driven by hatred and a desire for revenge, whereas Sade is driven by[3] loyalty and love for her father.

Of the two,[4] Kaninda seems more traumatised by his experiences. This is perhaps because[5] Sade has her brother, and at least a hope of seeing her father again. Kaninda has also seen the horrors of war, while[6] Sade has not been directly involved in conflict.

In terms of themes, both novels involve conflict, but of different kinds.[7] *Little Soldier* compares tribal and gang warfare, but[8] in *The Other Side of Truth* the conflict is more between the individual and the authorities. However, both also involve inner conflict in the form of guilt: Laura's in relation to the car accident, and Sade's over the shop-lifting incident. In addition, both ultimately[9] focus on the main characters learning from their problems.

1. Starts with what the plots have in common

2. Signals change of direction from preceding sentence

3. Signals comparison; repeating 'is driven by' highlights similarity *and* difference

4. Signals character comparison

5. Suggests explanation

6. Another comparing word

7. Topic sentence introduces new angle – similarity and difference in themes

8. Simple conjunction for comparison

9. Signals final (perhaps most important) similarity

1. How is comparing texts helpful?
2. What does 'However' at the start of a sentence indicate to the reader?
3. What does the word 'whereas' suggest?
4. Where is a 'topic sentence' normally placed?

Progress Check

25 3.9 Dialogue and stage directions in a play

How plays differ from novels

How plays are structured

Whereas novels are usually divided into chapters, plays are divided into Acts. A Shakespeare play, for example, always has five Acts. Each Act is divided further into scenes, usually with each change of scene shifting the action to a new setting. The stage directions say briefly where each scene is set.

Limitations on settings

A novel can describe characters moving rapidly from one place to another and can put characters in any setting they can make readers imagine. A play has to show its action on stage, so it is more limited. Some things would be difficult to show on stage. For example, it would be hard to have a horserace on the stage. However, it could be suggested by showing people watching the race and with sound effects. Alternatively, events can be reported by a character who has seen them.

The main ways in which plays differ from novels are:

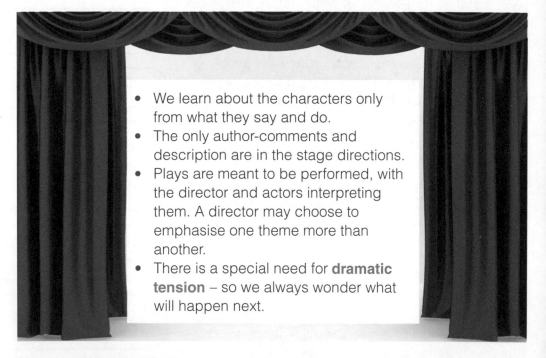

- We learn about the characters only from what they say and do.
- The only author-comments and description are in the stage directions.
- Plays are meant to be performed, with the director and actors interpreting them. A director may choose to emphasise one theme more than another.
- There is a special need for **dramatic tension** – so we always wonder what will happen next.

Dramatic tension

When reading a scene in a play, ask yourself:

- What could the characters be thinking or feeling?
- What are they hiding?
- What do they want?
- What could develop from the current situation?

Now ask yourself these questions in relation to the extract.

Reading a play

Plays are usually set out on the page as in the extract below.

In this extract, Laura plans to run away from home because she feels guilty about being involved in a hit-and-run car accident. Kaninda intends to stow away aboard a ship back to Africa. He has just passed a test ('the run') to get into a local gang. At the end of it, Laura saved his life.

LAURA	Troubles I got. Look at me! All dressed up for running off, hitching a lift in a lorry somewhere – but I've got no plan how.
	Kaninda puts a hand on her shoulder.
KANINDA	(*looking across at the sugar ship and back again*) What troubles you got?
LAURA	Big troubles.
	She waves them away.
	And Kaninda, I didn't know about the run.
KANINDA	Gets me what I want, just.
	*Kaninda takes a tissue from his pocket with which he wipes the tears from **Laura's** cheeks.*
LAURA	(*staring at **Kaninda** she has a sudden change of mind*) No, I'd better go back.
	*She takes the tissue from **Kaninda**.*
	But I can't go back home like this, can I?
	She cleans off her make-up with her own tears.
	Thank you, Kaninda.
KANINDA	(*helping her*) It's me who thanks.
LAURA	You're not upset about what I did to you?
	Kaninda shakes his head, shrugs.
KANINDA	I thank you always.
LAURA	Always? For saving you?
	Breaking away, looking across at the ship.
	I've made up my mind, Kaninda. When you go off on your ship to Mozambique, on whatever tide…
KANINDA	Who said this?
LAURA	I'm coming with you.

Bernard Ashley, *The Play of Little Soldier*

> Read the extract aloud, ideally with a partner, emphasising different possible interpretations. For example, how much does Kaninda like Laura? Could a romance develop, or is he anxious to get rid of her? Is she using him, or does he really like him? Act out the scene following the stage directions, and adding body language to fit your interpretation.

Progress Check

1. How do we learn about the characters in a play performance?
2. How does the playwright (author) indicate how characters should speak and move?
3. Why is dramatic tension necessary?

Worked questions

Read the following extract and then answer the questions that follow.

They held him with his back against the wall, pinning his arms. Kevin came up close, until his breath was on Elliot's face.

'Hello, Elliot. Were you thinking we'd forgotten you?'

He said nothing. Responding could only make it worse.

'Answer when you're spoken to.'

'No.'

'No what?'

'No – I hadn't forgotten you.'

'You're a loser, Elliot, you know that?'

'I...know that.'

Kevin smiled. 'There's a place for people like you, Elliot. It's called the rubbish tip. Why do you keep on turning up for school? You know we're always going to be waiting, ready to put you back where you belong.' He reached forward and ripped the front breast pocket of Elliot's blazer. It hung like a dead tongue.

Then he did the same to the other pockets.

For a moment, Elliot felt nothing. Then something inside him shifted. Suddenly, terrifyingly, like nothing he'd experienced before, white-hot rage erupted. It consumed him, uncontrollable, an exploding fire-storm, lunatic fury. He tore free of the hands pinning him and hurled himself at Kevin and hit him, hit him again, again, again –

'I'll *kill* you, I'll *kill* you, *kill* you, *kill* you!'

They wrenched him off and threw him against the wall. The back of his head smashed against the tiles, and he felt sick.

Slowly Kevin got up. He wiped blood off his mouth.

'You're going to wish you never did that.'

Elliot's rage was gone. Instead, he was blissfully numb. Everything was clear to him now. He would be dead very soon. But really, they'd already killed him a long time ago. So they couldn't hurt him any more.

'You can't kill me,' he said. 'I'm already dead.'

Graham Gardner, *Inventing Elliot*

1. **What impression of Kevin do you get in the extract, and how?** *(4 marks)*

Kevin seems to enjoy his power over Elliot, even though he apparently needs other bullies to back him up. The way he comes right up close <u>suggests a kind of intimacy in their relationship</u>,[1] although it is based on Kevin's power and Elliot's fear. He likes to think that perhaps their latest attack has shattered Elliot's hopes of being left in peace.

> 1. Subtle interpretation of detail

Kevin's 'Answer when you're spoken to' <u>shows that he is demanding the kind of respect that someone in authority has</u>.[2] He smiles because he is enjoying himself, and because he feels confident that Elliot cannot fight back. He enjoys his power, as shown when he rips his pockets.

> 2. Interprets the actual words Kevin speaks

When Elliot actually does fight back, Kevin does not seem unnerved. He gets up 'slowly', probably because he still feels in charge and is therefore in no hurry. His threat, 'You're going to wish you never did that,' <u>suggests that he enjoys the psychological power as much as actually hurting Elliot</u>.[3]

> 3. Good interpretation

2. **What is the narrative viewpoint, and why do you think the author chooses it?** *(3 marks)*

The viewpoint is third person, but from Elliot's perspective. This means that the author can show us Elliot's thoughts and feelings, as in <u>'For a moment, Elliot felt nothing.'</u>[1] We are encouraged to identify with Elliot, the <u>protagonist</u>[2] of the novel. We are not led to identify in the same way with Kevin: we only see his actions and hear his words.

> 1. Uses evidence
>
> 2. Uses correct technical term

3. **Describe what three stages Elliot passes through, and how we know.** *(6 marks)*

The only sign of what Elliot is thinking or feeling at first is in 'Responding could only make it worse,' which implies that he just wants to keep his pain and humiliation to a minimum. There is no mention of fear or shock, <u>perhaps because he is used to this</u>.[1] The sentence 'For a moment, Elliot felt nothing' belongs to this first phase: he is numbly resigned to being bullied.

> 1. Reasonable interpretation

<u>The next stage is signalled by 'Then something inside him shifted.'</u>[2] He is suddenly overcome by fury. The word <u>'terrifyingly' suggests that even he is shocked by this, afraid of his own anger</u>.[3] The phrase 'lunatic fury' adds to this sense of his being out of control, but also implies that he is mad to retaliate, because, as Kevin warns him, he will soon regret it.

> 2. Topic sentence showing how the text works
>
> 3. Focus on meaning of one important word choice

In the third stage, following on from his head smashing against the tiles, Elliot feels 'blissfully numb'. He has expressed his anger, and now he feels nothing, as if he is <u>so resigned to his fate that he is under anaesthetic</u>.[4] To say that he is 'already dead' is a very extreme statement of this resignation.

> 4. Good interpretation, well expressed

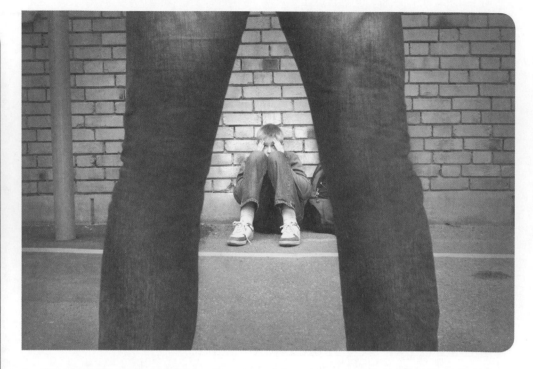

4. Comment on how the author uses language to bring to life what the characters do. *(6 marks)*

1. Makes point about form of text, then explains how it works

2. Refers to simile succinctly with embedded quote

3. Awareness of how paragraphing affects impact

4. Topic sentence

5. Infers meaning

6. Effective use of evidence

The author emphasises Kevin's relaxed attitude to tormenting Elliot by <u>slowing down the pace before Elliot attacks him. This is achieved by</u>[1] describing his actions in detail: 'He reached forward...'. The short sentence with <u>the 'dead tongue' simile</u>[2] also slows the pace down, as the moment itself is hanging, motionless, like a dead tongue. Finally, the line 'Then he did the same to the other pockets,' <u>a paragraph on its own</u>,[3] slows the pace even further, emphasising Kevin's slow, deliberate manner. After this, Elliot's sudden retaliation is even more dramatic.

<u>The language is most vivid in describing Elliot's retaliation</u>.[4] The phrase 'white-hot rage erupted' suggests the intense heat of a <u>volcano erupting</u>[5] – an uncontrollable force. The language is violent, but it also implies Elliot being taken over, not actually being in control: 'It consumed him'. It is as if he is being burned up by his own anger. The author chooses several powerful verbs to convey violence on both sides: <u>'tore', 'hurled', 'hit', 'wrenched' and 'smashed'</u>.[6]

5. The extract occurs at the start of the novel. What themes do you think the novel is likely to explore? *(4 marks)*

1. Makes an obvious point well

2. Expands on first point based on language

The extract suggests that the novel is <u>likely to focus on the theme of bullying</u>,[1] perhaps more widely exploring power and self-control, particularly because of the language, <u>such as 'erupted'</u>,[2] suggesting that Elliot can only defend himself if he loses control. How the basic bullying theme is developed will depend on how Elliot's character develops.

Practice questions

1. Read the extract below carefully, then answer the questions which follow.

Sade (pronounced Shad-deh) is on her way home from school when Marcia and Donna step out from behind her.

'There's something we want to show you,' declared Donna, once again linking her arm into Sade's.

'Yeah, it's important!' Marcia sidled up on her other side.

'I don't want to see anything. Excuse me,' Sade said tensely, making her limbs rigid as she felt herself being turned around. An elderly man hobbled past and a group of older Avon students were approaching them. Surely these two girls couldn't force her to go with them in full view of everyone?

'Excuse me!' Donna's voice tinkled with laughter as if Sade had just told a great joke.

'Look here, we were only going to do you a favour. Show you something. Help you pass the test.' Marcia was matter-of-fact as she twirled one of her slim braids between her fingers.

'I told you she wouldn't know about the test!' Donna bantered. 'Even if you don't come with us, you'll still have to do it, you know!'

The Avon students had passed by them, absorbed in conversation, taking no notice of Marcia, Donna and Sade.

'Test?' Sade mumbled. 'What test?'

'Right, Marcie! Let's show her. Top speed. We don't want to be late for Morrissy, do we, Sha-day-aday?' Donna giggled. Sade was propelled around and found herself being marched so rapidly that they were practically jogging down the road. She was being towed between the two girls, almost like a rag doll.

Beverley Naidoo, *The Other Side of Truth*

a) What do the verbs 'declared' and 'sidled' suggest about the mood and attitude of Donna and Marcia in the first two paragraphs? *(2 marks)*

b) What is implied about Donna and Marcia in the fourth, fifth and sixth paragraphs (beginning 'Excuse me!', 'Look here' and 'I told you')? *(2 marks)*

c) How does the language suggest who is in control in the final paragraph? *(3 marks)*

d) What is Sade's reaction to Donna and Marcia throughout the extract, and how is it revealed? *(3 marks)*

Learning Summary

After completing this chapter you should know:
- about rhythm, metre and poetic form
- how poets use similes, metaphors and personification
- about rhyme and other sound effects
- what a poem's 'voice' is
- how to write about poems.

26

4.1 What is a poem?

Poems were originally meant to be **sung**, or at least **spoken aloud**. Reading poems on the page is a relatively recent development. This tells us that the sound of a poem is very important. In fact, in a good poem, the sound, form and literal meaning of the words all combine to create the whole meaning of the poem.

A famous poet was once asked what one of his poems 'meant'. He answered that if he could explain that, it would not have been necessary to write the poem. So never treat reading a poem as a translation exercise. Remember:
- Every element of the poem contributes to the meaning.
- A poem can have many meanings, or layers of meaning.
- Your response to a poem is valid, if you can back it up with evidence from the poem.

If you had to define a poem, you could say that it is a piece of writing expressing ideas and emotions, and which tries to do so in a fresh way that makes them come alive for the reader, and in which the poet has chosen every word carefully for meaning and sound, to create an impact as part of a whole structure of words.

Approaching a poem

When you first read a poem, you may be baffled by it, and wonder what you could possibly find to say about it. So, here is an approach to reading a poem.

1. Read it aloud at least once, then again silently. Listen to how it sounds – the individual words and the rhythm. Notice how it looks on the page. Notice how the poet has divided the lines, but read to the punctuation, not just the end of each line.
2. Now read it highlighting words or phrases that particularly interest or appeal to you, or which seem significant.
3. Ask yourself what overall emotional mood or tone the word suggests. For example, does the poet seem happy, angry, mournful, in love? Does the tone or mood change as the poem progresses?

4. Ask yourself if the poem has a particular 'voice': is the poet just expressing his own ideas and feelings as himself, or is there a **persona** – an imagined speaker?

5. Are there any images (word pictures in the form of similes or metaphors) that strike you, and that suggest a mood or tone?

6. Is the poem in a particular form – e.g. a **sonnet**?

7. Finally, what does it seem to be about? Is there a 'message'? For example, if it is about a battle, does the poet seem to feel that war is glorious, or tragic? Does the poem tell a story?

Practising on a poem

Read the following poem, approaching it in the way suggested above. When you have read it once, read it again, paying attention to the notes. Ozymandias is a name for the ancient Egyptian pharaoh Ramesses II.

'Ozymandias', by Percy, Bysshe Shelley (1792–1822)

I met a traveller from an antique land[1]
Who said: 'Two vast and trunkless legs of stone
Stand in the desert.[2] Near them on the sand,
Half sunk, a shattered visage[3] lies, whose frown
And wrinkled lip and sneer of cold command
Tell that its sculptor well those passions read
Which yet survive, stamped on these lifeless things,
The hand that mocked[4] them and the heart that fed.[5]
And on the pedestal these words appear:
"My name is Ozymandias, King of Kings:
Look on my works, ye mighty, and despair!"[6]
Nothing beside remains.[7] Round the decay
Of that colossal wreck, boundless and bare,
The lone and level sands stretch far away.'[8]

1. He says this is a traveller's tale. What is the effect of this, and the phrase 'antique land', in place of a country name?

2. What is your first impression of what is being described? Is it frightening, mysterious, funny?

3. *Visage* means face. Whose face? How would 'smashed up face' have a different effect?

4. *Mocked* here means 'copied', but with a hint of the modern meaning. The 'passions…survive' (outlive) the sculptor, in the sculpture itself.

5. Does this mean the sculptor's heart 'fed' on his master, or 'fed' the artistic work of the sculpture – or both?

6. A voice within a voice – the words inscribed on the statue's base. What did Ozymandias mean?

7. What is the effect of this short, plain line, coming straight after Ozymandias's words?

8. What feeling do you get from this ending? Does it contain a message?

Stand, and read the final five lines of the Shelley poem aloud. Put suitable expression into your voice. Use gestures to add to the meaning.

Writing about a poem

If you have worked your way through the stages under 'Approaching a poem', and made some notes on the poem itself, you could then produce a **mind map** or **spidergram** to help you plan a response to a poem. For 'Ozymandias' it might begin like this.

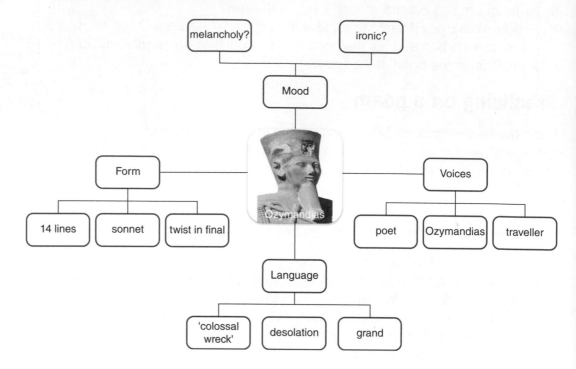

Write about each aspect in turn, perhaps with a paragraph on each. Make sure you provide evidence for what you say. You could use the **PEE** (Point, Evidence, Explanation) technique.

Example

Shelley leaves us with a view of the landscape around the broken statue which creates a mood of desolation and despair. The words 'decay', 'wreck', 'bare' and 'lone' give an impression of the destruction left by time, and the bleak emptiness of the desert. This is in ironic contrast to Ozymandias's self-image as 'King of Kings'. His greatness has been reduced to nothing.

Progress Check

1. Why should you read poems aloud?
2. What creates the 'meaning' of a poem?
3. How many 'voices' are there in 'Ozymandias'?
4. What should you always provide when writing about a poem?

4.2 Rhythm, metre and poetic form

Rhythm

You are already familiar with the concept of **rhythm**. Any piece of music has a rhythm: it is a quality of timing and repeated emphasis, or beats. In poetry, the rhythm is created by the stressed and unstressed syllables.

When we speak, we naturally stress some words, or **syllables** (pronounceable bits of words) more than others. If we did not do this we would sound like robots! Try saying the lines below naturally. As you do, notice how you emphasise some words and parts of words. You may notice this as your voice rising up on some words or syllables.

- I want a banana.
- We used to sing and dance about.
- I have a cousin in Australia.

Rhythm in poetry uses the natural rhythms of speech, but repeats particular rhythms for effect. One of the commonest rhythms is **iambic pentameter**, which has five pairs of unstressed and stressed syllables in each line. Shelley's poem 'Ozymandias' is in iambic pentameter. Here is a line with the stresses marked. Speak it aloud and tap out the stresses to hear them for yourself.

I <u>met</u> a <u>tra</u>veller <u>from</u> an <u>an</u>tique <u>land</u>

Why do poets use rhythm?

Poets use rhythm to give shape to the poem, and to make its emotion easier to absorb. Sometimes, too, the rhythm echoes the subject or mood of the poem. See if you think this is true of the following poem by modern poet Adrian Mitchell.

> Shakespeare uses iambic pentameter. See Topic 1.6 for a more detailed explanation.

Stufferation

Lovers lie around in it
Broken glass is found in it
Grass
I like that stuff

Tuna fish get trapped in it
Legs come wrapped in it
Nylon
I like that stuff

Eskimos and tramps chew it
Madame Tussaud gave status to it
Wax
I like that stuff

Elephants get sprayed with it
Scotch is made with it
Water
I like that stuff

Breaking the rhythm

Poets do not use rhythm in a completely regular, predictable way. From time to time, they break the rhythm in a way that contributes to the meaning and emotional impact of the poem. Look again at part of Shelley's poem:

> And on the pedestal these words appear:
>
> 'My name is Ozymandias, King of Kings:
> Look on my works, ye mighty, and despair!'
> Nothing beside remains.

Here the smooth iambic rhythm is suddenly broken. You could interpret this as happening with 'Look', but it definitely happens with 'Nothing'. Try reading this line with the normal iambic stresses:

> No<u>thing</u> be<u>side</u> re<u>mains</u>.

This would sound odd. Instead, the sense makes us stress it like this:

> <u>Noth</u>ing be<u>side</u> re<u>mains</u>.

This makes a strong break in sense, contrasting the boastful words of Ozymandias – a great Egyptian pharaoh – with the fact that his great 'works', his city and empire, have vanished almost without trace. There is even a possible double meaning here: 'Nothing *else* remains' and 'There is nothing here *but* remains.' The break in the rhythm helps to slow us down to take in that possibility.

Metre and verse form

A poem's **metre** is any set structure that its rhythm makes. So, 'Ozymandias' is in iambic pentameter, the metre being one of repeated lines of five feet each, a foot here being a pair of syllables.

Read Mitchell's poem 'Stufferation' again. Is this in the same rhythm as 'Ozymandias'? Is it in the same metre? If you're on your own, not on the school bus or a library, try singing it, beating out the rhythm. You will find that it has a definite rhythmic pattern, repeated in each verse – a metre.

Some poems are written in a particular **verse form**. Shelley's 'Ozymandias' is a **sonnet**: a poem with 14 lines of iambic pentameter in which the first 8 lines (the **octave**) establish an idea, and then the final six lines (the **sestet**) comment on it, or develop it. See if that is true in 'Ozymandias'.

Another verse form is the **ballad**. This is a traditional form, originally used in songs. Samuel Taylor Coleridge (1772–1834) used it in his *The Rime of the Ancient Mariner* because he wanted to write in a 'folk' style, in something like the language of ordinary people. It is about an old sailor who had a terrible experience at sea, being left the only man alive on his ship.

Here is one famous verse of Coleridge's poem:

> Water, water, every where,
> And all the boards did shrink;
> Water, water, every where,
> Nor any drop to drink.

Tap this out as you say it aloud. You will find that it is also in an iambic rhythm, but that it has only four pairs of syllables in a line.

> Some poems, like Adrian Mitchell's 'Stufferation', use rhyme and rhythm to reinforce each other. See Topic 4.5.

Progress Check

1. How many pairs of syllables are there in a line of iambic pentameter?
2. What is a poem's metre?
3. What is the verse form of Shelley's poem 'Ozymandias'?

4.3 Similes and metaphors

Similes and metaphors are both types of **imagery**. They can also be referred to as examples of **figurative language**. They create vivid **word pictures** by comparing one thing to something else.

Similes

Similes are more obvious, because they always use 'like', 'as' or 'than' in the comparison.

Similes in an older poem

Coleridge in *The Rime of the Ancient Mariner* uses a number of similes:

> Day after day, day after day,
> We stuck, nor breath nor motion;
> As idle as a painted ship
> Upon a painted ocean.

This vividly describes the ship being becalmed when there is no wind. Painters in Coleridge's day often painted ships, so his readers would understand this simile easily. The repetition of 'day after day' and 'painted' also adds to this sense of things being the same from one day to the next.

A little further on, Coleridge uses another simile to describe a strange, frightening, supernatural effect on the sea, this time using the word 'like':

> About, about, in reel and rout
> The death-fires danced at night;
> The water, like a witch's oils,
> Burnt green, and blue and white.

This makes us imagine 'oils' that a witch might use in a spell, or perhaps as in oil painting. The association with witchcraft certainly suggests that there is something unnatural and evil going on.

A final simile in this poem uses 'than'. The sailors find they are dumb, from thirst and perhaps from being cursed:

> And every tongue, through utter drought,
> Was withered at the root;
> We could not speak, no more than if
> We had been choked with soot.

This simile makes us imagine how the sailors felt, because it so vividly appeals to the senses. Can you imagine being 'choked with soot'? It would have been even easier for Coleridge's readers, in the days of coal fires.

Similes in a more modern poem

Modern poets also use similes. See how Ted Hughes uses them:

1. As if the 'depth' of water is huge to a fish, like the sky to us

2. Cosy – hibernating?

3. Combines a metaphor and a simile (sees the night as a 'starry aeroplane'); stars like nuts, echoing opening lines

4. Wandering

5. Pale-faced (a barn owl?), motionless, looking down

The Warm and the Cold

Freezing dusk is closing
  Like a slow trap of steel
On trees and roads and hills and all
  That can no longer feel.
    <u>But the carp is in its depth</u>
      <u>Like the planet in its heaven.</u>[1]
    And the badger in its bedding
      <u>Like a loaf in the oven.</u>[2]
    And the butterfly in its mummy
      Like a viol in its case.
    And the owl in its feathers
      Like a doll in its lace.
<u>Freezing dusk has tightened</u>
  <u>Like a nut screwed tight</u>
<u>On the starry aeroplane</u>
  <u>Of the soaring night.</u>[3]
    But the trout is in its hole
      Like a chuckle in a sleeper.
    <u>The hare strays down the highway</u>
      <u>Like a root going deeper.</u>[4]
    The snail is dry in the outhouse
      Like a seed in a sunflower.
    <u>The owl is pale on the gatepost</u>
      <u>Like a clock on its tower.</u>[5]

Ted Hughes

How do they fit?

All these similes make comparisons that make the thing described more vivid. Notice how all the comparisons hold true only in some ways. For example, 'freezing dusk' is like 'a slow trap of steel' in more than one way:

- Steel is cold and not comforting.
- Freezing dusk gradually makes water seize up by freezing it; it 'traps' it.
- The trap is 'slow' because the temperature gradually drops.
- It is a trap because it cannot be escaped.

However, there are obvious differences too. This brings the comparison into focus.

Metaphors

Metaphors are similar to similes, but more condensed. Instead of using 'like', 'as' or 'than', they speak of one thing as if it actually *is* another thing.

For example, John Donne wrote of his mistress:

She's all states, and all princes I.

He compares her to all the countries in the world, and himself to their rulers.

Andrew Marvell in 'To His Coy Mistress' wrote:

And yonder all before us lie
Deserts of vast eternity.

Here, Marvell uses a metaphor to speak of eternity – the future – as a desert. In other words he speaks of time as space.

Shakespeare uses three related metaphors in one of his sonnets in which he speaks of himself as an old man:

> Find a number of objects in your room. Examine them closely. How could you use them in similes or metaphors for something quite different? For example, how could a closed book be like a person?

Sonnet 73

That time of year thou mayst in me behold
When yellow leaves, or none, or few, do hang
Upon those boughs which shake against the cold,
Bare ruin'd choirs, where late the sweet birds sang.[1]
In me thou seest the twilight of such day
As after sunset fadeth in the west,
Which by and by black night doth take away,
Death's second self, that seals up all in rest.[2]
In me thou see'st the glowing of such fire
That on the ashes of his youth doth lie,
As the death-bed whereon it must expire
Consumed with that which it was nourish'd by.[3]
    This thou perceivest, which makes thy love more strong,
    To love that well which thou must leave ere long.[4]

1. Sees himself as winter, characterised by bare, birdless branches

2. Sees himself as the end of a day with night, like death, approaching

3. Sees himself as a dying fire sinking down to ashes

4. Concludes that as he has little life left, his lover should make the most of him now!

---

1. Similes always use one of three words to signal comparison. What are they?
2. How is a metaphor different from a simile?
3. What three things does Shakespeare compare himself to in the Sonnet 73 metaphors?

Progress Check

4.4 Personification

Personification is a technique similar to metaphor, in which something abstract, such as time, life, love or war is described as if it were **a person, a god or an animal**. It is found more often in older poems, but poets do still use it today.

Time

Time is often personified. In Andrew Marvell's poem 'To His Coy Mistress', quoted in Topic 4.3, he portrays time like this:

> *But at my back I always hear*
> *Time's wingèd chariot hurrying near.*

This is a poem in which he is urging the woman he loves to enjoy their love before it is too late. It is appropriate to describe time as driving a winged chariot, because that would move quickly. In a way, time here is almost seen as the same thing as death.

War

War is often associated with savage dogs. William Wordsworth in 'The Female Vagrant' writes that anything is better than making one's living from the suffering of war:

1. Pictures Want (Poverty) as living in a lonely cave

2. Does not want to be like a dog at the heels of its master (war), wading in blood

3. Pictures the rest of the 'brood' of dogs feeding on war

...better far
In <u>Want's</u>[1] most lonely cave till death to pine,
Unseen, unheard, unwatched by any star;
Or in the streets and walks where proud men are,
Better our dying bodies to obtrude,
Than dog-like, <u>wading at the heels of war</u>,[2]
Protract a curst existence, with the brood
That lap (their very nourishment!) <u>their brother's blood</u>.[3]

Nature

Shelley in 'Ode to the West Wind' addresses the wind as a chariot-driving god whose sister is Spring:

> O thou
> Who chariotest to their dark wintry bed
> The wingèd seeds, where they lie cold and low,
> Each like a corpse within its grave, until
> Thine azure sister of the Spring shall blow
> Her clarion o'er the dreaming earth.

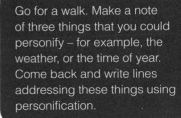

Go for a walk. Make a note of three things that you could personify – for example, the weather, or the time of year. Come back and write lines addressing these things using personification.

Progress Check

1. What type of image is personification similar to?
2. What is personification?
3. How does Wordsworth personify war?

4.5 Rhyme

 30

It is hard to define **rhyme**, but essentially it is an appealing combination of **similarity** and **difference** in sound when two words are heard close together. This combination creates a sense of harmony. At one time, when poems were sung or recited, rhyme helped the poets to **remember** the poem. There is also a strange quality about rhyme: it gives the words a sort of **authority**, as if they must be true.

Many poems rhyme, but it is certainly not essential. Some of the best poems, especially modern ones, do not rhyme. When you read a poem, do not focus closely on the rhyme, or regard each rhyme as the end of a sentence: simply read according to sense and punctuation.

Rhyme schemes

Poets use rhyme to structure their poems, often using a **rhyme scheme**, which is a pattern of rhyme. A rhyme scheme can be indicated using letters, like this:

Twas brillig, and the slithy toves	A
Did gyre and gimble in the wabe:	B
All mimsy were the borogoves,	A
And the mome raths outgrabe.	B

A new letter is used to indicate each new rhyme. In this fantasy ballad by Lewis Carroll, the rhymes help to make us 'believe' in his made-up words.

Different verse forms have set rhyme schemes. For example, if you look back at Shakespeare's sonnet on page 75, you will see that its rhyme scheme is ABAB, CDCD, etc., until it ends with a **rhyming couplet**, a pair of rhyming lines that give a sense of completion.

Within the rhyme scheme, poets use rhyme as part of the structure of the poem. They also use it to give emphasis to particular words. In the poem below, Emily Brontë uses rhyme to reinforce the power of the **refrain** repeated, with a slight variation, in each verse. She also uses a **half-rhyme** in the final verse to give a sense of unease. Read it out. Which words *almost* rhyme, but not quite?

Draw a picture suggesting the key elements of the poem 'Spellbound'. ('Wastes' means moorland.)

Spellbound

The night is darkening round me,
The wild winds coldly blow;
But a tyrant spell has bound me
And I cannot, cannot go.

The giant trees are bending
Their bare boughs weighed with snow.
And the storm is fast descending,
And yet I cannot go.

Clouds beyond clouds above me,
Wastes beyond wastes below;
But nothing drear can move me;
I will not, cannot go.

Progress Check

1. What two main elements does a rhyme contain?
2. What is a 'rhyme scheme', and how can it be indicated?
3. What is a rhyming couplet, and how is it used at the end of some poems?
4. What is a half-rhyme and how does Emily Brontë use one?

4.6 Alliteration and assonance 31

Alliteration

Alliteration is the technique of repeating **consonant** (non-vowel) sounds, especially at the beginnings of words. It can simply give a sense of pleasing harmony, often adding to the sense of harmony created by rhyme. It can also be used to help convey the sense of the poem.

See how John Keats uses alliteration in the first verse of his 'Ode to a Nightingale'. He is trying to give us a sense of how the song of the nightingale makes him feel as if he has drunk hemlock, or taken opium a minute ago and fallen into the River Lethe, the river of forgetfulness.

> My heart aches, and a drowsy numbness pains
>   My sense, as though of hemlock I had drunk,
> Or emptied some dull opiate to the drains
>   One minute past, and Lethe-wards had sunk:
> 'Tis not through envy of thy happy lot,
>   But being too happy in thine happiness,—
>   That thou, light-winged Dryad of the trees
>   In some melodious plot
> Of beechen green, and shadows numberless,
>   Singest of summer in full-throated ease.

Where can you find 'd' sounds in the first three lines that add to the sense of dull, muffled drowsiness? Where can you find 'h' sounds connecting two words in these lines? What sound is repeated in the final line, and what feeling does it create?

Assonance

Assonance, often used with **alliteration**, is the **repetition of vowel sounds**, especially in the middle of words. It usually creates a sense of harmony, though it can also make a connection between two or more words. Edgar Allan Poe (1809–49) uses it in 'The Bells'. See the highlighted vowel sounds. Read the verse out, listening for the assonance.

> Hear the m<u>e</u>llow w<u>e</u>dding b<u>e</u>lls,
>   Golden b<u>e</u>lls!
> What a world of happiness their
> <u>ha</u>rmony foretells!
>   Through the <u>ba</u>lmy air of night
>   How they ring out their delight!
>   From the m<u>o</u>lten-g<u>o</u>lden n<u>o</u>tes,
>   And all in tune,
>   What a liquid ditty floats
> To the turtle-dove that listens, while
> she gloats
>   On the moon!

Progress Check

1. What kind of sounds is alliteration applied to – consonants or vowels?
2. What technique is used in the line 'The flute tutor snoozing in his tomb'?
3. How does Keats use 'd' sounds in 'Ode to a Nightingale'?
4. What is the commonest effect of assonance?

4.7 The poem's 'voice'

The **voice** of a poem can refer to the tone in which the poet speaks. For example, in 'Ode to a Nightingale' (page 79) Keats speaks in a dreamlike but intimate way, sharing his feelings with us. However, it can also refer to a **persona**, a created character that we are supposed to imagine speaking the lines, as in the following poem.

The persona is that of a working man who has enlisted in the army just because he is out of work and has already sold his possessions. A simple man, he seems to accept that you have to kill an enemy in war. Yet he says it is 'quaint and curious' that he had to kill a man very much like himself.

Hardy's poem is not as simple as it seems. He uses the persona to make a political point: the working-class poor on both sides of a war have a lot in common, and no real reason to kill each other. This might be more effective than simply writing an obviously anti-war poem.

Read the Hardy poem aloud in a local working-class accent. Imagine you are the man sitting casually telling someone about the experience. Act out his tone and body language.

The Man He Killed, by Thomas Hardy

'Had he and I but met
    By some old ancient inn,
We should have sat us down to <u>wet</u>
    <u>Right many a nipperkin</u>!¹

    'But ranged as infantry,
    And staring face to face,
I shot at him as he at me,
    And killed him in his <u>place</u>.²

    'I shot him dead because —
    Because he was my foe,
Just so: my foe of course he was;
    <u>That's clear enough</u>;³ although

    'He thought he'd '<u>list, perhaps,</u>
    <u>Off-hand like</u>⁴ — just as I —
Was out of work — had sold his traps —
    No other reason why.

    'Yes; quaint and curious war is!
    You shoot a fellow down
You'd treat if met where any bar is,
    Or <u>help to half-a-crown</u>.'⁵

1. Working man; uses slang, such as *nipperkin* (a half-pint jar): they would have drunk beer together

2. Simple language and rhymes suggest he is a simple man

3. Does not question the simple argument: you have to kill an enemy

4. Begins to see enemy as like himself; enlisted casually, out of work

5. Generous. Says he might have lent the man money in other circumstances. Half-a-crown was a coin, equivalent to an eighth of a pound

1. What two things can the voice of a poem be?
2. How does Hardy use language to create a persona?
3. What point is Hardy making?

Progress Check

Worked questions

1. **Read the poem below and comment on how the poet uses rhythm, rhyme and language techniques to bring his subject to life.** *(12 marks)*

Sea Fever, John Masefield

I must go down to the seas again, to the lonely sea and the sky,
And all I ask is a tall ship and a star to steer her by,
And the wheel's kick and the wind's song and the white sail's shaking,
And a grey mist on the sea's face, and a grey dawn breaking.

I must go down to the seas again, for the call of the running tide
Is a wild call and a clear call that may not be denied;
And all I ask is a windy day with the white clouds flying,
And the flung spray and the blown spume, and the sea-gulls crying.

I must go down to the seas again, to the vagrant gypsy life,
To the gull's way and the whale's way, where the wind's like a whetted
    knife;
And all I ask is a merry yarn from a laughing fellow-rover,
And quiet sleep and a sweet dream when the long trick's over.

The poem expresses the poet's <u>love of the sea and his desire to be a sea wanderer,</u>[1] living 'the vagrant gypsy life' again. The strong, rolling rhythm suggests the motion of the sea, or the breaking of waves. It also conveys his enthusiasm for the sea.

Each stanza begins with the same phrase, suggesting compulsion, particularly in the words 'I must'. <u>This is echoed by the poet saying that the sea's 'call' 'cannot be denied': he has no choice</u>.[2] There is further repetition in 'And all I ask', suggesting that the sea offers everything he could need: the ship and a star to steer by, windy weather, and the company of fellow sailors.

<u>The poem's language creates a strong impression of the sea, and how Masefield regards it</u>.[3] What appeals to him is the sea's energy, reflected in the rhythm. He wants 'the wheel's kick and the wind's song' – the energy of the waves transferring itself into the 'kick' of the steering wheel, and the noise of the wind sounding like a song to a man who loves it. <u>The alliteration of 'wheel', 'wind's' and 'white' add to the sense of energy, as if the wind is whipping a sail repeatedly</u>.[4] There is a similar use of alliteration in the second stanza: 'windy day...white', and again in the third, with the repeated 'way', 'wind's' and 'whetted'.

<u>Masefield's view of the sea could be seen as rather idealised</u>.[5] The phrase 'vagrant gypsy life' suggests that he just wants to wander, not work or sail anywhere for a purpose. Similarly the idea of 'a merry yarn from a laughing fellow-rover' is one-sided – not at all like Coleridge's view of the sailor's life in *The Rime of the Ancient Mariner*. <u>Masefield uses assonance in 'merry...fellow' and 'yarn...laughing' to add to the feeling of harmony that he expects to find.</u>[6]

<u>Despite this</u>,[7] there is another side to the poem. The sea is 'lonely', and there is something mysterious in its personification with 'grey mist' on its face. There is also a sadness in the way rhythm breaks down at the end of each stanza, and in the actual words ending each stanza: 'breaking', 'crying' and 'over'. <u>In addition, the simile describing the wind as 'like a whetted knife' suggests discomfort. It is as if this is part of the sea's appeal</u>.[8]

---

1. Leads into commentary by summing up theme

2. Develops idea with a further point and evidence, then explains

3. Topic sentence: remainder of paragraph provides evidence

4. PEE, with imaginative interpretation

5. Topic sentence introducing new, slightly critical idea

6. Points out technique and explains effect

7. Signals a contradiction

8. Perfect PEE with embedded quote

Practice questions

1. **Read the following poem by Rudyard Kipling (1864–1936).**

The Way Through the Woods

They shut the road through the woods
Seventy years ago.
Weather and rain have undone it again,
And now you would never know
There was once a road through the woods
Before they planted the trees.
It is underneath the coppice and heath,
And the thin anemones.
Only the keeper sees
That, where the ring-dove broods,
And the badgers roll at ease,
There was once a road through the woods.

Yet, if you enter the woods
Of a summer evening late,
When the night-air cools on the trout-ringed pools
Where the otter whistles his mate,
(They fear not men in the woods,
Because they see so few.)
You will hear the beat of a horse's feet,
And the swish of a skirt in the dew,
Steadily cantering through
The misty solitudes,
As though they perfectly knew
The old lost road through the woods.
But there is no road through the woods.

Comment on how the poet uses language to create a sense of place and atmosphere. *(8 marks)*

2. **Read the following poem by Thomas Hardy (1840–1928).**

> **The Voice**
>
> Woman much missed, how you call to me, call to me,
> Saying that now you are not as you were
> When you had changed from the one who was all to me,
> But as at first, when our day was fair.
>
> Can it be you that I hear? Let me view you, then,
> Standing as when I drew near to the town
> Where you would wait for me: yes, as I knew you then,
> Even to the original air-blue gown!
>
> Or is it only the breeze, in its listlessness
> Travelling across the wet mead to me here,
> You being ever dissolved to wan wistlessness,
> Heard no more again far or near?
>
>   Thus I; faltering forward,
>   Leaves around me falling,
> Wind oozing thin through the thorn from norward,
>   And the woman calling.

Comment on how Hardy uses language and form to create mood and atmosphere.   *(8 marks)*

3. **Read the following poem by Siegfried Sassoon (1886–1967). It celebrates the end of the First World War.**

> **Everyone Sang**
>
> Everyone suddenly burst out singing;
> And I was filled with such delight
> As prisoned birds must find in freedom,
> Winging wildly across the white
> Orchards and dark-green fields; on – on – and out of sight.
>
> Everyone's voice was suddenly lifted;
> And beauty came like the setting sun:
> My heart was shaken with tears; and horror
> Drifted away ... O, but Everyone
> Was a bird; and the song was wordless; the singing will never be done.

Comment on how Sassoon uses language and form to convey joy and relief in this poem.

(8 marks)

Learning Summary

After completing this chapter you should know:
- what a sentence is
- how to use simple, coordinated and subordinated sentences
- how to vary your sentences for impact
- how to order information in a sentence
- how to write precisely and grammatically.

 33 **5.1** What is a sentence?

Defining a sentence

If you understand what a sentence is, you need never make the mistake of using a comma when you should start a new sentence, as in *The boat sank. We had to swim to shore.* See Topic 6.1.

In simple, non-technical terms, a **sentence** is a statement giving (or requesting) a piece of information that makes sense in itself. It should begin with a capital letter and end with a full stop, an exclamation mark or a question mark.

The following are all sentences:
- Would the boat float? (Question)
- It sank. (Statement)
- Jump! (Command)
- Help! (Exclamation)

You might say that 'It sank' makes no sense on its own. However, the slightly more technical definition of a statement sentence is:

Subject	+	Predicate		=	Sentence
What the sentence is about		Information about the subject, including a verb			
It (The boat)		*sank.*			

The word 'It' is a **pronoun**: a word which stands in for a **noun**, so it can be the subject.

So, 'It' is not a sentence on its own, and nor is 'sank', but together they make a sentence.

Progress Check

1. What is a *subject* in a sentence?
2. What is a *predicate*?
3. What punctuation should a *command* sentence end with?
4. What is a *pronoun*?

5.2 Using simple sentences 34

What is a simple sentence?

A **simple sentence** that is a statement consists of a **subject** and a **predicate**.

Simple sentences can be very effective, but if you use too many together they can make your writing sound jerky:

Liza went to the well. She fetched a bucket of water. She brought it back to the house. The floor was dirty. Liza mopped it. She did it thoroughly. It was as if her life depended on it.

This would be better reworded and punctuated:

Liza went to the well and fetched a bucket of water, and brought it back to the house. The floor was dirty, so she mopped it thoroughly – as if her life depended on it.

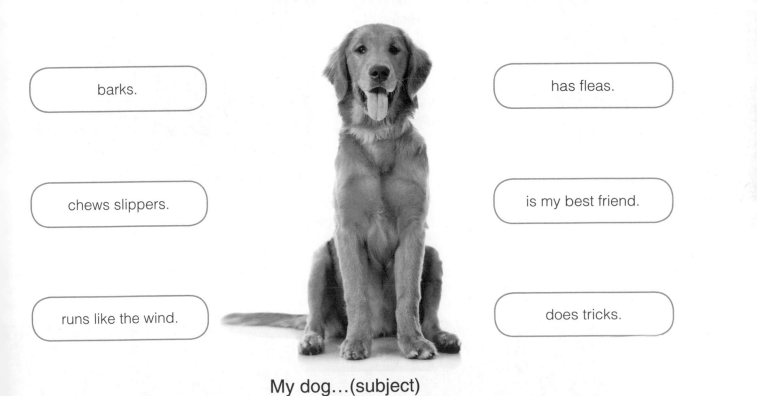

barks.

has fleas.

chews slippers.

is my best friend.

runs like the wind.

does tricks.

My dog…(subject)

Using simple sentences for dramatic impact

Short simple sentences often have a dramatic impact. How do they express the speaker's tone and mood here?

'I'm tired of saying this. Don't leave dirty clothes on the floor. The floor is for walking on. Dirty clothes go in the washing basket. Clean clothes go in the drawer. Is that clear?'

Simple sentences can also be used to increase tension and pace in narrative:

> *She threw open the tent flap. The rifle was gone. She could hear grunts and pounding feet getting closer. The bear was in the clearing now. She turned to face it. The bear came to a sudden halt.*

Minor sentences

A **minor sentence** is a special type of simple sentence. It is punctuated like a normal sentence but is grammatically incomplete. Use these sparingly to create tension, or to give an impression of thoughts rushing through a character's mind:

She held her breath and listened. Silence. Just a soft sighing in the highest tree branches. Was the bear still lurking in the shadows? Waiting?

Which three of these are minor sentences? Rewrite them as grammatically complete sentences. Is this an improvement?

Stand up and close your eyes. Carefully move round your room, hands outstretched, till you have touched two or three objects. Make up simple sentences describing them as if you were a character in a novel. Include at least one minor sentence. Example: 'He felt something soft and warm. The cat!'

Progress Check

1. What does a simple sentence consist of?
2. What is the likely effect of using too many simple sentences in a row?
3. For what effect can a minor sentence be used?

5.3 Using coordinated sentences

A **coordinated sentence** (also called a *compound sentence*) joins two simple sentences using a **conjunction**. Examples of conjuctions are:

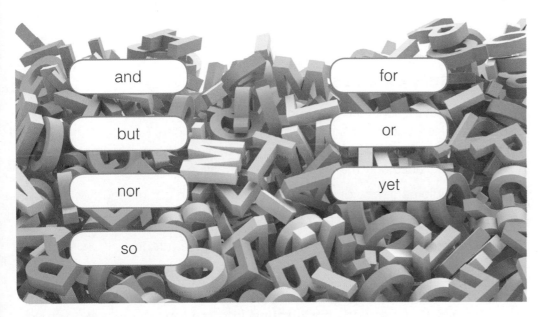

and	for
but	or
nor	yet
so	

Examples

- It's illegal **and** you could go to prison for it.
- I enjoy music **but** I can't play an instrument.
- The panda is an endangered species, **yet** they are still hunted.
- It's going to snow, **so** you'd better take a warm coat.

As you will see from the examples, the conjunction shows a relationship between the two parts of the sentence. For example, 'so' indicates a logical consequence; 'or' suggests an alternative; and 'but' implies a contradiction.

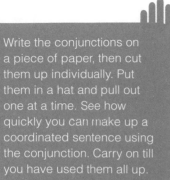

Have a go

See if you can join these simple sentences together using conjunctions from the list on page 89.

She finds maths challenging	make time to do it.
A pizza is not the ultimate in health food	he still eats junk food.
Learning to swim could save your life	he gets away with treating her badly.
Derren goes to the gym	she loves English.
She's devoted to Derren	I could put you under arrest.
You can come voluntarily	it makes a quick and easy meal.

Progress Check

1. What type of word joins the two halves of a coordinated sentence?
2. What does a word like *or* do as well as simply joining the two sentence halves?
3. Fill in with a conjunction: Van Gogh's paintings sell for millions, _____ he died in poverty.

36 | **5.4** # Using subordinated sentences

Subordinate clauses

A simple statement sentence (see Topic 5.2) could also be called a **clause**. A clause contains a subject (what it is about) and a predicate (a statement about the subject). A **subordinated sentence** is one containing a **subordinate clause**. A subordinate clause only makes sense in connection with the main clause.

Here is a simple sentence giving us some information about Mandy:

Mandy is running a marathon next week.

Here is the same sentence with a subordinate clause added:

Mandy, who used to pride herself on never exercising, is running a marathon next week.

The subordinate clause adds **background information**. This is true wherever it appears in the sentence. It could be at the beginning, like this:

Thinking that nothing was coming, he stepped out into the road.

Here, 'Thinking that nothing was coming' is not a sentence in itself because it does not contain a **finite verb**. In 'He thought that nothing was coming…', 'thought' is a finite verb; 'thinking' is not.

A subordinate clause could also go after the main clause:

She didn't invite Dan, assuming that he'd be too busy to come.

1. 1st subordinate clause, relating to Amir

A sentence can even use more than one subordinate clause:

She decided not to invite Amir, who would have talked about himself all evening,[1] which meant that she couldn't invite his friend Alfie either.[2]

2. 2nd subordinate clause, relating to her decision

Why use subordinated sentences?

Using a lot of simple or even coordinated sentences in a row can make your writing jerky. It can be more enjoyable to read, and more flowing in its sense, if you use a mixture of sentence types, including **subordinated sentences**.

Read the following passage and notice how the author uses a variety of sentence types, including subordinated sentences, to give a sense of a complex action.

The animals have taken over the farm, but the men try to recapture it. A pig, Napoleon, leads the defence from the rear.

It was a savage, bitter battle.[1] The men fired again and again, and, when the animals got to close quarters,[2] lashed out with their sticks and their heavy boots. A cow, three sheep, and two geese were killed, and nearly everyone was wounded. Even Napoleon, who was directing operations from the rear,[3] had the tip of his tail chipped by a pellet. But the men did not go unscathed either.[4] Three of them had their heads broken by blows from Boxer's hoofs; another was gored in the belly by a cow's horn; another had his trousers nearly torn off by Jessie and Bluebell. And when[5] the nine dogs of Napoleon's own bodyguard, whom he had instructed to make a detour under cover of the hedge,[6] suddenly appeared on the men's flank, baying ferociously, panic overtook them.[7] They saw that they were in danger of being surrounded. Frederick shouted to his men to get out while the going was good, and the next moment the cowardly enemy was running for dear life.

George Orwell, *Animal Farm*

Write four simple sentences on separate pieces of paper. Then write subordinate clauses adding information to them otn pieces of paper. Shuffle them and try to match them to make subordinated sentences. For example: 'The animals put up a brave fight', 'who love their farm'.

1. Simple statement sentence introduces the battle

2. Subordinate clause saying *when* they 'lashed out'

3. Subordinate clause giving information about Napoleon

4. Simple sentence introducing remainder of paragraph

5. Introduces subordinated sentence saying when 'panic overtook them'

6. Subordinate clause introduced by 'whom' because the dogs are the *object* of 'instructed'

7. Main clause – even though at end of sentence

---

1. What does a clause contain?
2. What kind of information does a subordinate clause provide?
3. A sentence can contain more than one subordinate clause. True or false?
4. Can a subordinated sentence contain two main clauses?

Progress Check

37

5.5 Varying sentence lengths for impact

Any piece of writing becomes boring if all the sentences are of the same length and type. However, sentence lengths can be varied for particular sorts of impact as well.

Short sentences for impact

Short sentences often have a dramatic impact, especially in dialogue. They can help to quicken the pace and create tension.

Read this example from Shakespeare's *Macbeth*. Macbeth and his wife are tense because Macbeth has just carried out their plan to murder King Duncan in his sleep. Notice the short sentences and questions, giving a sense of uncertainty.

> **MACBETH** I have done the deed. Didst thou not hear a noise?
>
> **LADY MACBETH** I heard the owl scream and the crickets cry. Did not you speak?
>
> **MACBETH** When?
>
> **LADY MACBETH** Now.
>
> **MACBETH** As I descended?
>
> **LADY MACBETH** Ay.
>
> **MACBETH** Hark! Who lies i' the second chamber?
>
> **LADY MACBETH** Donalbain.
>
> **MACBETH** (*looking on his hands*) This is a sorry sight.
>
> **LADY MACBETH** A foolish thought, to say a sorry sight.

Moving from short sentences to longer ones

One effective technique is to begin a paragraph or section of text with a short sentence announcing the topic – the subject. The next sentence is a little longer, expanding on this. Then the next sentence is longer still, bringing the section to a mini-climax. In this way, a rhythm is created. See how this is done in the extract below, and how the mini-climax expresses the author's feelings.

Mark Twain (1835–1910), *Old Times on the Mississippi*

Mark Twain, recalling his boyhood, remembers how jealous he was of another boy who got a job on a steamboat. It seemed unfair to him, as he had been 'good' whereas the boy had not.

<u>By and by one of our boys went away.</u>[1] He was not heard of for a long time. <u>At last he turned up as apprentice engineer or 'striker' on a steamboat</u>.[2] This thing shook the bottom out of all my Sunday-school teachings. <u>That boy had been notoriously worldly, and I just the reverse, yet he was exalted to this eminence, and I left in obscurity and misery</u>.[3] There was nothing generous about this fellow in his greatness. He would always manage to have a rusty bolt to scrub while his boat tarried at our town, and he would sit on the inside guard and scrub it, where we could all see him and envy him and loathe him.

exalted to this eminence: raised up to this height (of good fortune)

1. Short introductory topic sentence

2. Longer sentence developing story

3. Long coordinated sentence creates climax of Twain's indignation; exaggerated language matches sentence length

Take a ruler and measure the lengths of all the sentences in at least one paragraph of a novel where you think there is a sense of mounting tension or feeling. Record the lengths as a bar chart. Alternatively, count the words. What does your bar chart show?

1. Name two reasons to vary sentence lengths.
2. What is the likely effect of short sentences in dialogue?
3. Is a *topic sentence* normally short, medium-length, long, or of no particular length?
4. How can sentence lengths be used to create a 'mini-climax'?
5. Write a three-sentence play speech in which one person tells another that they either do, or do not, like them. Bring it to a climax.

Progress Check

5.6 Ordering information in a sentence

In a simple sentence there is **only one order** in which to present the information (unless you make the sentence passive):

The dog bit the postman.

If you wrote, 'The postman bit the dog', that would mean something quite different.

However, if you write a **coordinated** or **subordinated sentence**, there are more options for ordering the information. These have an effect on the sentence's impact. Consider:

* The dog has bitten a terrified newspaper boy, chased a postman, and barked at neighbours.
* The dog has barked at neighbours, chased a postman, and bitten a terrified newspaper boy.

Which do you think would have more impact in court if the dog owner were being ordered to restrain the dog?

The second probably has more impact, because the information is given in order of mounting seriousness, so that 'bitten a terrified newspaper boy' comes as a climax. We see this as the dog's worst offence because (a) being bitten is worse than being chased or barked at, (b) it is a boy, not an adult, and (c) the boy was terrified.

What about the following?

* The dog has barked at neighbours but he has never bitten them.
* The dog has never bitten neighbours but he has barked at them.

Say these two coordinated sentences aloud. Which would you use in the dog's defence?

Changing a sentence from active to passive ('The postman *was bitten by* the dog') is another option that changes the emphasis. This is dealt with in Topic 5.7.

Have a go

Try to write a sentence with the triplets of things pictured here.

Here is an example to start you off:

Aimee climbed the tree in an attempt to reach the cat.

Ordering clauses in a subordinated sentence

Subordinated sentences give you many options for ordering information.

Notice the different effects of these sentences:

- Recognising a friend, Ella left Dan's side, and started to cross the room.

(Friend – Dan – room)

- Leaving Dan's side as she recognised a friend, Ella started to cross the room.

(Dan – friend – room)

- Ella recognised a friend and started to cross the room, leaving Dan's side.

(Friend – room – Dan)

- Ella left Dan's side, starting to cross the room as she recognised a friend.

(Dan – room – friend)

- Ella started to cross the room as she recognised a friend, leaving Dan's side.

(Room – friend – Dan)

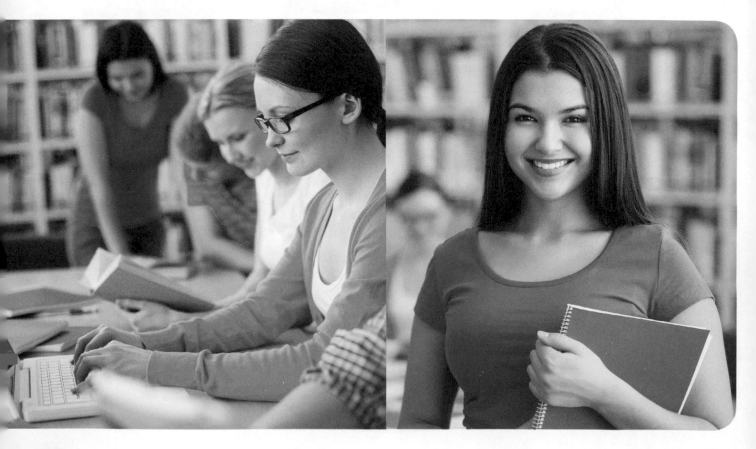

Power and emphasis

Which you choose depends on (a) what information you want to emphasise, and (b) what comes next. A general rule is that the most powerful places in a sentence are the beginning and end, so this is where to put information that you want to emphasise.

Look at the options on page 96. Which would you choose if:

- the key point was that it was not safe for Ella to leave Dan's side?
- the key point is that Dan is really upset that Ella has wandered off?
- the next sentence is 'She was almost halfway there when the whole room began to tremble, and lumps of plaster began to rain down from the ceiling'?

Burying information

It follows that if the beginning and end of a sentence are powerful, the middle is the place to put things you do not want to emphasise, sometimes known as **burying information**:

- The National Order Party has made Britain a safer place, despite a few people going missing, and has made Britain a country in which everyone gets what they deserve.

Write the names of three objects on three separate pieces of paper. (You could use objects from the pictures opposite.) Turn them over, shuffle them, read them, and write a sentence for each new order. Consider the different impact of each ordering.

---

1. In how many orders can you present a simple sentence without changing its meaning or making it a passive sentence?
2. Which are the most powerful places for information in a sentence?
3. Where is the place of *least* emphasis in a sentence?
4. What type of sentence gives most opportunities for changing the order of information?

Progress Check

5.7 Active and passive sentences

39

Here is an **active sentence**:

Elizabeth I ruled England for 45 years.

You could change this into a **passive sentence** like this:

England was ruled by Elizabeth I for 45 years.

The first version emphasises the career of Elizabeth I; the second emphasises what was happening in England. After the first version, you might go on to write: 'This was a remarkable achievement.' After the second version, you might write: 'This was a time of growing wealth for the country.'

What differences are there in the following sentences?

- The worm is eaten by the blackbird.
- The blackbird eats the worm.

Which would you use in a nature documentary on blackbirds? Or one on worms?

Victim status

The **passive** form suggests someone or something not acting, but instead being an object of an action. So, a news report focusing on the plight of victims of crime might say:

*A pensioner **was attacked** by a gang of youths in Newport last night.*

How would you rephrase this in the active form? How would the emphasis shift?

Disclaiming responsibility

The passive form is also used sometimes to avoid saying exactly who did something:

The prime minister admitted that mistakes had been made.

Why might the passive form be used here?

The passive form can also be used to avoid the need to say who *will* do something, as in this image:

Which form to use

It is normally better to use active sentences unless you want to achieve a particular effect, as shown above.

If this ladder is misused again, steps will be taken

Shut your eyes and point in a random direction. Open your eyes and see what you are pointing at. Write an active sentence about this thing (as in, 'My sister broke the mug') and then a passive one ('The mug was broken by my sister'). Compare the effect.

1. Is 'I was taken to the park' an active or passive sentence?
2. What is emphasised in 'The car was driven by Lewis Hamilton'?
3. How might you state that something had been done without saying *who* had done it? Write a sentence like this.
4. Which form should you use unless you want to achieve a special effect?

Progress Check

5.8 Cumulative sentences

🎧 **40**

A **cumulative sentence** is one in which a number of sub-clauses add information to a main clause. This can be a powerful way to present information:

Imran strode towards the wicket,[1] bat swinging lightly in his gloved hand, pads gleaming white, cap sitting squarely on his head, a faint agitation fluttering beneath his calm exterior.

It is called 'cumulative' because the information **accumulates**.

1. Main clause

Placing the main clause

The main clause can be placed at the start of the sentence, as above, or at the end:

Checking the seals of her air-tight suit, smiling a little nervously at her fellow travellers, breathing deeply to maintain her inner calm, <u>Irma waves a last goodbye to Planet Earth</u>.[1]

You can identify the main clause because it is the only part of the sentence that would **make complete sense on its own**.

A cumulative sentence is a special type of subordinated sentence. See Topic 5.4. for more on these.

1. Main clause

The main clause could even come **in the middle** of the sentence:

> *Breathing hard, legs pumping, his face strained, Peters sprints towards the goal, the goal that has eluded him all season, the goal that will make or break him, the goal at which he now aims his best kick.*

Can you identify the main clause here?

Using repetition

In the example above, placing the main clause in the middle works because the focus of the sentence changes to the goal after it. Repetition can be used at any point after the main clause:

> *Sonia remembered her father, a father who had always been there for his children, a father who believed in them, a father who had taught them the value of trust.*

This builds up a strong sense of the subject – the father.

Repetition could be used to **take the reader by surprise** with the final detail:

> *He was the brother I had always respected, the brother I had tried to be like, the brother I would have died for, **the brother who had now betrayed me**.*

Study the pictures opposite. Then stand up and begin a sentence with a main clause about one of them. Speak it out loud and walk forward. With each step, add a new detail to form a cumulative sentence. Then stop and write it down.

Progress Check

1. Why is a *cumulative* sentence called this?
2. How can you identify the main clause in a cumulative sentence?
3. How can a cumulative sentence take the reader by surprise?

5.9 Paragraphing

Paragraphs break up a text into manageable sections for the reader. A new paragraph should normally be indented, although in some books – such as this one – paragraphs are spaced instead.

Dialogue

In **dialogue**, you should begin a new paragraph whenever there is a change of speaker:

> *Malachai came over and sat with Rita.*
>
> *'So, where have you been?' she asked.*
>
> *'Here and there,' he replied.*

Non-fiction

In non-fiction, the general rule is to start a new paragraph whenever there is a shift in subject. If you plan an essay, perhaps using a mind map, spidergram or list, it may work well to start a new paragraph for each new main point.

Here is a plan for a short essay on 'Why I prefer holidays in Britain':

1. Lots of places to visit and things to do in Britain

2. Saves on travel time

3. Less hassle – airports, passports, etc.

4. Air travel makes global warming worse

5. No language problems

6. Come home when you've had enough

Topic Sentences

It can be very helpful for the reader if you begin each paragraph with a **topic sentence**. This is a sentence introducing the subject of the paragraph. Here are the first four paragraphs of the holidays essay, but not yet divided into four. Can you find the topic sentences, which should come at the start of the second, third and fourth paragraphs?

1. Topic sentence for first main point

<u>I really cannot see the appeal of foreign holidays when there is so much to do and see in Britain</u>.[1] Our wonderful coastline offers sandy beaches, rugged coastal paths, and safe swimming free of sharks and jellyfish. Inland destinations range from the inspiring peaks of Snowdonia to the lazy waterways of the Norfolk Broads, and from camping or self-catering to luxury hotels. When you go on a foreign holiday, you can easily spend an entire day getting there. This can include an exhausting car journey, the lengthy business of negotiating the airport – perhaps including a long wait if your flight is delayed, and probably further travel by train, taxi or expensive hire-car when your plane touches down. With a UK holiday you could be relaxing just a few hours after leaving home. In addition, there is the general stress of going abroad, made worse now by increased airport security. You have to book your flight, which may leave at some unearthly hour, pack your luggage bearing in mind weight restrictions, and get to the airport two hours early for security clearance. You have to make sure your passport is up to date, take it, and know exactly where it is when you get to the airport. You have to queue to check in your baggage, and again to get past customs, probably removing the contents of your pockets and your shoes. You are likely to be exhausted by the time you sit down in your cramped little seat and remember that the book you wanted to read is still in your suitcase, in the luggage hold! To make matters worse, flying massively increases your 'carbon footprint'. Planes fill the atmosphere with tons of polluting gases, accelerating global warming and using up scarce resources. If you stay in Britain, you save money and help to save the planet as well.

Fiction

With fiction the rules for paragraphing are more flexible – apart from dialogue. There is usually a new paragraph when there is a time shift. Modern stories and novels may well use some very short paragraphs for dramatic impact. Read the following and see how the short paragraphs create suspense.

Torak, a stone-age boy, is stalking a roe deer with his companion, a wolf cub.

> Torak glanced about for signs of a stream. West through the hazel, about thirty paces off the trail, he glimpsed a clump of alders. Alders only grow near water. That was where the buck must be heading.
>
> Softly, he and the cub moved through the undergrowth. Cupping his hand to his ear, he caught a faint ripple of water.
>
> Suddenly, Wolf froze: ears rammed forwards, one forepaw raised.
>
> Yes. There. Through the alders. The buck stooping to drink.
>
> Carefully Torak took aim.
>
> The buck raised its head, water dripping from its muzzle.
>
> Torak watched it snuff the air and fluff out its pale rump fur in alarm. Another heartbeat and it would be gone. He loosed his arrow.
>
> Michelle Paver, *Wolf Brother*

For more on dialogue, see Topic 3.3. For more on how short sentences create impact, see Topic 5.5.

Shut your eyes and imagine yourself stalking an animal – with a bow and arrow or a camera. Picture four or five separate stages of this process. Then write a number of short dramatic paragraphs like Michelle Paver's sequence.

Giving a sentence its own paragraph gives it more importance, especially if it is a short sentence. Notice, too, how in the extract there is even one paragraph that does not contain a grammatically complete sentence. Find it and think about its dramatic impact.

1. What do paragraphs do?
2. When should you begin a new paragraph in dialogue?
3. When should you begin a new paragraph in non-fiction?
4. What is the effect of Michelle Paver's short paragraphs?

Progress Check

42 5.10 Using tenses correctly and effectively

The **tense** of a verb refers to the timing of the action it describes. The main tenses are:

> Past ← Present → Future

However, there are also some variations within these three main divisions.

Past

Simple past	I did my homework.
Past continuous	I **was doing** my homework, when I heard a noise.
Perfect (tense)	'I **have done** my homework,' I lied.
Past perfect	I **had done** my homework, so I sat down to watch TV.

Present

Simple present	She **walks** to the door.
Present continuous	She is **looking** straight ahead.

Future

Simple future	He **will be** worried.
Future perfect	He **will have been** waiting for three hours by then.

Using tenses in a story

If you are writing a story, or describing events in your own life, you can choose to write in the **past** tense or (more unusually) in the **present** tense.

If you are writing in the past tense and you want to **look back at a time before the time you are writing about**, you need to use the past perfect, like this:

> *I ate my lunch alone. I **had made** the sandwiches that morning.*

This is completely acceptable. However, if you go on using the past perfect for a long time, it can become boring for readers: they will start to want to know what happens *now*!

If you are writing in the **present** tense, you still **go back one stage in time to refer to an earlier time**:

> *I **walk** to the door. I **locked** it this morning, but someone has left it open.*

It is important to be consistent. You will confuse the reader if you wander between tenses. If you are unsure about tenses, it may be safer to use the past.

The conditional tense

The **conditional tense** is a special tense using **would, could, should or might**. It imagines what would, could or might be. Here are some examples.

> *She smiled happily. In just a few hours she **would** be lying on a tropical beach.*

> *I **should** finish decorating my room by this evening.*

> *I **could** walk to school, or I could catch the bus. Decisions!*

> *I **might** be asleep later. Wake me up if you have to.*

If you want to be really sophisticated, you could use some variations, like these:

> *She **could have** been lying on a beach, but instead she was stuck in an airport!*

> *I **should have** finished it, but it all went wrong.*

> *I **could have** caught the bus if only I'd remembered to bring some bus fare.*

> *If I **had** only **listened** I **might have** been rich and famous.*

Write the verbs 'be', 'walk', 'make' and 'take' on pieces of paper. Then write 'Simple past', 'Past continuous', 'Perfect tense' and 'Past perfect' on pieces of paper. Lay the two groups separately, face down. Take a word and a tense at random and make up an interesting sentence using them. Repeat till you have used all verbs and tenses.

'I could have been…'

'Instead I was…'

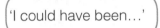

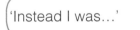

1. What are the three main tenses?
2. What tense is 'He was walking towards the bus stop'?
3. What two main tenses could you write a story in?
4. Give an example of the past perfect tense.

Progress Check

43 **5.11** # Subject–verb agreement

Students often make mistakes in **subject–verb agreement**. A verb has to agree with the subject to which it applies. If the subject is singular, so must the verb be; if the subject is plural, so must the verb be:

1. Ahmed **go** to school. ✘	Ahmed **goes** to school. ✔
2. The fans **cheers** their team. ✘	The fans **cheer** their team. ✔
3. They **was** laughing at me. ✘	They **were** laughing at me. ✔

Speech and writing

In speech, people sometimes use non-standard grammar, as in 'They was kicking the ball,' but in written English you should always use standard grammar, as in 'They were playing football.' The only exception to this is in dialogue in a story. In a story a character could be the sort of person who uses non-standard grammar, at least in an informal situation.

Collective nouns

A **collective noun** is a noun for a group of the same thing; for example:

- a flock of sheep
- a herd of elephants
- the staff (referring to workers in one place)
- the class (referring to students in school).

It can be tricky to work out what verb form to use with collective nouns. The general rule is to use a singular verb:

*There **was a herd** of elephants charging towards me!*

However, at times sticking to the rule can sound strange. For example, which would you say?

*Dear Sir, the class **hopes** you will recover from your accident soon.*

*Dear Sir, the class **hope** you will recover from your accident soon.*

If you are really thinking of a number of individuals, it will probably sound more natural to use the plural verb form – **hope**. Certainly it would sound more natural if you were writing, 'The class **all hope** you will…'. The word 'all' makes the reader think of a group of individuals.

Money and measurements

It is normal to treat money and measurements as singular:

*I'm sure you will agree that £1,000 **is** a lot of money to pay.*

*Ten miles **was** a long way to walk.*

Progress Check

1. Should you write 'We was joking' or 'We were joking'?
2. Should you write 'We are tired' or 'We is tired'?
3. In writing, should you use standard or non-standard grammar?
4. What general rule should you follow when applying a verb to a collective noun?

5.12 Using pronouns

A pronoun takes the place of a noun in a sentence. It saves you having to name the noun every time you refer to it.

The cat was stuck up a tree. The fireman climbed up to try to get the cat down, but the cat climbed higher and higher. Eventually the fireman got close to the cat. The fireman almost fell off when the fireman reached for the cat and the cat scratched the fireman.

This is easier to read (and to write) using pronouns:

*The cat was stuck up a tree. The fireman climbed up to try to get **her** down, but **she** climbed higher and higher. Eventually the fireman got close to **her**. He almost fell off when **he** reached for **her** and she scratched him.*

Notice that there are two forms of pronoun here:
- he and him
- she and her.

You should use **he/she** for the **subject** of a clause and **him/her** if the thing referred to is the **object** – having something done to it. (Look again at 'she [subject] scratched him [object]'.)

You can also use **it**, which remains unchanged as subject or object.

Possessive pronouns

A **possessive pronoun** is one which states **ownership**:

That is your CD. **Mine** is here.

This is my coat. **Yours** is on the peg.

This is not her lunch. It is **his**.

This is not his seat. It is **hers**.

This is not our car. **Ours** is blue.

It is not our money. It is **theirs**.

It's mine!

Relative pronouns

A **relative pronoun** is commonly used in a subordinated sentence, in a clause referring to the main clause:

- Iqbal, **who** rarely misses school, was absent today.
- Hockey, **which** is my favourite sport, is now banned.

The **possessive form** of who or which is **whose**:

- I don't know **whose** sock this is, but I don't want it.
- Who can tell me **whose** this is? (What person can tell me to whom this belongs?)

Pronoun confusion

Although pronouns save you having to repeat the subject of a sentence, you do have to make sure the reader can always tell to whom they refer. Sometimes confusion can arise:

Nicole asked her mother if she could make her a cup of tea.

Is Nicole being kind or lazy? Reword the sentence for each possibility.

Note that *its* does not need an **apostrophe** when used as a possessive. For more on apostrophes, see Topic 6.5.

Do not confuse 'their' with 'there' or 'they're', or 'whose' with 'who's'. See Topics 6.5 and 9.3.

Write all the pronouns from this section in a circle on a large piece of paper. Spin a knife or other object in the centre so that it points at one pronoun. Then make up a sentence using that pronoun. For added challenge, turn your sentences into a story.

Progress Check

1. 'Dan looked at Dan's car. Dan's car was new and Dan was proud of his car.' Rewrite using pronouns.
2. 'Yours' and 'mine' are what kind of pronoun?
3. In what kind of sentence is a relative pronoun commonly used?
4. 'I know the girl whose/who's sister wrote this song.' Which is it?

Worked questions

1. **Write three or four paragraphs about your likes and dislikes.**
   In these paragraphs try to do the following: *(12 marks)*

   - Use a variety of sentence types and lengths for impact.
   - Order information effectively.
   - Use active and passive sentences.
   - Use paragraphing effectively.

<u>You could say that I'm mostly a people person</u>.[1] I like school mostly because it gives me an opportunity to meet my friends. <u>As I live some distance from school, I take the bus every day, which means that I get to see some of my friends even before the school day starts</u>.[2] My friends and I get on when the bus is almost empty, so we usually occupy the seats right at the back. <u>We talk, exchange jokes, swap gossip, and even – strange though it may seem – compare notes on homework</u>.[3] English is one of the subjects I like, so I enjoy reading my friends' stories and getting their feedback on mine.

<u>Like most of my generation, I spend quite a lot of my time watching TV</u>.[4] Sometimes I just watch whatever happens to be on. This may sound pointless, but in fact it means I come across a wide variety of programmes. <u>I find myself watching a cross-section of everything that television has to offer, from wildlife programmes about stampeding elephants, to historical battle re-enactments, to celebrity cookery shows</u>.[5] I love gathering information from here and there like this. In fact, I have <u>been told</u>[6] that I should work in the media.

Of course there are a lot of seemingly random things that I like. These include <u>winter sunsets, toffee ice cream, the smell of my dad's aftershave, that moment in a swimming pool before anyone gets in and the water is almost motionless</u>.[7] However, nothing quite beats staying in bed with my i-Pod on a Saturday morning.

My dislikes are fairly few. However, I do hate bullying in any form. <u>It's cowardly. It shows human beings at their lowest level. It comes from a pathetic failure of imagination – and inability to see the victim as a fellow human being</u>.[8] Luckily, I have never been bullied. I have occasionally been called names, but that I can ignore.

1. Simple topic sentence

2. Effective subordinated sentence

3. Good list ordering information, with last piece held back for effect

4. Short subordinated topic sentence (first part adds interest)

5. Longest of three sentences gradually increasing in length to mini-climax

6. Appropriate passive sentence

7. List building up to most interesting item

8. Short, medium and long sentence building in strength

2. **Write an opening to a story. Vary your sentences and paragraph lengths for effect. Use a cumulative sentence. Use tenses and pronouns effectively.** *(12 marks)*

1. Pronoun leaves man anonymous

2. Good use of past conditional tense

3. Effective use of past perfect

4. Past perfect phrase introducing paragraph, explaining background

5. Cumulative sentence emphasises his problems

6. First short sentence building tension; clever use of 'his'

7. Short minor sentence in short paragraph creates tension

_He_[1] was in what his old commanding officer _would have called_[2] a 'tight spot'. It was a low-lying, tiny island in a wide river, with floodwater rising rapidly. The enemy were ranged only a couple of hundred yards away, beyond the bushes. In the light of a full moon he could see slight movements. Once, an unsuspecting enemy soldier _had come down_[3] to the river to fetch water. He had heard the man cough, seen the glint of moonlight on his bucket. Too close for comfort.

He had arrived here by canoe,[4] having become detached from his regiment. Now he was in effect a prisoner on this shrinking island. He was undetected as yet – but for how long?

He sat wondering what to do, the cold beginning to gnaw into his bones, his wet feet starting to go numb, hunger already beginning to make him light-headed and perhaps impair his judgement.[5]

As he considered how to make his escape, before dawn revealed his position, two of the enemy came to the riverbank a hundred yards downstream. He almost held his breath. _He watched while they walked upstream towards 'his' island._[6] Now they were no more than twenty yards away. He could hear their quiet conversation.

A ripple of moonlight, like waving silk, as the two men entered the water. He could hear his heart. _Like a drum._[7]

3. **Write three or four paragraphs of an essay comparing life in Britain in Victorian times, now and 150 years from now. In these paragraphs try to do the following:**

   - use paragraphing correctly
   - order information effectively
   - show your grasp of different tenses. *(12 marks)*

1. Subordinate clause in present tense used to set scene

2. Correct use of past conditional tense

3. Past conditional tense continued, with well ordered information

4. Good topic sentence, with shift into past tense

5. Good use of past perfect tense

As I remove my toast from the electric toaster,[1] choose from a host of TV channels, take the milk from the fridge and sit down to enjoy breakfast, I think for a moment how different all this _might have been had I been born_[2] in the middle of the nineteenth century.

If my family had been among the poverty-stricken masses moving to the fast-growing cities to find work, _I would have been lucky to find myself in a tiny terraced house, probably with several people sharing a bedroom, and even a bed._[3] A winter's day would have begun with getting a fire going in the living room, if we could afford coal. Breakfast might have been a piece of bread, or some thin gruel.

Even for the better-off, life in Victorian times was very different from now.[4] Lighting was by candles or oil lamps, and homes were heated by coal.

Shopping had to be done on a daily basis as there was no easy way to keep food cool. Cooking was a lot more difficult too: with no gas or electricity, people depended on fires or coal-fired stoves. _Gas stoves had been invented_[5] by 1850, but they were not widely used till much later, especially outside of the big cities.

Practice questions

1. Rewrite the following paragraphs in the past tense. *(10 marks)*

I am feeling pretty pleased with myself. I have just got my first Saturday job, in a greengrocer's, and already I have been congratulated on my hard work and positive attitude. Now, however, a rather grumpy-looking customer enters the shop, an elderly lady with her hair in a bun.

'Young lady,' she says, 'I want two pounds of potatoes, a bunch of asparagus, and a quarter of mushrooms. And make it snappy.'

'Certainly,' I say, trying hard to be polite. After all, isn't the customer always right?

I give her the veg, take her £10 note and give her the change.

'I gave you a £20 note,' she says.

My positive mood is fading fast. This woman is a shop assistant's nightmare. She looks at me steely-eyed, like my old head teacher in primary school. Her hand is held out. I know for sure that she only gave me £10. I wonder if I should call for the manager.

Instead I decide to stick to my guns. 'It was a ten,' I say, quietly but firmly.

2. **Rewrite the following paragraphs using pronouns.** *(10 marks)*

> The two boys were strolling through the park kicking cans, wondering how to spend the rest of the two boys' day. When the two boys came to the boating lake, the two boys were surprised to see an empty boat, with the boat's oars pulled just out of the water. The boat was just sitting there. The taller boy smiled.
>
> 'Terry,' the taller boy said, 'do you fancy a boat trip?'
>
> Terry grinned. Terry had never had the money to go on a boat trip. This was Terry's big chance.
>
> 'Give us a hand, Lee,' Terry said as Terry clambered in.
>
> Terry and Lee were in the middle of the lake when Terry and Lee realised that there was a problem with the boat. The boat was filling up with water.

3. **The following paragraphs are a continuation of the essay on page 110. Imagine that you are now living in the 22nd century. Rewrite these paragraphs, changing the tenses and whatever else is necessary to present them from a 22nd-century perspective.** *(10 marks)*

So, you might begin, 'In the early 21st century, most people lived ...' Assume that the predictions in the second paragraph come true.

> Nowadays, most of us live in centrally heated and well-insulated houses. We can shop once a week if we want, and put food in the fridge or freezer. We have sophisticated ovens and, if we are really lazy, we can pop ready-meals in the microwave and have them on the table in a few minutes. Then we can eat them in front of the TV or DVD, or listening to music on our MP3 players, or even while playing games on our Xbox or texting a friend. Our opportunities for technology use and media consumption are endless.
>
> The pace of change is constantly increasing. In the 22nd century, life will probably be even easier, with developments in technology that we can barely imagine now. Perhaps we will control our devices by thought power and even communicate by telepathy. Instead of watching flat TV screens, we could be enjoying lifelike 3-D hologrammatic presentations, with sound effects. We may even hook up to simulators that make us feel immersed in the illusion of other 'realities'. Travel, too, is likely to be very different. It could be solar-powered and we could abandon the wheel: flying saucers could become everyday items.

4. **Now write a final paragraph using the future tense to predict what might happen instead if climate change is not stopped.** *(5 marks)*

Using punctuation for clarity and effect

6

Learning Summary

After completing this chapter you should know:
- how to use capital letters and full stops
- how to use commas and dashes
- how to use colons and semicolons
- how to use speech marks
- how to use apostrophes.

6.1 Ending and beginning sentences

🎧 45

Use a **capital letter** to start a new sentence and a full stop to end one, unless it is a question, or an order or exclamation. A questions ends with a question mark. Orders (commands) and exclamations end with a single exclamation mark:
- Get out, now!
- Ouch!

You should start a new sentence when you have written a complete sentence and are not adding a dependent **clause** to make a subordinated sentence:

- Dad's hobby is tropical fish. He has a huge tank full of them. ✓
- Mum goes rock-climbing, she says it keeps her fit. ✗ **(Two complete sentences)**
- My sister does karate, which is a form of martial art. ✓
- My brother plays rugby. Which I hate. ✗ **(One subordinated sentence)**

A **comma splice** is an incorrect use of a comma when there should be a full stop and new sentence.

> For many students, the problem is knowing when to end a sentence. For what a sentence is, see Topic 5.1.

Progress Check

1. What punctuation marks can end a sentence?
2. What mark follows an order?
3. What is the problem with this sentence? 'Dave is tall, he has to stoop in doorways.'

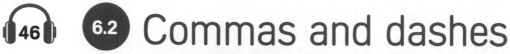

46 **6.2** Commas and dashes

Commas and clauses

Correct use of commas helps your reader to understand your meaning. Compare the following:

- After eating, Gary, Lyn and Kevin went skating.
- After eating Gary, Lyn and Kevin went skating.

Unless Lyn and Kevin are cannibals, which is correct? Why?

In this example, the comma comes after a **subordinate clause**. This is a phrase that adds information to the main clause ('Gary, Lyn and Kevin went skating'). This is an important use of commas. Here are more examples. Notice that the subordinate clause can come at the beginning, the end or the middle of the sentence. The commas help the reader to understand the sentence.

*Black Elk, **a Lakota medicine man**, visited England and met Queen Victoria.*

***A lifelong teetotaller**, Granddad says he does not need alcohol to have a good time.*

*I met her in a café, **a grimy little place on the King's Road**.*

*She works for a living, **which is more than can be said for you**.*

Commas in lists

Commas also break up the items in a list:

I enjoy French, Welsh and English.

I bought salad, crisps, cheese and mustard.

Without the comma, the reader might think, at least for a moment, that you could buy 'salad crisps'. Note that in simple lists the final comma is usually left out because the 'and' replaces it. However, in some lists a comma still helps the sense:

I brought orange juice, apple pie, and a huge tub of ice cream for my aunt.

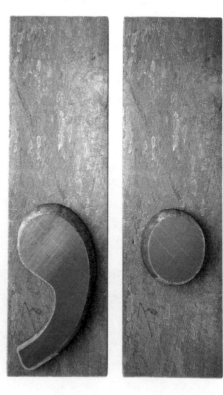

Commas with people and names

See these examples where the comma, or lack of it, helps make the sense clear. In each case the subject of the sentence is emboldened.

- **The builder**, who is a vegetarian, brings his own lunch.
- **The builder who is a vegetarian** drinks tea, but the other builder prefers coffee.

You do not need a comma in these sentences:

- My cousin Wilf lives in Devon.
- My brother Jack is a mechanic.

However, commas do help here:

- The tallest boy in the class, Nigel, was able to reach the ball.

Using dashes

Some people use dashes lazily, in place of other punctuation. However, they are effective when used properly. A dash **shows a break in the flow of ideas**, as in an 'aside' or a passing explanation:

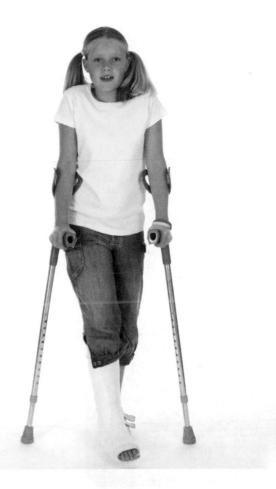

Lynda was on crutches – she had broken her leg – and could only walk a short distance.

(Saves having to say '*because* she had broken her leg'.)

Shakespeare was the son of a glove maker – a commoner.

(Explains a significant point.)

The other woman – a dancer – was slim but muscular.

(Adds information, partly to explain; saves saying '*who was* a dancer')

A dash can also be used in **dialogue** to show a sentence that is left incomplete:

Liam turned pale. 'But what about –'

'No time for that,' I answered, pushing him through the door.

Arrange a collection of items in front of you. Make up two sentences using them in lists and two with subordinate clauses.

---

1. Where do the commas go? 'I love Canada which has cold winters and hot summers most of all.'
2. Why is a comma not usually used before the last item of a list?
3. I have two cousins. Should I say, 'My cousin who lives in Ely…' or 'My cousin, who lives in Ely…'?
4. What does a dash show?

Progress Check

6.3 Colons and semicolons

A **colon** (:) is used in two situations:
1. To 'announce' something, especially a list (like this one)
2. To show that a piece of information follows on as a consequence or explanation of what comes before the colon.

The prize-winners arc: Derek James, Amir Baz and Jane Taggart.

There is one extraordinary fact about rock-climber James Cameron: he is blind.

A **semicolon** (;) is also used in two ways:

1. To break up items in a list where commas are needed within one or more items (often with a colon in front)
2. As a slightly stronger mark than the comma, but where there is a special connection between two statements, so that a full stop and new sentence might seem too much.

The school sports groups will be divided into: football, rugby and hockey; swimming, cycling and running; and table tennis, squash and badminton.

Losing your homework once could be careless; losing it twice is suspicious.

Older texts are more likely to use the semicolon than modern ones, although it is still a very useful punctuation mark. See how the semicolon is used here:

> Devise body language for each type of punctuation mark – for example, a downward chop of the hand for a full stop. What do you think would be appropriate for a semicolon? Stand up and read the passage above aloud using these gestures.

Mary Seacole, a black British nurse, attended soldiers during the Crimean War (1853–56)

It was a fearful scene; but why repeat this remark. All death is trying to witness – even that of the good man who lays down his life hopefully and peacefully; but on the battlefield, when the poor body is torn and rent in hideous ways, and the scared spirit struggles to loose itself from the still strong frame that holds it tightly to the last, death is fearful indeed. It had come peacefully enough to some. They lay with half-opened eyes, and a quiet smile about the lips that showed their end to have been painless; others it had arrested in the heat of passion, and frozen on their pallid faces a glare of hatred and defiance that made your warm blood run cold.

Progress Check

1. Which punctuation mark can be used to 'announce' a list?
2. Which punctuation mark could be used to divide two related statements?
3. When might you use semicolons in a list?

6.4 Quotation marks

Quoting from another text

Use **quotation marks** round any text that is **taken directly from another text**:

1. The poet John Keats called autumn a 'season of mists and mellow fruitfulness'.

2. Hamlet tells Ophelia, 'Get thee to a nunnery!'

3. Orsino likes music: 'If music be the food of love, play on.'

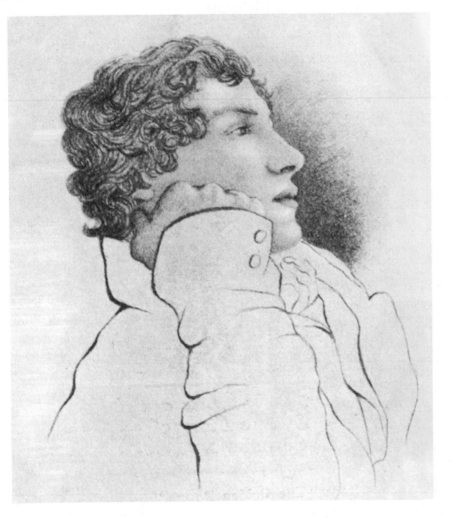

Where the quotation marks go in relation to other marks

If you are just quoting a phrase – not a full sentence, just use the quotation marks and put the final full stop outside them. (Example 1 above)

If you are quoting a full sentence that runs on from your own sentence, use a comma first, and put the final punctuation marks inside the quotation mark. (Example 2 above)

If you are quoting a sentence that is meant to be evidence for your statement, use a colon before the opening quotation mark. (Example 3 above)

Do not use quotation marks around **reported speech**:

Orsino tells the musicians to keep on playing.

Quoting to show a special use, or for irony

You can also use quotation marks to make the reader aware that you are **using a word or phrase in a special way**, perhaps as used elsewhere, but not in a particular text:

- Do Britain and America still have a 'special relationship'?
- It seems that Iraq possessed no 'weapons of mass destruction' after all.

Quotation marks can also be used **ironically**, to show that the writer does not agree with what the word suggests:

So, you're my 'friend' are you? With 'friends' like you, who needs enemies?

Quotation marks in dialogue

In a story, you should always use quotation marks round anything a character actually says. As with all quotation marks, it is up to you whether you use doubles ("…") or singles ('…'). However, it is now more normal to use single quotation marks, then doubles for anything quoted within them.

Here is how it works:
- She glared at me. 'So, you're my "friend" are you?'
- Jem admitted that he had been scared: 'He told me I would be "punished" if I breathed a word of it to anyone.'

You can also break a line of dialogue:
- Harry appeared puzzled. 'If that's true,' he said, 'why did you swallow the pill?'
  (Here the comma belongs to Harry's actual sentence, so it goes inside the first closing quotation mark.)

> Remember to begin a new paragraph with every change of speaker. For more on paragraphs, see Topic 5.9.

> Record or note down some dialogue from a TV drama. Write it first as a script (see Topic 3.9), then as dialogue in a story. Add the necessary text to the actual words spoken. For example, 'Don't look at me like that,' said Vic, frowning.

- Gemma looked hard at Harry. 'He promised me', she explained, 'that it would be all right.' (Here, Gemma's actual words are 'He promised me that it would be all right.' There is no comma, so in the dialogue the comma goes after the quotation mark.)

Notice that the second part of the quoted sentence does not begin with a capital letter.

Progress Check

1. Add quotation marks: *When Lady Macbeth dies, Macbeth calls life a tale told by an idiot.*
2. Add quotation marks: *He told me not to tell anyone. If you do, he said, you'll regret it.*
3. Why are quotation marks used here? *This show is the kind of 'entertainment' I can do without.*

6.5 Apostrophes for possession and omission 🎧49

Apostrophes should only ever be used to show possession (ownership) or **omission** (that something has been left out). **Never use an apostrophe just because a word ends in 's'.**

> My **brother's** room is a tip. ✔
> (**Possession** – the room belonging to my brother.)

> I **don't** want to go to bed at nine **o'clock**. ✔
> (I do not want to go to bed at nine of the clock.)

> I enjoy eating **carrot's** and **tomatoe's**. ✘
> (Wrong: these words are just plurals.)

> **It's** time for bed. ✔
> (Short for 'It is')

> The roof leaks because **it's** tiles are falling off. ✘
> (Wrong: 'its' is like 'his' and 'her'.)

Possession – singular and plural

Place the apostrophe before the 's' for a singular noun, and after it for a plural:

> The cat's dinner is on the floor.
> (One cat)

> The dogs' leads are hanging up on the door.
> (More than one dog)

Names

Most cases are straightforward:

Emily's hair is dark brown.

If someone's name ends with 's', you normally add the 's' and still put the apostrophe before it, like this:

James's eyes are grey.

If two people own something, it is normal nowadays to add the apostrophe only after the second name:

Paul and Sarah's house is on the hill.

Plural nouns

Place apostrophes in plural nouns like this:

The children's clothes were wet.

More on omission

A number of verb forms can be **contracted**, and frequently are in speech and dialogue. This means that they are shortened by leaving something out. Examples:

wouldn't	won't
negatives	
can't	shouldn't
don't	

you're
I'm   he's
Pronouns and the verb 'to be'
they're   she's
we're

> Find several photos of people, in a magazine or family album, etc. Write a sentence for at least one individual and one pair or group of people that uses an apostrophe for possession and an apostrophe for omission. Example: My sisters' hair couldn't get much longer.

Do not confuse *they're* with *their* or *there*, or *you're* with *your*.

Apostrophes are sometimes used in dialogue to show the way a character speaks:

We're a huntin' shootin' an' fishin' family, don't y'know.

You could try this in your own dialogue, but use it sparingly: it is hard to keep it up convincingly.

Progress Check

1. I have one sister who has two hamsters. How should I punctuate this? *My sisters hamsters cage needs cleaning.*
2. Punctuate this: *Should I should put my countrys needs before both my parents happiness?*
3. Add apostrophes: *I cant read who theyre addressed to. Does that say OConnor or OBrien?*

Worked questions

1. **Punctuate the following paragraph, breaking it into sentences, with capitals and full stops, and adding commas where necessary. Also, decide on a good place to split it into two paragraphs.** *(12 marks)*

it was a perfect day for the beach the sky was the colour of a robin's egg and the sea which had warmed over the last week or so to the temperature of a warm bath was gently undulating it wouldn't have been any good for surfers but Sue and Errol were just here to swim and sunbathe a family nearby were playing with a beachball but the children were well behaved anyway they kept their distance when Errol started to feel quite toasted by the sun's rays he suggested a swim Sue agreed and they ran down to the water lying on their backs in the gentle waves they could see gulls a kite and someone hang-gliding in the distance that was when sue suddenly became aware of a dark fin slicing through the water towards them it was getting nearer every second

1. A topic sentence

2. Comma needed to avoid reader thinking the sky was the colour of the sea, as well as a robin's egg

3. Subordinate clause split off with commas

4. Comma here because the information after 'but' is about the children, not the whole family

5. Needs to be a new sentence

6. Comma splits off a subordinate clause indicating a time shift – a good place for a new paragraph

7. Commas in list; third one, after 'and', makes it clear that only the hang-glider is 'in the distance'

8. Has to be a new sentence unless you delete 'It was'

It was a perfect day for the beach.[1] The sky was the colour of a robin's egg,[2] and the sea, which had warmed over the last week or so to the temperature of a warm bath,[3] was gently undulating. It wouldn't have been any good for surfers, but Sue and Errol were just here to swim and sunbathe. A family nearby were playing with a beachball,[4] but the children were well behaved. Anyway, they kept their distance.[5]

When Errol started to feel quite toasted by the sun's rays,[6] he suggested a swim. Sue agreed and they ran down to the water. Lying on their backs in the gentle waves, they could see gulls, a kite, and someone hang-gliding in the distance.[7] That was when Sue suddenly became aware of a dark fin slicing through the water towards them. It[8] was getting nearer every second.

2. **Add apostrophes to the following passage.** *(12 marks)*

Its already twelve oclock. The guests will be here before long, and I havent even chopped the carrots and tomatoes. And then Shaun doesnt eat meat, so Ive got that vegetarian dish to do. And its still in its foil container. Id better put Shauns dish in the microwave to thaw. Luckily my younger sisters friend Jed has brought some salad – hes thoughtful like that, but my brothers wives are always so fussy. Wait till theyve got childrens parties to organise! Itll be a miracle if they dont find something to complain about. Oh no – theres the doorbell!

1. It is

2. Omission ('of the clock')

3. have not

4. No apostrophes needed!

5. 'it's' = it is; 'its' is a possessive pronoun

6. I had

7. One sister, so apostrophe before the 's'

8. Must be more than one brother, so apostrophe after the 's'

9. 'children' is already plural, so apostrophe before the 's'

10. there is: do not confuse with 'theirs'

It's[1] already twelve o'clock.[2] The guests will be here before long, and I haven't[3] even chopped the carrots and tomatoes.[4] And then Shaun doesn't eat meat, so I've got that vegetarian dish to do. And it's still in its[5] foil container. I'd[6] better put Shaun's dish in the microwave to thaw. Luckily my younger sister's[7] friend Jed has brought some salad – he's thoughtful like that, but my brothers' wives[8] are always so fussy. Wait till they've got children's[9] parties to organise! It'll be a miracle if they don't find something to complain about. Oh no – there's[10] the doorbell!

Practice questions

1. **Add commas to the following:**

    a) All things considered it's a good result I think. *(2 marks)*

    b) Unlike Scotland which has North Sea oil Wales has few mineral resources now. *(2 marks)*

    c) I have the people's respect which is more than can be said for my opponent the labour candidate. *(2 marks)*

    d) The soldiers seeing themselves outnumbered beat a hasty retreat. *(2 marks)*

2. **Add colons and semicolons to the following:**

    a) There's no need to speak I know everything. *(2 marks)*

    b) There's only one reason we're not dead they need us alive. *(2 marks)*

    c) To lose one parent may be regarded as a misfortune to lose both looks like carelessness. (Oscar Wilde) *(2 marks)*

    d) Moses only saw the Promised Land Aaron entered it. *(2 marks)*

    e) We need to take the following a two-man tent, with tent pegs our sleeping bags, and maybe pillows a cooking stove, with spare gas cylinders and matches and a torch. *(2 marks)*

3. **Add quotation marks to the following:**

    a) Dickens, through his narrator, Pip, calls Miss Havisham the strangest lady I have ever seen, or shall ever see. *(2 marks)*

    b) Martin Luther King's famous I have a dream speech is a masterpiece of rhetorical language. *(2 marks)*

    c) Sir Andrew Aguecheek in *Twelfth Night* says, I was adored once too. *(2 marks)*

    d) She looked at the sky. I think she said I might come inside after all. *(2 marks)*

    e) I don't think I'll get the job, he said sadly. They called me a talentless idiot with no ideas. That can't be good, can it? *(2 marks)*

4. **Add apostrophes to the following:**

    a) Its time we gave the school its due. Theyve done all they can to improve Kevins concentration. *(3 marks)*

    b) Karens a star. She doesnt know how to sing in tune, but her cakes cant be faulted. Hers are the only ones I dont wish I hadnt eaten. *(3 marks)*

    c) Cant you see, Ill make you famous. Youll be on every TV set in the land!' *(3 marks)*

    d) 'My little darlin, theres nuffin I wouldnt do for you.' *(3 marks)*

    e) There is a big audience out there, thanks to the bosss hard work and my two brothers publicity. But theyre here because were Britains finest. *(3 marks)*

After completing this chapter you should know:

- where English comes from
- how to choose words
- how to understand words from context
- how to improve your vocabulary and spelling
- key spelling rules
- how to avoid common spelling errors.

Learning Summary

7.1 Where English comes from 🎧50

English has been **developing** for centuries. If you have read some Shakespeare you will know that it has changed quite a lot in the 400 years since he was alive, but its history goes back much further.

Anglo-Saxon

The Angles, Saxons and Jutes were tribes from roughly the area we now call Germany and Denmark. They started to move to England in about 450 CE, after the Romans had left Britain to defend Rome. The words 'England' and 'English' come from 'Angles'. However, the language spoken, and sometimes written, by these earliest English has come to be known as **Anglo-Saxon**.

Some poems, histories and religious texts were written in Anglo-Saxon, but its main influence on modern English comes from spoken English. Although less than a thousand modern English words come from Anglo-Saxon, they are mostly ordinary, everyday words that we use a great deal.

Some examples are:

young	sister	wake
old	daughter	itch
man	cold	game
woman	house	door
husband	milk	alive
wife	moon	dead
brother		

Manuscript of *Beowulf*, an epic heroic poem in Anglo-Saxon alliterative verse from the 10th century

The Vikings

The **Vikings** started to invade England in 793CE. They gradually settled in many parts of England, especially in the North East, many marrying Saxon women. Hence there are many Viking words in place names and dialect in Yorkshire. The Viking words that have entered English and survived are, like the Anglo-Saxon ones, mostly 'everyday' words. Some examples:

anger	hit	scare	skirt	take	wrong
bag	knife	skin	sky	ugly	

The Normans

The one date that most British people know is 1066, the date of the **Norman Conquest**. This is when William the Conqueror and Norman knights defeated the Saxon King Harold at the Battle of Hastings. From that point, the Saxons, and those Vikings who had settled in England, were ruled by the **Normans**.

The Normans spoke Old French, which included a lot of words that originally came from **Latin**. It also included words that reflected the lifestyle and concerns of the Norman upper class. Examples are:

mansion	judge	beef	flower
money	justice	art	spaniel
court	jury	beauty	terrier
castle	mutton	sculpture	nice
prison	pork	cushion	please

As the Normans gradually mixed with England's existing inhabitants, their languages combined to make Early English. However, an important difference remains even today. Many words that come from Norman French are regarded as being more **formal** and upper-class than words with similar meanings that come from Anglo-Saxon. This is because the Normans were once the ruling class.

This means that if you are trying to write in a formal style, you will probably find yourself using more words that have Norman origins.

See how the Norman words in the table below are more formal in tone, even now.

Anglo-Saxon	Norman
husband/wife	spouse
want	desire
friend	companion
dead	deceased
eat	dine
sleep	repose
sea	ocean

Anglo-Saxon	Norman
climb	ascend
king	monarch
sickness	malaise
buy	purchase
smell	odour
ask	enquire
beg	implore

Make up some sentences using one or more Norman words. Make the whole sentence formal. Speak it aloud in an appropriate tone of voice. Then do the same with some Anglo-Saxon words.

Newer words

New words enter English either from foreign languages or by invention. This happens all the time, and gradually these words are included in dictionaries.

Some foreign words that have entered English

bungalow	juggernaut	shampoo
pundit (an expert)	alfresco (in the open air)	kangaroo
pizza	yoghurt	fracas

Invented words

radar	gazump
scuba	serendipity (fortunate accidental discovery)
internet	prequel

1. What does the word 'English' come from?
2. What kind of words have survived from Anglo-Saxon?
3. What ethnic group gave English the words 'skin', 'sky' and 'skirt'?
4. How are the words 'friend' and 'companion' different in origin and tone?

Progress Check

51

7.2 # Making word choices

Writing precisely

Writing precisely means choosing your words with care to say exactly what you mean, and with as little room as possible for the reader to misunderstand you.

In English there are many words that are **broadly similar in meaning**, but which do not mean exactly the same. Look at the following words that all refer to being angry in some way. Which **adjective** best describes the woman pictured?

indignant – feels personally offended or unfairly judged
exasperated – feels highly frustrated, 'at the end of their tether'
irritable – easily made to 'snap'
outraged – very angry because of something morally offensive
furious – just very angry
resentful – angrily resistant to being expected to do something

> Stand up and act out the words above the picture opposite. You could improvise a line to go with your body language. Try to match the exact meaning of each word. You could also look up 'pleased' in a thesaurus and act out the similar words suggested.

You can increase your ability to write precisely by using a **thesaurus** and a **dictionary**, online or in book form. The thesaurus will give you a range of similar words for the one you look up; the dictionary will give you their exact meanings.

Have a go

Which of the words listed above do you think would work best in the following sentences?

* She was always _____ after a late night, especially before breakfast.
* Dear Sir, I am _____ at the Church's decision to appoint women bishops.
* Having tried for hours to make him see her point of view, she was now completely _____.
* At 14, Laura was _____ at being called a child.
* _____, I screamed at him to get out.
* I was _____ at the idea of having to share my room with a stranger.

Writing concisely

Writing concisely means expressing yourself without using unnecessary words. It is often more effective to think of a single word to replace two or more words. This may increase the impact of a sentence, as well as reducing the word count – for example, when writing a magazine article. A useful way to remember this is:

- Less is more.

For example, you can often make a more effective sentence by replacing a **verb** and **adverb** with a better verb:

- I ran quickly to the bus stop.
- I **sprinted** to the bus stop.

Similarly, you can sometimes replace a verb and adjective with one verb:

- The deckchairs were made pale by the sun.
- The deckchairs were **bleached** by the sun.

You can also often express a whole phrase with a single well-chosen **noun**:

- My brother pretends to be ill so he doesn't have to go to school.
- My brother is a **malingerer**.

Tautology

You should be careful to avoid using **tautology**. This means accidentally saying the same thing twice in two different ways, like this:

- Smartphones are a new innovation. (An *innovation* is something new.)
- He was a lazy layabout. (There are no hard-working layabouts!)
- There was frozen ice on the pond. (All ice is frozen.)
- I shouted loudly. (Can you shout quietly?)

1. What does 'writing precisely' mean?
2. Which should you write? 'I was shocked/riveted/astounded/aghast to hear that I had won first prize.'
3. How could you say 'He spoke very quietly in my ear' more concisely?
4. Of what kind of mistake is this an example? 'She was beautifully pretty.'

Progress Check

52

7.3 # Learning and using new words

The best way to expand your vocabulary is simply to read more. However, you will learn new words even more effectively if you make an effort to understand unfamiliar words.

Understanding words from their context

As young children, we learn language by hearing it spoken and working out for ourselves what it means. Then we experiment by using the words we hear. This is **learning by context**. When you read an unfamiliar text, there may be words that you do not fully understand. However, you can often work out their meaning, or at least get some idea of what they mean, from their context – how they are used in a sentence.

There are several ways in which the context of a word can help you:

- You can identify what **class** of word it is: **noun, verb, adjective, adverb**. You should be able to do this by the grammar of the sentence.
- It can be helpful to ask yourself what other words might replace the unfamiliar word and still fit the sentence grammatically.
- You may also recognise words as being similar to other words that you already know. For example, you may know the word *famine*, and guess that *famished* is related to it.

In the following passage, Charles Dickens argues that one of his characters, Jonas, is completely realistic in his psychology and the way he treats his father. Dickens believed that our characters are strongly formed by our background and upbringing. Read the passage and try to work out the meaning of the underlined words using the notes.

When you have a rough idea of what this passage means, look up the words in a dictionary. Then see if you can rewrite the passage in your own words.

Using your new words

There is a risk that you may forget your new words if you do not use them. You can help to prevent this by making a note of the words and their meaning in a small notebook which you divide up into letters of the alphabet. Writing them down will also help you to memorise their spelling.

Then make an effort to use your new words in speech or writing as soon as possible.

...the <u>sordid coarseness</u>[1] and brutality of Jonas would be unnatural, if there had been nothing in his early education, and in the <u>precept</u>[2] and example always before him, to <u>engender</u>[3] and develop the <u>vices</u>[4] that make him <u>odious</u>.[5] But, so born and so bred, admired for that which made him hateful, and justified from his cradle in cunning, treachery, and <u>avarice</u>;[6] I claim him as the <u>legitimate issue</u>[7] of the father upon whom those vices are seen to <u>recoil</u>.[8] And I <u>submit</u>[9] that their recoil upon that old man, in his unhonoured age, is not a mere piece of poetical justice, but is the extreme <u>exposition</u>[10] of a direct truth.

Charles Dickens, Preface to *Martin Chuzzlewit*

1. Would 'coarse' sandpaper be rough or smooth? You may have also heard of 'coarse language'. So, is 'sordid' going to mean 'lovely'? (Especially followed closely by 'brutality'.)

2. Related to 'concept' (an idea) and 'example' (as in to 'set an example').

3. Related to 'generate'. What do 'generators' do?

4. From the same root as 'vicious'; so, will 'vices' be good or bad qualities?

5. The '-ious' ending suggests that this is an adjective. Is it likely to be positive or negative in meaning?

6. If 'avarice' is listed after two bad qualities, what sort of meaning will it have?

7. 'Legitimate' is related to 'legal'; an 'issue' is something that comes out (e.g. a magazine).

8. A 'coil' is a spring; it stretches, it then springs back.

9. On some websites you click 'Submit' to send a form containing information.

10. Related to 'expose'; must relate to a direct truth.

Progress Check

1. What is the best way to increase your vocabulary?
2. How can knowing the *class* of a word (or what *part of speech* it is) help you to work out its meaning?
3. What should you do with the new words you learn?

53 **7.4** # Using a dictionary or thesaurus

Using an online dictionary

If you are working on a computer with internet access, you can look up a word online. In fact you can obtain a definition of most words just by typing the word into Google. For many words, a definition will appear at the top of the search results; for others you will have to click on a link, such as www.collinsdictionary.com.

If using an online dictionary like the *Collins English Dictionary*, you may have to scroll down to see numbered alternative meanings. The commonest meanings are usually given first. You should be able to work out which one fits the word in the sentence you are trying to understand, especially if you read the example phrases that are often provided.

For example, if you look up the word *vice* in the *Collins English Dictionary*, you will see three main meanings for the word used as a noun. Under the first (1), six slight variations are given, beginning with 'an immoral, wicked, or evil habit, action, or trait'.

If you scroll down, you will find, under (2) and (3), two completely different meanings for the word as a noun.

So, *vice* as a noun could mean:
- 'an immoral, wicked, or evil habit, action, or trait'
- 'an appliance for holding an object while work is done upon it, usually having a pair of jaws'
- 'a person who serves as a deputy to another'.

In the Dickens phrase 'develop the vices that make him odious', which of these meanings is likely to be correct?

Some online dictionaries, including the *Collins English Dictionary*, also enable you to click on a speaker icon to hear the word pronounced. For example, how do you think the words 'engender' and 'avarice' are pronounced? The *Collins English Dictionary* will tell you.

Some online dictionaries, including the *Collins English Dictionary*, will also give you the word's **derivation** (where it comes from). For example, for 'avarice', you will find:

> C13: from Old French, from Latin *avaritia,* from *avārus* covetous, from *avēre* to crave.

This means that the word was first used in the 13th century, and came from Norman French. It entered Norman French from Latin, and came originally from a Latin verb meaning 'to crave'. The line marked over the 'e' tells us that the Latin word is pronounced with a long vowel, like the sound in *bear*, not *berry*.

Using a dictionary in book form

You may find more information in a dictionary in book form than in an online one, especially if you use a large one such as the *Collins English Dictionary* or the *Concise Oxford Dictionary*. Some of this is given in abbreviated form.

Examples are:
- *n.* (noun)
- *v.* (verb)
- *adj.* (adjective)
- *adv.* (adverb)

You will find all abbreviations used at the front of the dictionary. You should also find a guide to the way that pronunciation is shown.

To use a book-form dictionary, you will need to understand **alphabetisation**. First, you need to know the order of the alphabet. Then you need to apply it letter by letter:
- harm
- harmful
- harmless
- harmonica
- harmonise
- harmony

Making better word choices will enable you to write precisely and concisely. See Topic 7.2.

You can speed up your search if you know that the first complete word entry for a verso (left-hand) page is given at the top-left of that page, and the last word of a recto (right-hand) page is given at the top-right of the page. This means you can tell at a glance what the alphabetical range of the two pages will be.

Look up the following words in a dictionary: epistle, eradicate, voracious, amiable. Write sentences containing them. Then use a thesaurus to find alternatives for each word.

Using a thesaurus to find synonyms and related words

Using a thesaurus is one of the best ways to increase your vocabulary, giving you a wider range of words to choose from, and helping you to be more precise. A thesaurus, online or in book form, will give you a range of words that are *close* in meaning to the one you look up. If they mean exactly the same thing – although the tone may be different, as in *ask* and *enquire* – they are **synonyms**. However, the words listed in the thesaurus may only be broadly similar.

For example, if you look up *ask* in the Collins online *English Thesaurus*, the first list of related meanings is:

- inquire, question, quiz, query, interrogate.

This could be useful if you wanted a replacement word because you had already used *ask* a lot, or if you wanted to be more precise. However, you cannot just substitute one word for another:

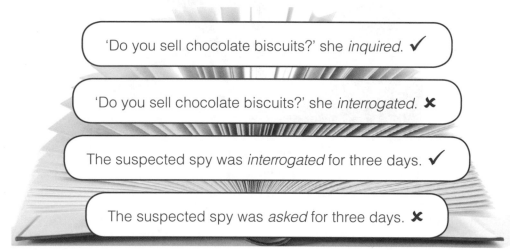

'Do you sell chocolate biscuits?' she *inquired*. ✓

'Do you sell chocolate biscuits?' she *interrogated*. ✗

The suspected spy was *interrogated* for three days. ✓

The suspected spy was *asked* for three days. ✗

Antonyms – opposites

Antonyms are the opposites of words. Not all words have opposites. Many opposites can be formed using **prefixes** (see Topic 7.5). Other opposites are completely different words, not formed using prefixes or suffixes, as in:

- beautiful – ugly
- clever – stupid
- relaxed – tense.

Again, these just have to be learned. However, some books of antonyms are available, and the *Collins English Thesaurus* (www.collinsdictionary.com/dictionary/english-thesaurus) offers opposites beneath the meanings for many words.

Progress Check

1. What is meant by the *derivation* of a word?
2. Put in alphabetical order: absolutely, aardvark, abstain, acute, absolve, accessory, ace
3. What are *synonyms* and *antonyms*?
4. Why must you take care in using a thesaurus to find replacement words?

7.5 Prefixes

A **prefix** goes at the beginning of a word to change its meaning. There are numerous prefixes, some of which are listed below.

Prefix	Meaning	Example
anti	opposing, against	anti-aircraft, antibiotic, antisocial, anticlimax
de	removal, reversal	demystify, defrost, decompose
out	exceeding, external	outweigh, outnumber, outdo, outboard
over	too much, top	overconfident, overjoyed, overcoat, oversee
micro	small-scale	microphone, microscope, micro-organism
pre	before	prehistoric, previous, prefix
re	again	return, reawake, rewrite, rebuild
semi	partly	semi-invalid, semi-detached, semicircle
sub	under	submarine, sub-standard, subterranean
super	beyond, extra	supernatural, supersonic, super-size

Can you think of other prefixes, or other examples of those shown above?

Forming opposites with prefixes

In many cases, the easiest way to form the **antonym** (opposite) of a word is to use a **prefix** to reverse its meaning.

Common prefixes forming opposites (especially for adjectives) are:

    un-   in-   im-   il-   ir-

You need to learn or look up which prefixes to use with which words. However, there are rules for *im-*, *il-* and *ir-*:

> *im-* comes before 'b', 'm' or 'p': imbalance, immeasurable, impossible, impolite, immoral

> *il-* comes before 'l': illegal, illegitimate, illiterate, illegible, illicit

> *ir-* comes before 'r': irrelevant, irregular, irrational, irreligious, irreducible

Un- and *in-* words

These just have to be learned, though the more you read, the more you will get used to seeing the correct form, and therefore remember it. Most of these words are adjectives. There are a few exceptions, such as *unburden* and *unzip* (verbs).

• ungroomed

imbalance

Words taking *un-* to form their opposite	Opposites with *in-*, *im-*, *il-* or *ir-*
available	inactive
balanced	imbalance
certain	incoherent
delivered	indifferent
educated	ineducable
friendly	inferior
grateful	ingratitude
heroic	inhuman
interesting	inimitable
just	injustice
knit	
lawful	illegal
marked	impossible
noticed	innocuous
opened	inoperative
promising	imperishable
questionable	
registered	irresponsible
stable	insensitive
talented	intolerant
used	
ventilated	invisible
washed	involuntary
yielding	
zip	

Hyphens with prefixes

Some prefixes are normally followed by a hyphen, especially those ending in a vowel, to avoid any confusion.

Some commonly hyphenated words with prefixes are:
- anti-inflammatory, anti-intellectual
- pre-loading, pre-Victorian
- ex-wife, ex-headmaster, ex-army, etc.

In addition, some prefixes are commonly added to a variety of words, as if they were actually separate words. The prefixes 'semi', 'pro' and 'ex' are used in this way, to mean 'almost', 'in favour of' and 'former'. In these cases, they are rarely printed without a hyphen.

Examples are:
- semi-literate, semi-official
- pro-independence, pro-EU
- ex-pupil, ex-minister.

Forming verb opposites using *de-* and *dis-*

Many verbs can be turned into their opposite (or almost their opposite) using the prefixes *de-* or *dis-*, though it is not always as simple as adding the prefix. Some are shown below.

De-	Dis-
deactivate	disagree
decelerate (opp. accelerate)	disappear
decontaminate	disapprove
deform	disband
dehumanise	discolour
dematerialise	dishearten
destabilise	disinfect

Write six prefixes on a piece of paper. Put them in a hat and practise picking out one at a time and thinking of a sentence containing a word that uses the prefix.

Making adjectives and nouns from prefixed words

• deformation

Some of these words using *de-* and *dis-* can be turned into adjectives by the addition of a **suffix**, as in 'deactivated', disagreeable' and 'disapproving'.

Some can also be turned into nouns: 'deactivation', 'disagreement', 'deceleration'.

Which others can be changed to adjectives or nouns in this way?

1. What do the prefixes *anti*, *pre* and *semi* mean?
2. Think of two words using the prefix *sub*.
3. Use prefixes to form the opposites of *grateful* and *gratitude*.
4. Do you *disactivate* the burglar alarm or *deactivate* it?

Progress Check

7.6 Suffixes

Suffixes go at the ends of words to change their meaning. They can be **grammatical** or **derivational**.

Grammatical suffixes are just the endings that change the grammatical form of a verb, as in:

- light<u>en</u>
- walk<u>ed</u>
- sleep<u>ing</u>
- small<u>est</u>

Derivational suffixes give a word a new meaning based on the original word, often one in a new word class. As with prefixes, there are many of these. Some are listed below.

Suffix	Word class formed	Example
-ation	Noun	exploration, hyphenation, commendation
-er		learner, walker, driver, plumber
-cian		musician, dietician, mathematician
-ness		goodness, nastiness, emptiness
-ment		enjoyment, predicament, merriment
-al	Adjective	musical, digital, minimal
-able		enjoyable, employable, manageable
-ible		defensible, incorrigible, edible, flexible, legible
-uble		soluble, voluble
-ly	Adverb	nicely, quietly, noisily, excitedly
-ise/ize	Verb	recognise, realise, materialise
-ate		originate, hesitate, elevate

Can you think of other suffixes, or other words formed using the ones above?

-able, -ible, -uble

These three suffixes all mean 'able to be'. So, *flexible* means 'able to be flexed'; *manageable* means 'able to be managed'. The third ending is rare, so you need not worry much about spelling words that use this suffix. The *-able* suffix is the commonest, but there are quite a few *-ible* words, so you will have to learn their spellings.

Opposites using suffixes

A suffix comes at the end of a word to modify its meaning. Some pairs of opposite adjectives can be made using the suffixes *-ful* and *-less*. See the examples below. Note that the spelling is *ful*, not *full*.

artful	artless
mindful	mindless
thoughtful	thoughtless
careful	careless
joyful	joyless
tasteful	tasteless
lawful	lawless
useful	useless

Use a dictionary to find opposites beginning with *in-*, *im-*, *il-* or *ir-*. Try to find four for each prefix. Write the original word (without the prefix) on the reverse (sticky side) of a sticky note and attach it to your wall. Then randomly turn over one at a time and see how quickly you can say the right prefix to make the opposite.

- joyful
- joyless
- careless
- careful

1. Which is correct? Enjoyable/enjoyible; flexible/flexable; edible/edable; regrettable/regrettible.
2. Using the correct prefixes, make the opposites of: forgiving, resolved (decided), polite, legible.
3. What are the opposites of joyful, fearless, careless?
4. What are the opposites of satisfaction, materialise, contented?

Progress Check

7.7 Nouns and noun phrases

A **noun** is a word for a thing.

Types of noun

A **proper noun** is a name, for example for a person, country or ship:

• **Pauline** sailed to **South Africa** on the *Queen Elizabeth*.

All other nouns are **common nouns** but these are sometimes divided into two types: concrete and abstract.

Concrete nouns are words for things in the physical world:

• table, banana, sheep, boy, gas, air, elephant

Abstract nouns are words for ideas, concepts or phenomena that are not part of the physical world:

• love, death, history, danger, certainty

Grammatically, both types of common noun are used in the same way. However, it is worth remembering that, although abstract nouns help you to write about ideas concisely and effectively, if you use too many abstract nouns you risk losing your readers' interest.

Which statement below do you find more appealing?

The expression of ideas in writing has more power than physical violence.

The pen is mightier than the sword.

Noun phrases

A **noun phrase** is a group of words that acts like a noun in a sentence. It can be the subject of a sentence, as below:

- **Going to sleep** is one way to avoid work.
- **His drinking** became a problem.
- **Being tired** can lead to accidents.

A noun phrase can also be the **predicate** of a sentence (what is said about the subject):

- My most appealing character trait is **being modest**.
- I just enjoy **messing about**.
- Parents hate **loud drum-playing**.

Place three objects in front of you. Make up a sentence for each that contains a noun phrase involving that object.

Nouns replacing phrases

Having a good noun vocabulary will help you to write concisely and with more impact. A group of words can often be replaced by a single well-chosen noun. See if you can match up the phrases below with the noun that could replace them. If in doubt, check your answers using a dictionary.

She is **someone who has aided her country's enemies**.	revolution
Antarctic wildlife is all part of a fragile **network of relationships in which different species depend on each other for survival**.	hypocrite
He is **someone who criticises others for the faults he has himself**.	hypothesis
London is the UK's **largest city and its administrative centre**.	traitor
If your **idea put forward as a basis of reasoning** is correct, then there must indeed be other intelligent life in the universe.	compromise
Any marriage involves **reaching agreements that both partners can accept even if neither sees them as ideal**.	ecosystem
He wanted to start a **process by which the social order is transformed or replaced**.	capital

Collective nouns

A **collective noun** is a word for a group of things, such as:

- flock, herd, pod (dolphins), school (whales), shoal (fish)

These are normally treated as singular in a sentence:

- The reindeer herd is galloping across the frozen steppes, but the wolf pack is gaining on them.

1. What do Dave, Canada and the *Titanic* have in common?
2. Is a common noun (a) vulgar, (b) much-used, (c) not a proper noun?
3. What is a noun phrase?
4. How is a collective noun usually treated grammatically in a sentence?

Progress Check

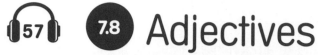

7.8 Adjectives

An **adjective** is a **describing word**: it provides information about a **noun** or **noun phrase**.

Where adjectives are most often used

You can use adjectives anywhere in a piece of writing to give more information about a noun. However, they are particularly important in a description of a person or place, particularly when they are first being described in a novel or story. See the following examples.

> Oh! But he was a tight-fisted hand at the grind-stone, Scrooge! A squeezing, wrenching, grasping, scraping, clutching, covetous, old sinner!
>
> Charles Dickens, *A Christmas Carol*

Here Dickens uses a series of adjectives to give us a quick insight into Scrooge's character. Notice that some of the words are adjectives formed from verbs.

> A few miles south of Soledad, the Salinas River drops in close to the hillside bank and runs deep and green. The water is warm too, for it has slipped twinkling over the yellow sands in the sunlight before reaching the narrow pool. On one side of the river the golden foothill slopes curve up to the strong and rocky Gabilan Mountains, but on the valley side the water is lined with trees – willows fresh and green with every spring, carrying in their lower leaf junctures the debris of the winter's flooding; and sycamores with mottled, white, recumbent limbs and branches that arch over the pool. On the sandy bank under the trees the leaves lie deep and so crisp that a lizard makes a great skittering if he runs among them.
>
> John Steinbeck, *Of Mice and Men*

Steinbeck uses a great many adjectives to paint a word picture of an important setting at the start of the novel. Sometimes he uses two adjectives to describe one noun, as in 'strong and rocky Gabilan Mountains'. On one occasion he even uses three: 'mottled, white, recumbent limbs'.

Wuthering Heights is the name of Mr Heathcliff's dwelling. 'Wuthering' being a significant provincial adjective, descriptive of the atmospheric tumult to which its station is exposed in stormy weather. Pure, bracing ventilation they must have up there at all times, indeed: one may guess the power of the north wind blowing over the edge, by the excessive slant of a few stunted firs at the end of the house; and by a range of gaunt thorns all stretching their limbs one way, as if craving alms of the sun. Happily, the architect had foresight to build it strong: the narrow windows are deeply set in the wall, and the corners defended with large jutting stones.

Emily Brontë, *Wuthering Heights*

Here Emily Brontë introduces the rugged house on the edge of the moors that is the main setting of the novel. The description is important as it suggests the wild emotions of the novel and the rugged character of one of the two main characters, Heathcliff. Find the adjectives. What do they suggest about the house and its inhabitants?

Use adjectives with care

Dickens uses a lot of adjectives to describe Scrooge, but this is quite unusual. *A Christmas Carol* is a fairly short book with a strong moral message, and Dickens wants to get on with telling us what Scrooge is like as quickly as possible. Notice that in the description from *Of Mice and Men*, the most adjectives Steinbeck uses at a time is three. Even this is quite a lot, and there is a general rule in modern fiction writing that you should not use more than three adjectives together. If you overuse adjectives, it can slow the writing down.

In your own writing, it is a good idea to look at any cases where you have used more than one adjective and ask yourself if it is really necessary. Often, your description will have more impact if you use only your most powerful adjective, or perhaps just two rather than three. This is especially true if two or more of the adjectives are close in meaning.

Look at these examples.

> *He was a moody, bad-tempered, irritable man who hated all children.*
Three closely related adjectives. Which one would you keep?

> *We strolled through the beautiful, colourful garden.*
Probably beautiful because it is colourful – so delete which?

> *They threw me into a deep, tomblike, depressing dungeon.*
Which adjective could you easily delete? (Which one goes without saying?) Which one could replace both of the others?

> *The crowd was angry, wound up to a fever pitch, baying for blood.*
One adjective and two adjectival phrases. Which would you definitely scrap?

Show, don't tell

The phrase 'Show, don't tell' is an important piece of advice in fiction writing. It is usually more enjoyable for a reader to find out about a character by what they do and say, or how they see things, than to be told. So, this means that at times it is better to have a character *show* what they are like rather than using adjectives to describe them.

Compare:
> *He was an irritable, unkind, violent man.*
> *'Out of my way!' he snarled, kicking the cat.*

Which version tells us more vividly what the man is like?

Think of six adjectives to describe the appearance of the man in the picture below.

Find a mirror. Look into it. Try to think yourself into four different moods, changing your expression to match each. For each mood write down three adjectives. Then choose one and write a third-person description of yourself in that mood.

Progress Check

1. When are adjectives particularly likely to be used in fiction?
2. What adjectives describe the sands, the pool and the foothill slopes in the *Of Mice and Men* extract?
3. What is the most adjectives you should normally use in a row?
4. How can you reveal character using fewer adjectives?

7.9 Verbs and adverbs

Verbs are **doing** words – words which describe an **action**. So, the following are all verbs:

run	think	laugh	sing	clap
play	pretend	cry	shout	

However, some verbs are not obviously active:

be	exist	conclude	begin	end	persist

Choosing vivid verbs can greatly improve your writing. Read the following action passage and see how well-chosen verbs bring it to life.

> Hord **swung** his axe at Torak's throat. Torak **ducked**. Wolf **sprang** at Hord, **sinking** his teeth into his wrist. Hord **bellowed** and **dropped** his axe, but with his free fist **rained** blows on Wolf's unprotected head.
>
> 'No!' **yelled** Torak, **drawing** his knife and **launching** himself at Hord. Hord **seized** Wolf by the scruff and **threw** him against the basalt, then **twisted** round and **lunged** for the Nanuak **swinging** from Torak's neck.
>
> Torak **jerked** out of reach. Hord **went for** his legs, **throwing** him backwards into the ice. But as Torak **went down**, he **tore** the pouch from his neck, and **hurled** it up the trail out of Hord's reach. Wolf **righted** himself with a shake and **leapt** for the pouch, **catching** it in mid-air, but **landing** perilously close to the edge of the ravine.
>
> 'Wolf!' **cried** Torak, **struggling** beneath Hord, who was **straddling** his chest, and kneeling on his arms.
>
> Wolf's hind paws **scrabbled** wildly at the edge. From just below him came a menacing growl – then the bear's black claws **sliced** the air, narrowly **missing** Wolf's paws…
>
> Michelle Paver, *Wolf Brother*

Notice that not all the verbs highlighted here are unusual. It is perfectly acceptable for some verbs in an account to be ordinary. For example, 'dropped' and 'threw' are ordinary, though the author uses a more exciting word for 'threw' a few lines later – 'hurled'. However, most of the words are chosen to give a vivid and precise impression of the action. See, for example:

- **bellowed** – indicates Hord's loud, angry, desperate cry, almost like an animal
- **rained** – indicates blows falling as thick and fast as rain
- **lunged** – says in one word 'threw himself forward trying to reach and grab'
- **straddling** – sitting on something with legs on both sides
- **scrabbled** – desperately tried to get his paws over the edge.

Notice that two verb phrases are highlighted in the extract:

- went down
- went for.

The verb 'went' (past tense of 'go') is quite ordinary, but it works well in these verb phrases to add a sense of action and excitement.

Adverbs

Adverbs **add information to a verb** or, less often, an **adjective**. They can be very useful, but you should use them sparingly in your writing. It is often more effective to use a really good verb. For example, why write, 'He shouted desperately' when you can write 'He screamed' or 'He yelled'?

The Michelle Paver extract uses very few adverbs with the verbs:

- scrabbled **wildly**
- **narrowly** missing.

In all these case, the adverbs are justified, adding valuable information or flavour.

Get up and tidy your room! Then think about what you have just done and write three sentences using interesting and vivid verbs to describe your actions.

Progress Check

1. Why use vivid verbs in your writing?
2. Should all your verb choices be unusual?
3. To which types of words do adverbs add information?
4. Why should you be sparing in your use of adverbs?

7.10 Improving your spelling 59

English spelling is just not consistent. A famous writer, George Bernard Shaw, who wanted spelling to be made easier, pointed this out by inventing a word:

ghoti

How would you pronounce this word?

Answer: 'fish'. Shaw explained it like this:

- *gh* as in *enough* (f)
- *o* as in *women* (i)
- *ti* as in *lotion* (sh).

Despite the inconsistencies of English spelling, the more you read, the more you will get used to seeing words spelled correctly. If you are lucky, you will not even need to make a special effort to learn spellings. However, most people have difficulty with a least a few spellings, so it is useful to know some techniques for improving your spelling.

Look, say, cover, spell, check

One simple but effective technique is to look at the word you want to learn, say it out loud, then cover it and attempt to write it down. If you cannot remember the spelling immediately, uncover one letter at a time until you can. Keep testing yourself on the word every so often till you always get it right.

look   cover

say   spell

Keep a spell book

Add to your 'Look, cover, spell' technique by writing words you get wrong in a small notebook. Use one or two pages for each letter of the alphabet. (Perhaps use just one page for X, Y, Z!) Make sure you write clearly enough to read your own handwriting, and make sure you copy the word correctly in the first place, or you will be learning a misspelling.

Say it silly

Many English words that have difficult spellings can be spoken aloud exactly as they appear, which may sound silly but may help you to remember. For example:

- congestion – con-ges-ti-on
- knight – k-nig-ht
- jeopardy (danger) – je-o-pardy.

Spelling common sounds

It is often helpful to learn spellings by grouping words together according the shared letter patterns and pronunciation. See some patterns in the table below.

eigh	igh	ough	augh	tion	sion
weigh	fight	rough	caught	attention	revision
eight	fright	tough	haughty	mention	television
neigh	light	enough	daughter	election	tension
neighbour	might	bought	taught	selection	fusion
freight	night	brought	slaughter	convection	confusion
	plight	though	laughter	addition	pretension
	tight	thought		correction	
	sight	through			
		fought			
		nought			
		sought			

Mnemonics

Mnemonics are **memory techniques**. They can be used to help you remember spellings. For example, you could make up sentences incorporating two or more words in the same letter pattern groups:

- Are you **rough** and **tough enough**?
- What do my **eight neighbours weigh**?
- I got into a **fight** at **night**.
- I **taught** your **haughty daughter**.
- Stand to **attention** when you **mention** your **detention**.
- Avoid **confusion** and **tension** in your **revision**.

Another type of mnemonic focuses on individual words, making up a sentence using words beginning with each letter:

- **B**ig **e**lephants **c**an **a**lways **u**nderstand **s**mall **e**lephants.

Look in your English exercise book and find three words that you have spelled incorrectly. Use the 'Look, say, cover, spell' technique on them. Can you also use the 'Say it silly' technique on them?

Progress Check

1. According to George Bernard Shaw, what did *ghoti* spell?
2. Complete the technique: Look…
3. What is a good mnemonic for the words *rough*, *tough* and *enough*?

7.11 Spelling rules

Although so many spellings seem inconsistent, there are some spelling rules.

The magic 'e'

English has five **vowels**: a, e, i, o, u. In addition, the letter 'y' is sometimes used to make the 'i' sound, as in *crystal*.

In the words *hat*, *met*, *win*, *lop* and *cut* the vowels are pronounced with a short sound – the same sound with which you probably pronounced them when first learning the alphabet. Adding an 'e' to them changes this to a long vowel sound:

hate

mete (as in 'mete out punishment')

wine

lope

cute

Doubling

A double letter can also change vowel sounds, and can overrule the **magic 'e'**.

* bat – batting – batted
* net – netting – netted
* bin – binning – binned
* hop – hopping – hopped
* but – butting – butted

How would these double-letter words be pronounced if the letters were not doubled?

'I before E except after C'

This is the best-known spelling rule. The full version is: 'I before E except after C, but only when the sound is EE'.

So, this rule applies to words such as:

relief	receipt
brief	deceive
belief	conceited (all after 'c', so spelled 'ei')
chief	neigh
thief	reign
field	neighbour
receive	weigh (the sound is 'ay', not 'ee')

The letter 'q'

The letter 'q' is always followed by 'u':

quiet

quite

queue

queen

enquire

require

queasy

question

Spelling plurals and verb endings

Words taking 'es'

Simple plurals are formed by adding 's', as in *cats* and *dogs*. Similarly, the third person singular, present tense of a word like 'wait' just takes an 's': *waits*.

In the case of a noun or verb ending in 's', 'ch', 'sh', 'x' or 'z', the plural or third person singular, present tense take 'es', as in the table below.

Noun singular	Noun plural	Verb	Verb 3rd person singular, present tense
gas	gases	surpass	surpasses
church	churches	screech	screeches
bush	bushes	buzz	buzzes
fox	foxes	fix	fixes
waltz	waltzes	fizz	fizzes

Nouns ending in 'y'

If a word ends in 'y' after a consonant (not a vowel), form the plural by replacing the 'y' with 'ies':

- fairy – fairies
- dairy – dairies
- diary – diaries
- ferry – ferries
- lily – lilies
- lolly – lollies
- bunny – bunnies

In the rare case of a noun ending in 'ey', as in *honey*, form the plural by adding 's' in the normal way.

Nouns or verbs ending in 'o'

If the word ends in 'o' after a vowel, just add 's' to form the plural:

* studio – studios
* radio – radios
* rodeo – rodeos

If the word ends in 'o' after a consonant, add 'es':

* potato – potatoes
* mango – mangoes
* tomato – tomatoes

Make up your own mnemonics for spelling rules, write them on cards or sheets of paper, and stick them on your wall.

Note: you should never use an **apostrophe** in these plurals. Greengrocers often make this mistake!

The greengrocer's apostrophe

English apple's
£1.30 kilo
59p lb

1. How does the letter 'e' change the word *cute*?
2. What rule is broken by the words *weird* and *seize*?
3. What is the plural of *birch*?
4. What is the plural of *poppy*?

Progress Check

7.12 # Homophones

The commonest type of spelling error is the **homophone**. *Homo-* is a prefix meaning 'same'; *-phone* is a suffix meaning 'sound'. So, a homophone is a word that has the same sound as another word but a different spelling and meaning, often leading to confusion.

Perhaps the most commonly confused homophones are those shown below.

there (as in 'over there')	their (as in 'their coats')	they're (they are)
to (towards)	too (as well, too much)	two (2)

Other homophones are shown in the next table.

aloud (out loud)	allowed (permitted)
bare (uncovered)	bear (animal)
cereal	serial
isle	aisle
it's (short for 'it is')	its (possessive adjective, as in 'The dog ate its dinner')
might (as in 'I might go to university')	mite (as in a tiny insect)
mist (noun: light fog)	missed (verb, as in 'I missed the bus')
past (noun: history)	passed (verb: 'We passed your house')
practice (noun)	practise (verb)
principle (a rule)	principal (most important, head)
stationery (writing paper, etc.)	stationary (motionless)
strait (narrow place or difficult situation)	straight (direct)
where (as in 'where we are')	wear (clothes)

Progress Check

1. What does the word *homophone* come from?
2. Spell the word that could be used for a head teacher.
3. What is the correct word for writing paper, envelopes, etc.?
4. Correct this: The too girls didn't know wear there practise room was.

Worked questions

1. **Rewrite the following passage using more vivid verbs to replace the underlined verbs and verb–adverb combinations.** *(20 marks)*

Water had been <u>slowly getting</u> into the boat for the last hour, and now she was <u>going down</u> fast. Now, with a groaning sound, the stern <u>suddenly went</u> into the depths, and the prow <u>went</u> up towards the grey sky.

'Jump!' <u>said</u> Ben <u>loudly</u>, already in the sea and <u>holding onto</u> a lifebuoy.

Lyn <u>held on to</u> the raised prow. She was <u>moving all over</u> with fear, yet could not bring herself to <u>jump</u> into the choppy sea. Finally she <u>moved in a wobbly way</u> forward and <u>fell</u> into the water, her arms <u>moving confusedly</u> over her head.

The cold water seemed to bring her to her senses and she began to swim towards Ben. Now and again a bigger wave <u>fell</u> onto her head and <u>wet</u> her, <u>making her unclear about her direction</u> for a moment. Then she <u>went on</u> again.

When she reached Ben, her lips were <u>wobbling</u> with the cold, and her teeth were <u>opening and closing rapidly</u>.

'Someone should get our radio signal and start looking for us,' Ben <u>said loudly</u> above the sound of the sea.

'We're going to die!' Lyn <u>said suddenly without thinking</u>.

'We'll be fine.'

Lyn <u>held on to</u> one side of the lifebuoy, but something made her <u>turn suddenly</u> in the water. As she <u>looked across</u> the waves, she saw it. A dark fin <u>coming</u> towards them <u>very fast</u>.

Water had been <u>seeping</u> into the boat for the last hour, and now she was <u>sinking</u> fast. Now, with a groaning sound, the stern <u>plunged</u> into the depths, and the prow <u>tilted</u> up towards the grey sky.

'Jump!' <u>yelled</u> Ben, already in the sea and <u>clutching</u> a lifebuoy.

Lyn <u>clung to</u> the raised prow. She was <u>shivering</u> with fear, yet could not bring herself to <u>leap</u> into the choppy sea. Finally she <u>staggered</u> forward and <u>toppled</u> into the water, her arms <u>flailing</u> over her head.

The cold water seemed to bring her to her senses and she began to swim towards Ben. Now and again a bigger wave <u>crashed</u> onto her head and <u>drenched</u> her, <u>disorientating her</u> for a moment. Then she <u>struck out</u> again.

When she reached Ben, her lips were <u>trembling</u> with the cold, and her teeth were <u>chattering</u>.

'Someone should get our radio signal and start looking for us,' Ben <u>shouted</u> above the sound of the sea.

'We're going to die!' Lyn <u>blurted out</u>.

'We'll be fine.'

Lyn <u>gripped</u> one side of the lifebuoy, but something made her <u>spin round</u> in the water. As she <u>scanned</u> the waves, she saw it. A dark fin <u>slicing</u> towards them.

2. **Rewrite the following passage using more vivid or interesting adjectives to replace those underlined. You may sometimes have to change 'a' to 'an' or 'an' to 'a'.** *(20 marks)*

Davies was a <u>nasty</u> and <u>completely unkind</u> criminal. His record included armed burglary, assault and arson. Now he had managed to get himself a job as caretaker at a comprehensive school by providing <u>pretend</u> ID documents. Although usually <u>rude</u> and <u>horrid</u> in his private life, he was able to put on a <u>nice, polite</u> manner when necessary. This is how he fooled Mrs Haynes, the head teacher, usually a very <u>clever</u> woman.

This <u>bad</u> man's <u>sneaky</u> plan was to make a spare set of keys and give them to his accomplices, 'Smasher' Harris and 'Ratty' Wilson. Harris was a jewel thief who had stolen numerous <u>bright</u> diamond necklaces and <u>very expensive</u> bracelets. Wilson was a <u>thin</u> man with <u>pointy</u> features. He was <u>a very good</u> safecracker, which would be useful, as Davies did not have the combination to the school safe. He had tried to get it from the school secretary but, although she was usually <u>very easy to convince of something being true</u>, she had proved <u>difficult to persuade</u> in this case. Davies had given her his <u>nicest</u> smile but it had been no use.

Davies was a <u>vicious</u> and <u>ruthless</u> criminal. His record included armed burglary, assault and arson. Now he had managed to get himself a job as caretaker at a comprehensive school by providing <u>fake</u> ID documents. Although usually <u>insulting</u> and <u>abusive</u> in his private life, he was able to put on a <u>charming, respectful</u> manner when necessary. This is how he fooled Mrs Haynes, the head teacher, usually a very <u>astute</u> woman.

This <u>evil</u> man's <u>devious</u> plan was to make a spare set of keys and give them to his accomplices, 'Smasher' Harris and 'Ratty' Wilson. Harris was a jewel thief who had stolen numerous <u>sparkling</u> diamond necklaces and <u>precious</u> bracelets. Wilson was a <u>lean</u> man with <u>sharp</u> features. He was an <u>expert</u> safecracker, which would be useful, as Davies did not have the combination to the school safe. He had tried to get it from the school secretary, but, although she was usually <u>credulous</u>, she had proved <u>intractable</u> in this case. Davies had given her his <u>most winning</u> smile, but it had been no use.

Practice questions

1. **Rewrite the following using single words to replace the underlined phrases.**

    a) He <u>ran quickly</u> for the bus. *(1 mark)*

    b) She <u>said she hadn't</u> done it. *(1 mark)*

    c) He was campaigning for Scotland's <u>right to rule itself</u>. *(1 mark)*

    d) He is a <u>person who does the things for which he criticises others</u>. *(1 mark)*

    e) I want to get a job in <u>producing goods in factories</u>. *(1 mark)*

2. **Rewrite the following paragraph, choosing the precise word where there are options, and making the other underlined phrases more concise.** *(9 marks)*

    Ewan was feeling rather [irritable/resentful/furious] about having to clean the car. His father had practically [required/ordered/demanded] him to do it. It was so [unethical/biased/unjust]. After all, it was not his car, and he only ever needed to be given lifts in it because his parents [took a stand/insisted/persisted] on living so far away from the town – in a <u>middle of nowhere</u> farmhouse. His parents treated him like their <u>person who has to do whatever they are told to do whether they like it or not</u>! He <u>walked heavily and slowly</u> to the tap to fetch another bucket of water, but then he remembered that there was a hose in the garden shed. He found it and <u>got it to connect</u> to the tap. This made the job considerably easier. He was spraying the car and listening to his i-Pod when the church band came <u>walking in step</u> up the road.

3. **Rewrite the following paragraph more concisely by choosing nouns or noun phrases to replace the underlined phrases.** *(10 marks)*

    I paced around my cell. If I did not find a way to escape, I would soon be facing a <u>group of men lined up to execute me by shooting me</u>. I did not think of myself as <u>someone who was easily overcome by fears</u>, but it was hard not to feel a sense of <u>giving in to negative thoughts</u> in the present circumstances.

    To calm my mind, I thought about how I had got to this point. True, I had joined the <u>process by which a country is socially transformed</u>, but I had done this for the best possible reasons. I was a man of <u>adherence</u> to a <u>moral code</u>; I was not a <u>man who undermines his country by supporting its enemies</u>. All I wanted was <u>everyone being treated equally and fairly</u>.

    In my <u>feeling of high emotional arousal</u>, I found that I was beating my fist on the cell wall. Imagine my <u>sense of being caught out by the unexpected</u> when I found that one of the stones was loose. I got my fingers round it and tugged. It came out. With some effort, I prised out the stone next to it. Had I found a way to gain my <u>state of freedom</u>?

4. **Rewrite the following paragraph with correct spellings.** *(25 marks)*

I had promised to do the supermarket shopping as Mum was two tired after work. Unfortunatly I had only left myself about half an our. Would it be enouhgh? Perhaps if I really hurried. First I had to get breakfast serial – I new that much. The trouble is, theirs to much choice. Also, I hadn't had a lot of practise. Wear are the cornflakes, I thought. An assistant pointed to an isle, but when I got their it was full of stationary and dairys.

After about ten minuets I was doing better. I had almost filled the basket. Still, the time was rushing passed, and I still had to find some iced lolies, potatos and tomatos. And I musn't forge to ask for a reciept, Mum said. Just then, as I looked down past the qeue of customers at the till, I noticed someone acting strangly. He was quitely tucking a bottle of wine up his sweatshirt. What should I do? I was in a hurry. It would be a releif to discover that it was just a misteak. Oh no! Now I recognisd him: it was our next-door nieghbor!

5. **Rewrite the following passage, applying the technique of 'Show, don't tell' (see page 142). Focus especially on the underlined sections.** *(25 marks)*

Shannon was very nervous and miserable at finding herself outside the Head Teacher's office. The other girl sitting next to her, Becky Davitt, had been to blame but the teacher had resolved to punish them both. The door opened and the Head appeared. First he looked at Becky Davitt. He was not at all surprised to see her. He told her that she was always in trouble and he was sick of having to deal with her bad behaviour. She was a tough sort of girl, used to being criticised by teachers, and barely responsive to their comments or to punishment.

When the Head looked at Shannon he was clearly surprised, and told her so. Shannon considered trying to explain the situation, and he seemed prepared to listen, but then she felt afraid of Becky and her gang and stopped.

The Head was puzzled and at a loss as to what to do. He did not want to punish both girls but he felt that he had to, or it would seem unfair. He hated this kind of decision but he knew he had to do it.

After completing this chapter you should know about:

- writing in a consistent register and tone
- writing to explain, recount or describe
- writing letters, stories and poems
- writing reviews.

Learning Summary

8.1 Writing in a consistent register and tone

🎧 **62**

Register

The most important aspect of **register** is level of **formality**. You should pitch your register according to your audience, purpose and form.

Compare it with the spoken word. If you were giving a speech to an audience of teachers and parents on the importance of combating global warming, which of the following would be more appropriate?

1. Hey – how y'doin'? Cool. Listen up everyone. I'm here to say a few words about something that's gonna be a big problem before you know it. The planet's heating up. That's right – we're all gonna fry before long! Watch out London, because when those ice caps melt that water's gotta go somewhere! You'll need more than wellies!

See, it's like this. What with cars, and factories and stuff like that belching out loads of pollution – the old carbon dioxide and all that, it's, like, these gases are wrapping our old planet up in a big puffa jacket. Yeah – greenhouse gases they're called. It's gonna suddenly go crazy, if you know what I mean. It'll be like hotter than hell in some places and like an ice box in others. Then there's stuff

2. Good evening, ladies and gentlemen. Thank you for attending my talk this evening. Its purpose is to alert you to a rapidly growing problem – the problem of global warming. Scientists are now convinced that all the evidence points to the fact that annual mean temperatures are increasing, with potentially catastrophic results for the planet.

The technology on which our lifestyle depends, including motor transport and industry, is creating carbon dioxide and other greenhouse gases which are insulating our planet and trapping the heat from the sun's rays. The evidence suggests that the planet will, perhaps by 2030, reach a 'tipping point', the point at which heating and associated problems

For more on register, see Topic 2.3.

Find a newspaper or magazine article that is written in either a formal or informal register. Underline words and phrases that particularly create this register. Then rewrite some of it – one or two paragraphs – in a very different register.

like tsunamis and typhoons. They reckon that's all down to this warming thing too. I ain't fooling.

So, what I'm saying is, ease off on the electric, take the bus, and take your holidays at Southend-on-Sea, not the Bahamas. That's all from me, folks.

will escalate with increasing speed. This will increase the frequency of extreme weather effects that we are already experiencing, such as tsunamis and typhoons.

We should therefore do all we can to conserve energy by reducing our energy consumption, take public transport where possible, and avoid non-essential air travel. Thank for your attention.

It should be obvious to you that the first is more informal than the second. In fact, it is inappropriately informal for a serious subject and an audience of adult strangers, who will probably expect a more serious, persuasive approach to the subject.

Spot the following characteristics in the first speech:
- **slang** and **colloquial** (chatty) expressions (e.g. 'gonna fry!', 'belching out loads')
- overly familiar tone towards the audience: 'Listen up everyone', 'folks', etc.
- inappropriate humour (reference to London flooding, etc.)
- colloquial and vague vocabulary; e.g. 'stuff', 'go crazy', 'this warming thing'
- **non-standard English**; e.g. 'They reckon that's all down to', 'ain't'.

How does the second speech compare with this?

The key thing to remember is that your register in a piece of writing should be appropriate to the audience, purpose and form, and consistent. It should not, for example, begin by being formal and gradually become chatty.

Tone

For examples of tone, see Topic 2.4.

Tone is related to register but is wider. It relates to:
- the mood of a piece of writing – for example, angry, humorous, enthusiastic
- the relationship that the writer is aiming to create with the reader – for example, distant or friendly.

Decide on what tone you want to create and then use language accordingly. For example, if you want to be upbeat and enthusiastic in order to persuade, then choose positive language:

This is a fantastic opportunity to get involved in a really worthwhile project. You'll be able to hone your people skills, be wildly creative, and get some good practical experience. And, what's more, you'll be doing a job that could transform the lives of people in need. Apply today for a chance to shine, and make a difference!

What words or phrases here are particularly positive?

Progress Check

1. What register is 'Good evening, ladies and gentlemen'?
2. What makes 'It's gonna suddenly go crazy' informal?
3. What three factors should influence your use of register?
4. What tone do the words 'fantastic opportunity' suggest?

8.2 Writing to explain

 63

There are a number of situations in which you might be writing to explain – in other words, produce a piece of **explanatory writing**. For example, you might want to explain:

- how to use a device, such as a mobile phone
- how to find your house
- how you got involved in a hobby and why it appeals to you.

Writing instructions

Here are some tips for writing instructions:

- Put yourself in the position of the reader – what will they know already, and need to know?
- Be methodical – explain step by step, in a logical order, perhaps using numbers to organise the steps.
- Give helpful markers to reassure readers that they have got it right so far.
- Use clear, unambiguous language (that cannot be taken in more than one way).
- Be **concise** – do not be unnecessarily wordy.
- Use simple imperatives, such as 'Spread', 'put' and 'sit'.
- Use precise adverbs if they are likely to help, as in 'Spread *evenly*'.

What special points might you have to consider in explaining any of these?

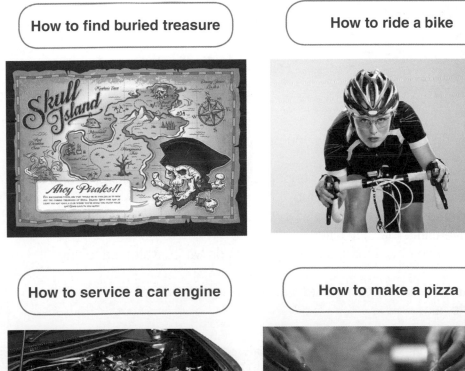

How to find buried treasure

How to ride a bike

How to service a car engine

How to make a pizza

Find a piece of technology that is difficult enough to require instructions, such as your phone. Remind yourself of what you have to do to carry out a basic procedure with it. Then write step-by-step instructions for it.

Explaining your hobby

This involves a different type of explanation from giving instructions. It is likely to be in three parts:

- the history of your becoming involved
- what the hobby is and what you do
- why it appeals to you.

An essay on, for example, how you became interested in canoeing might cover:

- living by a river and seeing canoeists going past, then talking to one who told you about a canoeing club
- your first efforts at canoeing – how you got on, what was difficult, and how you overcame the difficulties
- what you do now – for example, going off on 'white water' canoeing holidays
- why it appeals – exercise, fresh air, challenge, being on a river, wildlife, etc.

Progress Check

1. What is involved in putting yourself in the position of the reader?
2. How might you use numbers in instructions?
3. What is 'unambiguous' language?
4. In which of the pictured examples on page 157 would giving precise distances be important?

8.3 Recounting events

If you **recount events**, you tell someone what happened. If you recount events in writing, you are telling what happened to anyone who might read what you have written. What you say will depend on the intended **audience** and your **purpose** in recounting events.

Providing the key information

Imagine first that you were asked to provide a witness statement to the police because you had witnessed a robbery. The audience here would be the police, and perhaps eventually a judge and jury in court. The purpose would be to establish exactly what happened. Here is a list of the witness's comments.

- It was a lovely day.
- She hit him over the head with her handbag. It looked heavy.
- I live opposite Mrs Jones, at 61 Milverton Terrace, Hadnock.
- The man was about 6 feet tall, and thin. He looked a bit like my cousin Trevor.
- He didn't look to see if she was all right; he ran off towards the park.
- Poor Mrs Jones – such a nice lady. She's a retired nurse.
- There was a struggle.
- I saw a man I didn't recognise coming out of Mrs Jones's front door.
- Mrs Jones was walking home from bingo. She used to go on Thursdays at 2pm.
- She came through her gate just at the wrong moment.
- The daffodils in her garden were a sea of yellow.
- It's great that you've caught him.
- She fell and her head hit the garden wall. Then she stopped moving.
- He had short ginger hair and a rucksack.
- This was at about 4pm.
- He was wearing blue jeans and a short black leather jacket.
- I'm glad she's recovering.

Can you work out exactly what happened, and in what order? Which details are irrelevant to a witness statement?

Recounting personal events

If you are recounting personal events and they are *not* intended to be a witness statement – as in an autobiography – you still need to be selective. If you include every possible detail, your readers will be bored. Instead, you need to provide enough key information for them to imagine the events.

You need to give an idea of the order in which things happened, but it might make the story more interesting if you withhold some information and only reveal it later, for dramatic effect. This has a lot in common with writing a story.

You may sometimes be asked to respond to essay questions like this:
* Describe an event that had a big influence on you and why it did.

Here, you are not just being asked for facts: you are being asked to *describe*, which involves making it interesting for your reader.

Supposing you had witnessed the robbery detailed in the bullet list and you were describing it in response to this essay question. Which details would be irrelevant? Which ones would you develop? Which might you withhold for dramatic effect?

Your account might begin like this:

Go to a place where you can observe people – for example, a café, a shopping centre, a library, a playground. Find a vantage point from which you can watch what happens for a few minutes. Make notes if you think it will help you. Then recount what you have seen.

It was a warm afternoon in late spring. I was just admiring the sea of daffodils in Mrs Jones's garden across the street, when, to my surprise the front door opened. I thought she'd gone to bingo, the same as she usually did on a Thursday, but there was her door opening. Curious, I came closer to the window. I was even more baffled when I saw a rotund figure in a brown overcoat and red beret bustling along the street towards the front gate. It was Mrs Jones!

How has the writer of this paragraph withheld information to make it a better story? How might you continue it, using the information in the bullet list?

Personal opinion and feelings

Notice that the essay question is in two parts. The second part asks you to explain why the event had a big influence on you. Perhaps you witnessed the attack on Mrs Jones and this made you decide to join the police, or become a social worker, or move to the country, or help the elderly. You will have to explain this in an interesting way that the reader will relate to.

For example, this part of the essay might begin like this:

> For days I thought about the injustice in the world, and how people like Mrs Jones's attacker so often get away with their cowardly crimes. I also thought about Mrs Jones's courage in defending her home against this intruder. Eventually, I came to this conclusion…

How might you continue this part of the essay?

1. What factors should decide what information you give?
2. If writing a personal account, how will your selection of information be different from what you would provide in a witness statement?
3. In what ways might biographical writing be similar to a story or novel?

Progress Check

8.4 Describing a place

If you are describing a place, whether in a story or in non-fiction, you need to choose **details** well, and choose **language** that will make the place come to life for your readers. You also need to **sequence** the details in what seems like a natural order.

Describing a city

Here is a description of the centre of York.

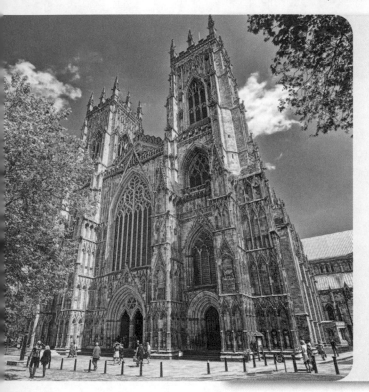

> The middle of York is lovely. It is full of old streets with funny names, and very old houses and shops. The Minster, which is really a big cathedral, is tall and impressive. Some of the shops look as if they have been there for a very long time. Some sell old sweets, some sell chocolates, and some sell other things. There are also posh modern restaurants. There are some bits with cobbles, and even a big Roman pillar that got dug up from somewhere. Guy Fawkes was born here, and there is a pub named after him. I like York. It is really great.

What would your English teacher think of this description? Hopefully, not a lot! This description does select some promising details, but the language used does very little to make the place interesting or exciting for readers. How would you improve it?

Here is one possible improved version.

> York's old medieval centre is a maze of narrow cobbled streets with names like Whipmawhopmagate and The Shambles. Black and white timbered Tudor buildings lean conspiratorially towards each other, the lower halves of many housing tiny Dickensian shops selling gobstoppers and mint humbugs, or opening into fancy upmarket restaurants. The smell of freshly made chocolate hangs on the air, inviting the wandering tourist inside.
>
> At the centre of these huddled streets, the cathedral tower soars into the sky like a lighthouse, overshadowing the Guy Fawkes public house, named after the notorious plotter who was born there. But an even more striking reminder of York's long history is a Roman pillar dug up in the cathedral grounds and now erected outside.

How does this version improve on the following phrases in the first version?

- The middle of York is lovely.
- old streets with funny names
- The Minster, which is really a big cathedral, is tall and impressive.
- Some sell old sweets, some sell chocolates, and some sell other things.
- posh modern restaurants
- bits with cobbles
- a big Roman pillar that got dug up from somewhere
- Guy Fawkes was born here…

Why has the paragraph break been added before 'At the centre…'?
How does this help the improved structure of the description?

What you should have noticed is:

- The language is more vivid (e.g. 'maze', 'huddled streets', 'soars').
- Some short sentences have been rearranged as subordinated sentences (like the second sentence).
- There is some imagery ('like a lighthouse').
- Selective examples are given to bring it to life (e.g. 'gobstoppers and mint humbugs').
- There is an appeal to the senses (the smell of chocolate).
- The paragraph has been broken into two, with the details relating to the Minster (the cathedral) going into the second paragraph.

Go outside. Consider what details of the surrounding area you could describe interestingly. Make a list. Write one or more paragraphs.

1. How should you treat the details in a description?
2. What is wrong with 'The middle of York is lovely' as an opening?
3. What is good about the phrase 'the smell of freshly made chocolate'?
4. What is wrong with 'old streets with funny names'?

Progress Check

8.5 Describing a person

Most of the advice given in Topic 8.4 about describing a place also applies to describing a person. However, there are some special options open to you:

- Make their physical appearance reflect their personality.
- Hint at their life history or character by referring to details – for example, a scar, a tattoo or a stooped posture.
- Reveal some things by what they say and do – in fact, in a story this is the most effective method.
- Indicate their character and interests by describing their clothes or possessions.
- Describe the way they move and speak – not just what they say, but their voice.

Describing a character in a story

Here is how Charles Dickens describes an escaped convict through his narrator Pip in *Great Expectations:*

> 'Hold your noise!' cried a terrible voice, as a man started up from among the graves at the side of the church porch. 'Keep still, you little devil, or I'll cut your throat!'
>
> A fearful man, all in coarse gray, with a great iron on his leg. A man with no hat, and with broken shoes, and with an old rag tied round his head. A man who had been soaked in water, and smothered in mud, and lamed by stones, and cut by flints, and stung by nettles, and torn by briars; who limped, and shivered, and glared, and growled; and whose teeth chattered in his head as he seized me by the chin.

The Medway marshes in Kent, where Pip meets the escaped convict, Magwitch

What impression do you get of this man? What do his words suggest, and his style of speech? How do you suspect his recent past has influenced his outlook and behaviour?

Notice that Dickens *shows* what the man is like: he does not *tell* us what his character is like, or what his current state of mind is.

Describing someone you know

If you are describing someone you know, you could begin by making a list, spidergram or mind map of details you want to include. Then select which details to focus on and work out an order in which to deal with them.

Some students make the mistake of just describing the person's physical appearance. This often makes for quite boring reading.

Others describe character traits without linking them to anything physical or to any examples:

> *My Auntie Nora is a nervous and impatient woman. She likes doing crossword puzzles. She can be quite irritable.*

This could be rewritten to be more interesting:

> *My Auntie Nora is a thin-faced woman with darting eyes. Never still, she sits tapping a pen on the table, frustrated by her inability to get the final clue of her crossword. I offer to help. 'Shh – I'm concentrating!' she snaps.*

Have a go

Look at the people pictured below. Choose one and imagine a personality and lifestyle to fit their looks. Make a table of details that you would include in a description.

Look at yourself in a mirror – preferably a full-length one. Make a list of details that you might describe, and that you could match to your character. Try to be objective. Describe yourself in the third person.

1. How could you improve on just describing someone's appearance?
2. How could you use someone's clothes or possessions in a description?
3. What would it suggest if someone was 'never still' and 'tapping'?

Progress Check

8.6 Writing letters

Nowadays people write emails more often than letters on paper. Most people expect emails to be less formal than paper letters, and to have shorter paragraphs to make them easy to read on-screen. However, both forms of communication should be clear and written in correct English.

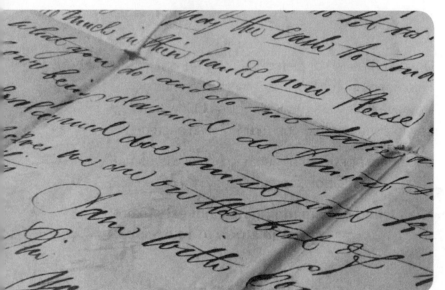

Any letter should:

- be written in an appropriate register – for example, fairly formal for a job application
- be structured – divided into well-sequenced paragraphs
- address the recipient in an appropriate way
- come to a conclusion
- be signed in an appropriate way – for example, 'Kind regards' or 'Yours sincerely'
- give your address and phone number (not necessary in an email).

Formal letters

A formal letter should be written in Standard English. See Topic 2.3.

This is the kind of letter you might write to apply for a job or work experience, or to complain about something in your area. This will probably be addressed to someone you have never met.

33 King's Terrace
Hedgerton
Bristol BS3 5LD
Tel. 01179 456789[1]

Councillor B. Goode
Council House
Frame St
Bristol BS1 3HB[2]

30.8.14[3]

Dear Councillor Goode[4]

I am writing to bring to your attention an increasing road traffic problem in Hedgerton.[5]

As you may know, drivers frequently use residential roads linking the A38 and B443 as short-cuts, especially during rush hour. Drivers speed past pedestrians, including children on their way to school in Victoria Park. As a resident of King's Terrace, one of the roads most often used, I have seen cars narrowly missing pedestrians on several occasions. I have also observed tensions between local drivers and commuters, in one case resulting in a serious 'road rage' incident.[6]

Like most local residents, I would like you to consider making some of these streets one-way, and perhaps cutting off the upper end of King's Rd. Failing this, speed bumps would at least improve the situation.[7]

I look forward to hearing your response to these proposals.[8]

Yours sincerely[9]

Aaron Lewis

Aaron Lewis[10]

1. Your address, with phone number if you wish

2. Address of person you are writing to, with postcode

3. Date (can also go above addressee's address)

4. Formal 'salutation' – only 'Sir or Madam' if you do not know the name

5. Introduces subject

6. Main body of letter; note formal language

7. Requests action

8. Conclusion (not essential, but in this case it encourages response)

9. A formal 'closing remark', or sign-off (use 'Yours faithfully' with 'Dear Sir or Madam')

10. In a typed and printed letter, type your name and sign by hand above

Ask a parent or guardian for a formal letter, for example from a bank. See if it conforms to these rules. Imagine you are dictating, to your secretary, a letter to a local councillor. Speak it aloud.

Progress Check

1. In what register should you write a job application?
2. How many addresses should there be on your letter?
3. What is the 'salutation' in a letter?
4. When should you use 'Yours faithfully'?

68 8.7 Writing a story

If your teacher asks you to write a story, you will usually be given a subject. Even if you have not been given one, or have decided to write a story yourself, you will need to think of a subject.

Below are listed some of the ingredients of most stories, on which you will have to decide before you start. Some of these are explained in detail in the part of this book dealing with reading, so the topics are listed here so that you can look them up. Appreciating other writers' stories is a good way to develop your own story-writing technique.

Ingredients of most stories

see Topic 3.1

See Topics 3.2 and 3.3

See Topic 3.2

See Topic 3.4

See Topic 3.5

See Topic 3.5

- Setting(s) – where the story takes place.

- One or more characters; if more than one, their relationship(s).

- Themes you wish to explore (for example, you might have been asked to write a story about 'Jealousy'.

- Plot and structure.

- Narrative viewpoint (third or first person, or third person but from one perspective).

- Tense (past or present).

Setting and atmosphere

Unless you are writing a novel, it would be unwise to use lots of settings, as this would confuse your readers. For a short story, one or two settings (perhaps three at most) should be enough.

It is a good idea to use settings that you know as your starting point. Of course, if you are writing science fiction this may be difficult! However, remember that you can modify these settings. Do not get stuck on describing a place you know exactly as it is. Use your imagination!

Settings are very important for creating atmosphere. This is described in Topic 3.1. For example, a dark pine wood at dusk could be a good setting for a frightening part of the story, or the whole story.

Characters

A story needs at least one character. A few excellent stories just have one character. For example, Jack London's *To Build a Fire*, which you can find online, is just about one man in the frozen north having to build a fire to keep himself alive. It works because of the tension and suspense. Will he keep the fire alive, and survive, or not?

Think of a character you could include in a story. Move about your room in the style of that character. What words could describe him or her?

However, you may prefer to write a story with two or more characters.

Remember that the best way to reveal character is by what a character does and says. If you are writing in the first person, or from one character's viewpoint, you could include what they think.

Actions + Speech + Thoughts = Character

This is the principle of 'show, don't tell'.

Themes, plot and structure

Themes

Your **themes** are likely to emerge from your characters and your plot. However, if you do want to explore a particular theme, you will have to think of a situation that will make this possible. For example, what situation could lead to jealousy arising in one or more of your characters? Perhaps character X has a close friend (Y) who becomes increasingly close to a newcomer (Z), and then X becomes jealous and plots to drive Y and Z apart.

Many of the rules for describing real people apply equally to fictional characters. See Topic 8.5.

Plot and structure

The Jealousy theme mentioned above could work well, as any plot needs **tension**, **conflict** and some **suspense**. Essentially, you need a situation, a conflict, and a path towards a resolution.

Ideally, your plot should develop out of your characters. Do not turn your characters into lifeless puppets acting out your plot. Instead, ask yourself, 'What would character X do in this situation?' They might surprise you. That would probably be a good thing, because it could surprise the reader too. Never be predictable!

Narrative viewpoint and tense

Be consistent in whatever tense you use. See Topic 5.10.

You need to choose the viewpoint from which to tell the story. This could be:
- First person – 'I went upstairs…'. This can be very immediate, making the reader relate to the narrator, but it limits what they can comment on; they cannot comment on what they cannot witness.
- Third person – 'Jed was not a humble man. He did not appreciate being criticised…'. This means that you can comment on whatever you want, including all your characters' thoughts and actions.
- Third person but from one person's viewpoint – 'He was stuck. What could he do? He tried to remember the code. What was it again?' This can offer you the best of both worlds.

Most stories are written in the past tense. You could try using the present tense to create a sense of immediacy.

Progress Check

1. Can you have a story with one character?
2. Why is setting important?
3. What is narrative viewpoint?
4. What three things does any plot need?

8.8 Writing a poem

Poets usually write poems because they have thought of an idea for a poem, and perhaps one or two lines they want to include. However, it is possible to inspire yourself. Here are some ideas.

Persona poems

Think of an object, or an animal, or something in the landscape, like a tree, or even an airport. Then imagine what it might say if it could speak.

For example, an airport might begin with:

> I am the place that never sleeps
>
> except when storms rage or fog creeps
>
> around my runways.
>
> Planes? Toys! I swallow them and spit them out
>
> over and over and over.

A good example of this kind of poem is Stevie Smith's 'River God', which is written, as you might guess, in the voice of a river god. It is easy to find online.

Character poems

Think of a character you know, or make one up, perhaps based on someone you have seen in passing. Or think of a famous person, living or dead. Then make a mind map, spidergram or list of details you could mention about them in a poem.

If you think of a simile or metaphor for one feature, you could include it at this stage. For example, someone might have a chin jutting out like the cliffs at Dover. You might take this as a sign of their determination.

This type of poem could be written in the first person, like a 'persona poem', or in the third person.

One way to spark your imagination and come up with a new angle is to put the character in an unusual setting and imagine how they would behave or be seen by others. For example:

- Napoleon goes to the local swimming baths.
- Beyoncé becomes a librarian.
- Detective Columbo (Peter Falk) goes undercover as the school caretaker.
- Your auntie appears on *The X-Factor.*

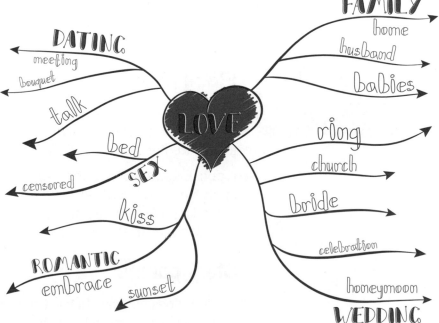

A variation on this idea would be for a character in a novel you have read to take on a new, independent life and address the author. For example, Stanley Yelnats in *Holes* could turn out to be guilty after all:

Sucker

I fooled you all along.

Those holes you made me dig –

each one I imagine you in it.

Innocent fool?

Wrong place, wrong time?

No way, Mr Sachar, no way.

> As with describing a person in prose, it is more interesting to link physical appearance to character. See Topic 8.5.

Place poems

You could begin with a place that inspires you. It does not have to be beautiful, but it should at least be interesting. Describe the details that interest or appeal to you. Perhaps use one or two metaphors or similes.

If possible, work towards an idea coming out of this place. For example, you might imagine how it will look in a hundred years' time, or you might think of the timelessness of nature, or how an underground car park is like the unconscious mind!

Story poems

A poem does not have to tell a story, but it can do. If it does, be very selective. Do not include every detail of the story: focus on the interesting or unusual things.

Setting out your poem

Here are some tips.

- You can decide where to break your lines; this does not need to be at the end of a sentence, or even at a comma. But remember that line breaks are one of the ways to get your meaning across. Putting a phrase on a line on its own breaks it off slightly from the next line.
- You can also decide where to start a new **stanza** – this is like a paragraph break in prose. Either do this regularly – say, after four lines, or when you move on to a new idea or detail.
- Your poem does not have to rhyme. You could use some rhymes, or none at all. It is up to you.
- Use punctuation as you would do normally. You do not need to begin each line with a capital, though some poems do – especially older ones. It is up to you.

Tennyson's poem 'The Charge of the Light Brigade' tells the story of a famous British cavalry charge in 1854. What details of the story can you pick out in the extract below? How many men were there and what were they ordered to do? What do you think the line 'Someone had blundered' refers to?

> Find two interesting objects. Move them around if possible. Feel them and look closely at them. Imagine the conversation they might have and write this as a poem. Start a new stanza for each change of speaker: no need for speech marks.

I
Half a league, half a league,
Half a league onward,
All in the valley of Death
    Rode the six hundred.
"Forward, the Light Brigade!
Charge for the guns!" he said.
Into the valley of Death
    Rode the six hundred.

II
"Forward, the Light Brigade!"
Was there a man dismayed?
Not though the soldier knew
    Someone had blundered.
    Theirs not to make reply,
    Theirs not to reason why,
    Theirs but to do and die.
Into the valley of Death
Rode the six hundred.

III
Cannon to right of them,
Cannon to left of them,
Cannon in front of them
    Volleyed and thundered;
Stormed at with shot and shell,
Boldly they rode and well,
Into the jaws of Death,
Into the mouth of hell
    Rode the six hundred.

IV
Flashed all their sabres bare,
Flashed as they turned in air
Sabring the gunners there,
Charging an army, while
    All the world wondered.
Plunged in the battery-smoke
Right through the line they broke;
Cossack and Russian
Reeled from the sabre stroke
    Shattered and sundered.
Then they rode back, but not
    Not the six hundred.

Progress Check

1. What 'person' should you write a 'persona poem' in?
2. How could you write a poem with an interesting new angle on a famous person?
3. What is a stanza?

70

8.9 Arguing your case

Writing to **argue** and writing to **persuade** are closely linked, and they often overlap. The main difference is this. Any piece of persuasive writing is a combination of two elements:

- *logos* – logical ideas, arguments
- *pathos* – emotional appeal.

These words are taken from ancient Greek **rhetoric** – the art of using words persuasively.

A mostly **argumentative** piece of writing will emphasise *logos*; a mostly **persuasive** piece of writing will emphasise *pathos*.

Using *logos* – developing your arguments

Any persuasive writing requires reasoning. Suppose you want to write an essay aimed at persuading people of your age to become vegetarian. Begin by arranging your reasons, or arguments. You could list them, but a more visual system such as a mind map or spidergram often works better because you can see it all at once and can easily add to it.

Here is the start of a possible plan:

Health - avoid meat additives

Kinder - animals want to live

Go veggie

Eco - soya uses less land, less rainforest cut down

Humanitarian - more efficient food production

Using *pathos*

Most people are swayed by their emotions at least as much as their minds. Advertisers and charity campaigners realise this and play on it. While you do not have to be emotionally manipulative, if you are arguing for something that has an emotional aspect, you should aim to reach your readers emotionally.

With the argument for vegetarianism, there are a number of ways that you might do this:

- Describe how animals are reared and slaughtered.
- Describe the possible effects of antibiotics, etc., present in meat.
- Paint a graphic picture of deforestation – trees cut down to make way for beef farming.
- Point out that our planet is worth saving for future generations.

However, your actual word choices are important here too.
For example, compare these sentences:

- Great swathes of virgin rainforest are slashed down every day, delicate ecosystems destroyed, so that a few ranchers can make profits out of beef farming.
- Large areas of unproductive jungle are harvested every day, making way for enterprising ranchers to use the land for beef farming.

Ordering your arguments

Next, think of how you could order your arguments so that one leads on naturally to the next. You may, for example, decide to put your strongest argument first, or you could build up to it. You might order your arguments like this:

1. Kinder – animals want to live. This is the most obvious, the one that most people will at least understand.

2. Health – avoid meat additives. Give evidence for vegetarianism being healthy, and link to the previous argument – people should be kind to *themselves*.
3. Humanitarian – more efficient food production. Be kind to humanity – easier to feed the world on vegetarian food.
4. Eco – soya uses less land – less rainforest cut down. Saving the planet is a logical next step from feeding the world's population.

KINDER → to animals → to self → to humanity → to planet

See more on arguing a case, and using link words, in Topic 2.7.

Counter-arguments

Include one or more **counter-arguments**. This means anticipating what an opponent might say in arguing against you. You should then dismiss the counter-argument with your own. Here is an example.

> Some meat-eaters claim that eating meat is 'natural', because humans have been doing it for thousands of years. However, the fact that we have always done something does not mean that we should carry on doing it. Humans have also used capital punishment for thousands of years, but in civilised societies we are now realising that it is wrong.

Notice how the word 'However' is used here to signal the start of the dismissal.

Writing your essay

If you have planned properly, you should find you can write your essay fairly easily. It may work for you to start a new paragraph for each main point in your plan.

You should always try to lead your reader through your arguments step by step. You can do this by using paragraphs well, and beginning each paragraph with a **topic sentence**. For example, you might write:

An even more compelling reason, however, is efficient land use.

The rest of the paragraph would go on to expand that idea and explain it.

Conclusion

Bring your ideas together without either repeating yourself or introducing a completely new idea. One way to do this is to refer back to the start of your essay. Another might be to look forward to the future in some way:

As global warming becomes an increasing threat, menacing the developing world and the entire planet, it makes increasing sense to be kind to animals, ourselves, humanity and the planet by switching to a vegetarian diet. Only by doing so can humanity look forward to surviving into the 22nd century.

Write out a list, or create a diagram, showing arguments against being vegetarian. Write the key words on separate cards or sticky notes. Move them around and consider different options for how to order them in an essay.

1. What is logos?
2. What is pathos, and how can you apply it to your language?
3. How should your arguments be organised?

Progress Check

71

8.10 Writing a review

A **review** should provide two things:

- information on the book, play, performance, etc., that you are reviewing
- your evaluation of it – what you think of it.

Information

The kind of information that readers want to know is:

- **novel** – author, title, its **genre**, if it has one (crime, thriller, comic, etc.), its plot (but don't give away the ending), main characters
- **play production** – author, title, director, where and when performed, plot, what company (e.g. Royal Shakespeare Company), names of leading actors and what characters they played
- **concert** – performer(s), when, where, type of music, what the performers looked like, what the audience response was, etc.

Evaluation

The reader wants to know your opinion so that they can decide whether to read the book, see the play, etc., or to compare it with their own opinion. Tell readers what you thought, and why. Do not just say 'It was wonderful' or 'It was terrible': use more interesting language and give your reasons:

Siobhan Redmond was superb as Lady Macbeth, giving a convincing portrayal of a woman whose power depended on her personal charisma more than on her role as queen.

Arranging information and evaluation

It makes for dull reading if you just give all the information, then all the evaluation. Ideally, begin to hint at your evaluation early on – perhaps even in the opening sentence.

It is confusing for the reader if you swing back and forth between positive comments and negative ones. Make your comments in blocks. For example, if you mostly enjoyed a novel, it might work to write two positive paragraphs, then a more critical one, then a conclusion in which you say that on balance you recommend it.

Tense

For more on reviews, with examples, see Topic 2.9.

Write a review of a novel in the present tense: 'Stanley finds it hard to settle in when he first arrives.' Also use present tense for a music album or film.

However, if writing a review of a specific performance of any kind, use the past tense, because it was a one-off: it happened on one occasion.

Progress Check

1. Give two reasons why people read reviews.
2. What two main elements should your review include?
3. In what tense should you review a novel?
4. In what tense should you review a play production?

8.11 Summarising

Summarising a text means writing a **shorter, more concise version** of it, including only the most important points.

A good way to begin is to make a bullet-point list of main points. Even at this stage, try to use your own words where possible. This will mean you really get to grips with the ideas, and don't just rework the original words.

Here is an extract to summarise, from an article about canoeing on the River Wye.

> It is often helpful to use concise subordinated sentences in a summary. See Topic 5.4.

The river has many and varied delights – the rapids at Symonds Yat, just exciting enough but not enough to be scary, the slow meandering stretches where we might stop for a picnic and swim, and the herons, cormorants, kingfishers and occasional leaping salmon. There's historic interest too – such as the old iron bridge at Redbrook or the now restored wharf at the former ship-building centre of Brockweir, once famed for its many taverns and sinful sailors.

> Read a newspaper story. Count off the main points on your fingers, summarising them out loud in short phrases, as in a bullet list.

Bullet list

You could write a bullet summary of the first paragraph as follows:
- The river is appealing in many ways.
- It can be rapid or slow.
- Offers wildlife and historic sites.

Notice how 'herons, cormorants, kingfishers and occasional leaping salmon' is summed up in one word: 'wildlife'.

Continuous prose

The bullets can then be written as continuous prose:

> *The river is appealing in many ways, with rapid and slow stretches, and a variety of wildlife and historic sites.*

Progress Check

1. What is the first stage of writing a summary?
2. What does 'concise' mean?
3. What sentence type is especially useful in summaries?

Worked questions

1. **Take the following key details (from Topic 8.3, now in chronological order) and turn them into a continuous account in response to the essay question 'Describe an event that had a big influence on you and why it did.'**

   (20 marks)

   - It was a lovely day.
   - Mrs Jones was walking home from bingo.
   - The daffodils in her garden were a sea of yellow.
   - I saw a man I didn't recognise coming out of Mrs Jones's front door.
   - He was about 6 feet tall, and thin.
   - He was wearing blue jeans and a short black leather jacket.
   - He had short ginger hair and a rucksack.
   - She came through her gate just at the wrong moment.
   - She hit him over the head with her handbag. It looked heavy.
   - There was a struggle.
   - She fell and her head hit the garden wall. Then she stopped moving.
   - He didn't look to see if she was all right; he ran off towards the park.

1. Sets scene, taking reader through own experience, rationing information

It was a warm afternoon in late spring. I was just admiring the sea of daffodils in Mrs Jones's garden across the street, when, to my surprise the front door opened. I thought she'd gone to bingo, the same as she usually did on a Thursday, but there was her door opening. Curious, I came closer to the window. I was even more baffled when I saw a rotund figure in a brown overcoat and red beret bustling along the street towards the front gate. It was Mrs Jones![1]

2. Effective narration, keeping us in suspense

At that moment a tall, thin ginger-haired man in jeans and a black leather jacket emerged furtively from Mrs Jones's front door. He was carrying what looked like a full rucksack. As bad luck would have it, he and Mrs Jones both reached the garden gate at the same moment. Any hopes I'd had that perhaps he was her long-lost son or nephew were shattered when I saw her jump back in shock, then quickly recover herself and swing her heavy handbag at him with all her might.[2]

3. Lively simile

4. Shares own feelings

She was only a small woman, and aged 70. Nonetheless, the man staggered back, almost dropping his rucksack. She swung again, looking for a moment like a small medieval knight wielding a mace,[3] but before she could connect, the man had righted himself. He caught her arm, and for a few seconds they struggled. I was, I am ashamed to say,[4] too surprised to act. By the time I thought of helping brave Mrs Jones, or at least phoning the police, she had fallen and hit her head hard on the wall.

Far from showing any sympathy or regret, the cowardly intruder rushed off down the street without a look back. Only then did I rush out to Mrs Jones, and then dial 999.

After several weeks, Mrs Jones, thankfully recovered and returned home in the summer.[5] As for the burglar, I was delighted to hear from the police that he had been caught after another attempted robbery a week later, and that my witness statement had helped to identify him.[6]

5. Summarises – no need for more details

6. Important stage in the explanation

This incident made me think long and hard about the state of our society, and the fact that so many crimes go unpunished. Perhaps the burglar had a deprived childhood, perhaps he was poor, but the fact is, nothing justifies breaking into an old woman's home and leaving her for dead. I knew that if I joined the police I could only make a small difference, but the fight against crime has to be worth it, even if it is never over.[7]

7. Convincing conclusion fully explaining significance of incident to the author

2. **Now summarise the account in question 1 to approximately half the number of words.** *(10 marks)*

<u>One afternoon in late spring I saw Mrs Jones's front door open.</u>[1] Curious because she was normally at bingo on Thursdays, I was then surprised to see Mrs Jones herself approaching her house.

1. Daffodils omitted

At that moment a tall, thin, <u>casually dressed</u>[2] ginger-haired man emerged from Mrs Jones's front door, carrying a seemingly full rucksack. He and Mrs Jones reached the garden gate <u>simultaneously</u>.[3] <u>Recoiling</u>,[4] then recovering, she swung her heavy handbag at him.

2. Sums up how he was dressed

3. Single word replaces phrase

4. Well chosen verb expresses sense succinctly

She was a small 70-year-old woman. Nonetheless, the man staggered back, almost dropping his rucksack. She swung again, but he caught her arm, and they struggled briefly. <u>I was too surprised to act</u>.[5] In a moment, she had fallen and hit her head hard on the wall.

5. Personal feelings (shame) omitted

<u>The intruder fled</u>[6] without looking back and I rushed out to Mrs Jones, then dialled 999.

6. 'Down the street' omitted as unnecessary

After several weeks, <u>Mrs Jones returned home</u>.[7] As for the burglar, he was caught after another attempted robbery a week later. My witness statement had helped to identify him.

7. Time of year (summer) omitted as unnecessary

This incident made me think about crime in our society. Perhaps the burglar had a deprived childhood, or was poor, but <u>nothing justifies his behaviour</u>.[8] I knew that if I joined the police I could make a small but worthwhile contribution to the fight against crime.

8. Repetition of crime details avoided by 'behaviour'

Practice questions

1. **Describe a place that means a lot to you, so as to make it come to life for the reader.** *(20 marks)*

Try to:
- select physical details well, to give readers a strong impression of what is important
- appeal to the senses, to help the reader's imagination
- use well-chosen adjectives and verbs
- be sure to explain why the place means a lot to you.

2. **Write a persuasive magazine article arguing either for or against becoming vegetarian.** *(20 marks)*

You could consider:
- Is it rational for meat-eaters to eat some animals but not others?
- Do human beings need to eat meat to remain healthy?
- What would happen to farm animals if everyone became vegetarian?
- Humans have eaten meat for thousands of years, so is it therefore justifiable?

Remember to use persuasive language techniques and to use linking words and phrases to join your arguments together.

3. **Summarise this paragraph: make a bullet list, then write a prose summary. Reduce it to 70 words or fewer.** *(10 marks)*

> **Canoeing on the River Wye**
>
> Of course, nothing quite compares with Tintern Abbey, and it is an especially exciting sight seen from the river. The only snag – one which results from the same phenomenon that made it possible for Brockweir to launch its ships – is the tide. The Wye is tidal as far as Bigsweir Bridge. Even at Llandogo, a strong incoming tide comes in faster than the river ever flows downstream at low tide. However, the tide has its uses. You can go online and check the tide times for Sharpness, and – making an allowance of half an hour or so – catch the incoming tide to wash you upstream to Bigsweir. As it turns, you come back down again with minimum effort. Likewise you can catch the tide going out, thus missing the rapids at Coed Ithel Weir, and pitch up at Tintern.

Drafting, editing and proofreading 9

After completing this chapter you should know about:
- improving your first draft
- editing your sentences
- proofreading your work.

9.1 Improving your first draft

When we speak of **drafting** we mean producing a first version of a text. It is hard to get a piece of writing exactly right first time. Even the best writers go back to their writing after the first attempt and improve on it. Here are some questions to ask:

- Does the **structure** makes sense, and does one paragraph follow on logically from the next?
- Can the **flow** be improved by adding any linking words or phrases like 'However'?
- Is everything that the reader needs to **understand** clear and sufficiently explained?
- Can individual words and phrases be made more **vivid** or **original**?
- In fiction, does the **continuity** work? For example, does a character have blue eyes in paragraph 1 and 'eyes like emeralds' later on?
- In **dialogue**, is it clear **who is speaking**?
- Are there sentences that would be better written in a more **concise** form?
- Are there short sentences that would be better combined to make **subordinated** ones?
- Are there any **comma splices** – where you should have started a new sentence?
- Are the **tone** and **register** consistent?

Find a first draft of your written work. Read it, bearing the checklist in mind. Mark or change things you could improve

Practice

Bearing in mind the list of questions, how could the following be improved?

Our last family camping trip was a bit of a nightmare. We had left the tent pegs behind we had to use rocks to hold the edges of the tent down. It was great that we were able to find rocks in the field. It was not so great that one was hidden in the grass right under where we pitched the tent. So I had to crawl under the tent in the middle of the night to dig it out and get rid of it.

We got stuck in traffic on the M5 on the way there. It was already getting dark when we got there. Roger was sick in the car, which did not help. Then we couldn't find the field and the farmer had gone to the pub.

It rained heavily on the first night and after a while the water started to pool on the roof and then leak in. I woke up with it running down my neck in the middle of the night. Still, the next day was sunny and everything dried out. We got some more tent pegs. Roger loved it and ran around fetching sticks and wagging his tail. In the end it was brill.

Here is a redrafted version of the first two paragraphs. Improvements are marked in the first paragraph. How has the second paragraph been improved? What would you put in the final paragraph?

1. Begins on note of anticipation

2. Gives some background information

3. Makes it clear that Roger is a dog!

4. Arouses reader's curiosity

5. Good word choice

6. Subordinated sentence combines information; good adverb of time: 'eventually'

<u>We had all been looking forward to the camping trip</u>[1] – <u>a week in a small secluded campsite in Devon</u>.[2] Even Roger the <u>dog</u>[3] seemed excited. Unfortunately, <u>not everything went to plan</u>.[4] First, we found ourselves stuck in a mile-long crocodile of cars on the M5 for two hours, and then we drove round and round the <u>maze</u>[5] of country lanes trying to find the site, <u>eventually arriving at dusk to find that the farmer who owned the field had gone to the pub</u>.[6]

This meant that we had to find a place to pitch our tent on our own, in gathering darkness. It was only when we tipped out the tent from its bag and tried to lay it out that we realised we had bungled: we had a tent, but no tent pegs. How could we hold it down? Eventually Dad hit on the idea of using rocks – of which there seemed to be plenty in our part of the field.

Progress Check

1. How could a word like 'However' improve your writing?
2. What is 'continuity' in a story?
3. How might a reader become confused reading first-draft dialogue?

9.2 Editing your sentences for impact

When you have **edited** your writing at the level of paragraphing, checking that the structure works well, and that your sentences are in the right order, you may need to zoom in on some **individual sentences**. Points to check are dealt with below.

Simple, coordinated and subordinated sentences

You should normally aim to use a variety of **sentence** types and lengths. Some of your **simple sentences** may be better joined into **coordinated** or **subordinated** ones. On the other hand, if you are trying to create tension in a story, you may find it helps to break some long sentences into short ones.

Look at these short simple sentences:

> I first came across Darren in 2013. It was when my family moved down south. I went to a new school. My father had been made redundant. He had got a job in a chemical factory. Darren came up to me. It was outside the school gates. He looked self-confident. He was in Year 10. He had a nice smile. His teeth were very white. He seemed to have heard about me. This was surprising. I wondered how he had.

This could be reworked to make the sentences flow more smoothly and with more variety:

> I first came across Darren in 2013, when my family moved down south and I went to a new school. My father had been made redundant and got a job in a chemical factory. Darren came up to me outside the school gates, a self-confident Year 10 with a nice smile and very white teeth. To my surprise, he seemed to have heard about me. I wondered how he had. Where had he heard it from?

Word and punctuation choices

The next stage is to improve the word and punctuation choices:

I first ~~came across~~ **encountered** Darren in 2013, when my family moved down south and I went to a new school. My father had been made redundant and ~~got~~ **found** a job in a chemical factory. Darren ~~came up to~~ **approached** me outside the school gates, a self-~~confident~~ **assured** Year 10 with ~~a nice~~ **an engaging** smile and ~~very white~~ **dazzling** teeth. To my surprise, he ~~seemed~~ **appeared** to have heard about me. I ~~wondered how he had~~ was **curious**~~. Where had he heard it from?~~: **what was his source**?

See more on sentence structure and types in Topics 5.1 to 5.5.

There are no huge changes here, but the overall impact is increased by using more interesting, more accurate or more concise words, and by one change in punctuation.

Progress Check

1. In what ways might you need to change some short simple sentences?
2. Why might you change some words in redrafting?
3. What other element might you change for greater impact or accuracy?

9.3 Proofreading

🎧 75

Proofreading is the final stage of **redrafting**, when you are checking for relatively small errors, especially in spelling, punctuation and grammar. At this stage you should not be needing to move paragraphs around to improve on the structure, or even add new sentences.

If you have typed your work, using a computer spellcheck will help, but it will not catch all word confusions. Similarly, a grammar checker is unlikely to be completely accurate.

Here is a proofreading checklist:

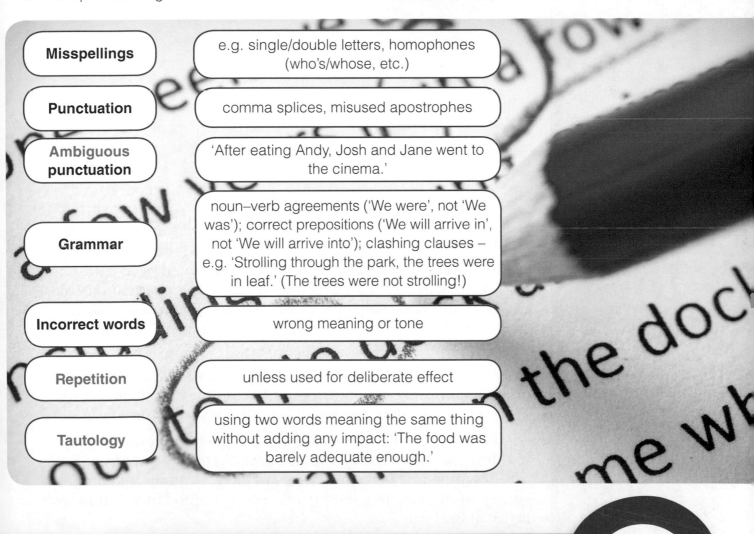

Misspellings	e.g. single/double letters, homophones (who's/whose, etc.)
Punctuation	comma splices, misused apostrophes
Ambiguous punctuation	'After eating Andy, Josh and Jane went to the cinema.'
Grammar	noun–verb agreements ('We were', not 'We was'); correct prepositions ('We will arrive in', not 'We will arrive into'); clashing clauses – e.g. 'Strolling through the park, the trees were in leaf.' (The trees were not strolling!)
Incorrect words	wrong meaning or tone
Repetition	unless used for deliberate effect
Tautology	using two words meaning the same thing without adding any impact: 'The food was barely adequate enough.'

Progress Check

1. At what stage of redrafting does proofreading come?
2. How can punctuation be 'ambiguous'?
3. What is 'tautology'?

Worked questions

1. Redraft the following passage, improving its structure, including sentence structure.

(20 marks)

> **Why we should eat meat**
>
> Vegetarians say we should not eat meat. I think we should. There are several persuasive reasons for this.
>
> Firstly it is tasty and makes us feel we have eaten a proper meal. Most people enjoy good, well-cooked meat.
>
> Next it is full of protein. We need that for growth and muscle tone. It can be part of a healthy diet. The Lakota Indians in North America lived mostly on a diet of buffalo meat. They were perfectly healthy. That was before they were put on reservations and got fat eating pasta.
>
> Next it is natural. We have canine teeth for eating meat. Our ancestors ate meat. Humans have done it for thousands of years. Even chimpanzees eat meat some of the time. They also eat fruit and vegetables. Farmers would not farm cattle just for milk. Anyway animals like cows and sheep would not be alive at all if they were not farmed for meat. Animals are killed for meat in humane ways.

1. Combines three simple sentences in one more streamlined coordinated sentence

2. More logical topic ordering, with effective subordinated sentences

3. Neatly slots in humane slaughter as logical extension of point about farming

4. Subordinate clause furthers the argument

5. Organises evidence effectively, with good use of a dash

6. Signals final point, while pointing out that it will be the most persuasive for many people

7. Strong final sentence

Vegetarians say we should not eat meat, but I think there are several persuasive reasons for doing so.[1]

Firstly, eating meat is natural. Humans have eaten meat for thousands of years. This is why our ancestors developed canine teeth, which we still have. Even our nearest relatives, the chimpanzees, supplement their fruit and vegetable diet with meat.[2]

It would be uneconomic for farmers to raise cattle just for milk, or sheep just for wool. These animals owe their lives to farming, and if we all became vegetarian they would become extinct. As it is, they live happy lives before eventually being humanely slaughtered.[3]

Meat is full of protein, which we need for growth and muscle tone,[4] and it is part of a healthy diet, as shown by the Lakota Indians in North America. Before they were put on reservations and got fat eating pasta, they lived mostly on a diet of buffalo meat – and were perfectly healthy.[5]

Last, but not least for most people,[6] meat is tasty and makes us feel we have eaten a proper meal. Most people enjoy good, well-cooked meat.[7]

Practice questions

1. **Rewrite the following, arranging it into a better structure at both paragraph and sentence level.** *(12 marks)*

Travel to Mars

People say that going to Mars fulfils a key human instinct. The instinct to explore. But I think this is misguided.

India recently sent a space rocket to Mars. This is a country which still has thousands of people in poverty. They are homeless and starving. Yet they still put money into space exploration. It seems to be more about international rivalry. Each country wants to assert its status by showing that it can take part in the space race. The USA and USSR began it in the 1960s. Yuri Gagarin was the first man in space.

We should be putting all the resources we can spare into combating global warming. This is a time when the whole of planet Earth is threatened. Pollution is causing global warming at an accelerating pace. The Amazon is being destroyed. The polar ice caps are melting.

We can explore in different ways. For example, we can find out more about how our fragile ecosystems on Earth work. We can study wildlife. We can do deep sea exploration.

2. **What errors can you find in the following restaurant review?** *(20 marks)*

Me and my grilfiend went out for a meal in a new restorant called Edmundos' last night, the food was expensive and over-priced and not really worth it. Their was a fountane in the middle of the floor, which was stone tiled so the place echoed quiet a lot and it wasnt always easy to here a conversasion. The food was tasty but barely adequate enough. I only had too potatos with my beef. Still walking around the plaice the other diners' seemed to be enjoying themselvs.

3. **Proofread and correct the following** *(20 marks)*

Strangly enough, one of my favorite place's is the local supermarket car park this is because I go skatebording their with my freinds. A manger at the supermarket used to complain sometimes and tell us to go somewhear else becos we was scaring of the customers and loosing the supermarket money but this was rubbish i talked to some of the customers and they used to like watching us. Anyway we was always careful to keep out of the way of cars. Anuther point is that the councils meant to be making us a skate park and theyve never got round to it. Using the car park keeps us of the streets. It also has some nice, gentle slops, and sheltered spots to just hang out and chat.

10 Spoken English

Learning Summary

After completing this chapter you should know about:
- Standard English
- using rhetorical devices in a speech
- speaking from notes
- preparing for a debate
- contributing to a discussion
- writing and rehearsing a playscript.

76

10.1 Spoken and written English

The main differences between written and spoken English are shown below.

Written English	Spoken English
More likely to use **Standard English**	**Colloquial** expressions, dialect and slang are common
Usually in complete sentences	Often uses incomplete sentences
Has to communicate just by what is on the page	Supplemented by facial expression, body language, and tone of voice
People can reread anything that is unclear	Listener cannot 'rewind' in a live situation
Mostly one-way communication	Discussion two-way; even with a speech, listeners may have a chance to ask questions

Standard and non-standard English

Even in speech, Standard English is more appropriate in formal situations such as:
- speeches
- debates
- interviews
- in court.

In fact, Standard English is appropriate in any situation in which you are mostly talking to strangers, in which it is particularly important that you are understood, or in which there is a lot at stake. However, it is important to realise that Standard English can be spoken in any accent.

Standard English is made up of two elements: **grammar** and **vocabulary**.

Standard grammar

Standard grammar is **conventional** grammar, as used by **newsreaders** because they want to be understood by as wide a section of listeners or viewers as possible. It excludes all variations of grammar that may be used by local dialect groups or social groups.

Non-standard grammar variations	Standard grammar
I ain't	I am not
we was	we were
me and Kevin	Kevin and I
give it I	give it to me
she weren't	she wasn't
we were sat there	we were sitting there

Standard vocabulary

Vocabulary refers to individual words. Most words in a dictionary are part of standard vocabulary. However, language is constantly developing, so words that are considered slang may well be in the dictionary in ten years' time.

Also note that some familiar words are still marked as being *colloquial* (abbreviation *colloq.*) in the dictionary and are therefore not quite part of standard vocabulary. An example of this is 'hassle'. This has been in use for at least 40 years, but it is still better to use 'inconvenience' or 'nuisance' in a formal situation.

Some other examples of standard and non-standard vocabulary are shown below.

> Cover up the standard grammar expressions in the table above. Read the non-standard ones and put the standard equivalents into sentences as quickly as you can.

Standard	Non-standard (slang or local dialect)
excellent	wicked, brill, ace, safe, boss, etc.
pleased	made up
police officer	copper
informer	grass
footpath	twitten
alcohol	booze
mend	fettle

1. How does face-to-face spoken communication depend less on the actual words than written communication?
2. Why would it be important for a politician giving a speech to be understood immediately?
3. Is 'We was sat down...' an example of Standard English, non-standard grammar or non-standard vocabulary?

Progress Check

10.2 Using rhetorical devices in a speech

Rhetoric, originally an ancient Greek concept, refers to the techniques of persuasive language. A **rhetorical device** is a **language technique**, especially one used to argue or persuade.

Some of the most common rhetorical devices are shown below.

Device (technique)	Example
Alliteration – the repetition of consonant sounds, usually at the start of words, for effect	The dead-dull detonations of distant grenades.
Antithesis – opposites or contrasts	It is better to die on your feet than to live on your knees. (Emiliano Zapata)
Exaggeration (**hyperbole**), usually for comic effect	Margo…let out a scream that any railway engine would have been proud to produce. (Gerald Durrell)
Irony – achieving a comic effect by saying, or hinting at, the opposite of what one really means, often to criticise through ridicule	It must be tough not knowing where your next million-pound bonus is coming from.
Lists	The hungry queue for food banks; the homeless huddle in doorways; people worry themselves sick over mounting debt.
Metaphor – an image (word picture) which speaks of a thing as if it were something similar	We shall prove ourselves once again able to defend our island home, to ride out the storm of war. (Winston Churchill)
Onomatopoeia – the use of words that sound like what they describe	Arrows whizzed past me and thudded into a tree a few feet away.
Oxymoron – two apparently contradictory metaphors or ideas used together	Dracula's eyes blaze with icy passion.
Parallelism – repetition of a phrase with a significant variation, often including a repeated grammatical structure	The hand that rocks the cradle is the hand that rules the world.
Personification – a kind of metaphor presenting an inanimate or abstract thing as a person, god or animal	The dogs of war are hard to call to heel.
Repetition	The will of the people brought me to power and it is the will of the people that I will serve.
Rhetorical question – one which expects no answer. (May express anger or criticism.)	Does this government think that it rules over a nation of idiots?
Simile – an image which compares one thing with another using *like*, *as* or *than*	He was crushed – like a ripe banana beneath the foot of King Kong.
Triple (also called a **triad** or **tricolon**) – using groups of three words or phrases, often with the third forming a mini-climax	This mission will be difficult, delicate and dangerous.

Barrack Obama's victory speech (2008)

If there is anyone out there <u>who still doubts that America is a place where all things are possible; who still wonders if the dream of our founders is alive in our time; who still questions the power of our democracy, tonight is your answer.</u>[1]

<u>It's the answer</u>[2] told by lines that stretched around schools and churches in numbers this nation has never seen; by people who waited three hours and four hours, many for the very first time in their lives, because they believed that this time must be different; that their voices could be that difference.

It's the answer spoken by <u>young and old, rich and poor, Democrat and Republican, black, white, Hispanic, Asian, Native American, gay, straight, disabled and not disabled</u>[3] – Americans who sent a message to the world that we have never been just a collection of individuals or a collection of Red States and Blue States: we are, and always will be, the United States of America.

It's the answer that led those who have been told for so long by so many to be cynical, and fearful, and doubtful of what we can achieve <u>to put their hands on the arc of history and bend it once more toward the hope of a better day.</u>[4]

It's been a long time coming, but tonight, because of what we did <u>on this day, in this election, at this defining moment,</u>[5] change has come to America.

1. Parallelism ('who still...') in a triple

2. Positive phrase repeated in next two paragraphs

3. List, rising to climax

4. Metaphor

5. Repetition of 'this', in a triple

Practise speaking all or part of President Obama's speech in front of a mirror, making appropriate gestures.

1. What is a *rhetorical device*?
2. What is a *triple* (or *triad*, or *tricolon*)?
3. What key positive phrase does Obama use in three paragraphs?

Progress Check

10.3 Speaking from notes or using a PowerPoint

It is usually more effective to **speak directly** to an audience than to read a speech. Speaking, rather than reading, gives the audience the sense that you are connecting to them, not just reading the words. Reading is likely to bore them.

Using notes or prompts

Not many people are such able and confident speakers that they can speak without having anything on paper to refer to. An effective compromise is to use notes or prompts. You should then only have to glance at them to remind yourself of what you want to say.

There are a few options for what kind of notes to use.

Conventional notes

You could use a list of key points, numbered or in bullet points. These really should be key points: if you write sentences or even complete phrases, it will be tempting to start reading them out, and you will end up reading out notes that were only meant to be memory joggers. Stick to key points.

Use highlighting for the most important bits if it helps you. It is all right to read out short quotations – for example, from a novel.

Make sure you can read your own handwriting. It is embarrassing to be struggling with this. Equally important, make sure your notes are in order by numbering or stapling them together: you do not want to be scrabbling about trying to find the right page. Stapling has the advantage that if you drop the pages, they will not get out of order.

For a short talk, you may be able to fit everything on one page, which is more manageable.

Cards

Some people use small postcard-size index cards. You could write three or four points on one card. When you have decided on a structure, number the cards. Again, make sure they are legible – and do not drop them!

You should have your cards in order and then put each one aside, or at the bottom of the pile, when you have used it.

Visual methods

Mind maps or **spidergrams** can be used for planning, and then as prompts for the talk. Use a large sheet of paper and let your plan spread out so that you can see it easily and add to it. Decide on the order when you have all your ideas on paper. Then number each one in a different colour from the text, to show you the order during the talk.

Small symbols may work better as prompts than words or phrases for some things. For example, if part of your talk on the play *Macbeth* is about revenge, you could draw a dagger to jog your memory.

Another good thing about visual methods is that you can see the whole plan at a glance, which will help you to feel in charge and see where you have got to, and to answer questions easily at the end.

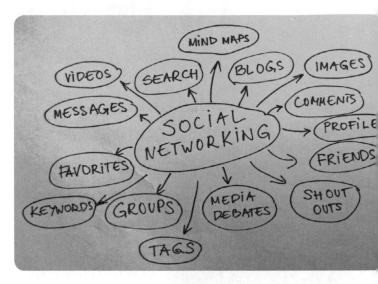

Using a PowerPoint

Choose a prompt method and use it to plan a short talk on speaking from notes. Deliver the talk and record it. Play it back. How were you?

This can be very helpful. However, do not make the mistake of putting all, or most, of your talk on the PowerPoint slides and then reading them out to your audience. This is boring! Just have two or three key points on each slide to help the audience focus, and to act as prompts for you. Images or diagrams can add interest – just one per slide.

If you use a PowerPoint, look round at it but then turn back and speak to the audience. Do not talk to the screen!

1. Why is it not a good option to read your whole talk?
2. What are two advantages of using a visual method to help you give a talk?
3. In which direction should you be facing most of the time if using a PowerPoint?

Progress Check

79

10.4 Preparing for a debate

A **debate** is a formal, structured discussion carried out with set rules. It leads to a vote, which normally decides who has won the debate. Debating is an established way to reach democratic decisions.

Structure

Your teacher will probably set the exact rules for your debate, but normally there is a resolution, worded something like this:

> *This house believes that wolves should be reintroduced to the Scottish Highlands.*

There will be two teams: an affirmative team supporting the resolution, and an opposing team opposing it. There will be two or three people on each team.

Conducting the debate

1. The affirmative team's first speaker will present their arguments.
2. The opposing team's first speaker will present their arguments.
3. Both second speakers in turn have a chance to add to the first speakers' arguments.
4. Each team then has an opportunity to offer a 'rebuttal' of the other side's arguments, and to sum up their own case.
5. There is usually then a vote and the proposal is either 'carried' or 'defeated'.

Your preparation

Preparation for a debate is similar to preparing for a talk, except that you have to prepare as a team and decide what areas each person will cover. You also have to listen carefully to the other team's arguments during the debate and prepare to argue against them. Your teacher may allow you time to prepare for this. You should also bear in mind any other details your teacher gives you on timing.

Essentially, you must know the subject very well in order to be fully prepared. This involves anticipating the other side's arguments and knowing how to counter them.

Even if you are not on one of the teams, you should have the opportunity to discuss the issues at some point.

Progress Check

1. How many teams are there in a debate?
2. What is a 'proposal' in a debate?
3. How is preparing for a debate different from preparing for a solo talk?

10.5 Contributing to a discussion  80

Whether or not you are formally assessed for speaking and listening, these are vital skills in English, and in later life. Contributing to a discussion can be broken down into a number of skills, most of which involve listening:

- putting forward your own views
- responding to the views of others
- moving the discussion on
- leading a discussion.

Putting forward your own views

There are many ways to do this. For example, you could begin:

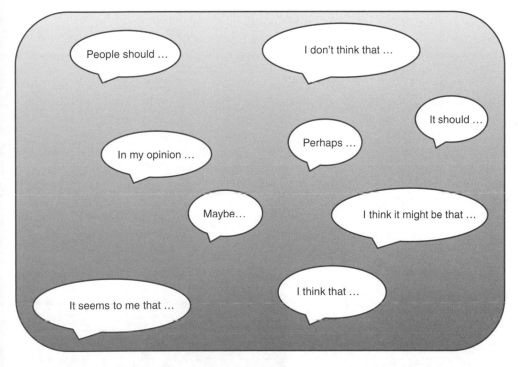

People should …

I don't think that …

It should …

In my opinion …

Perhaps …

Maybe…

I think it might be that …

It seems to me that …

I think that …

Some of these are more assertive and less open to other opinions than others. If you are still exploring the subject, a phrase like 'It seems to me that…' leaves you room to modify your views. It also invites others to comment.

If you are not confident about speaking out, you may have to be prepared to 'push in'. Speakers often overlap slightly. If you are already a confident speaker, remember that a discussion is not all about getting your views heard, or bulldozing others into accepting them. Listen to others, and be prepared to change your views.

Responding to the views of others

In order to respond, you will have to listen properly. This might be difficult if you are trying to hang on to an idea that you want to put forward, so it can be helpful to jot down your ideas so that you can then concentrate on what someone is saying.

You could respond to others in various ways:

- Agree completely, perhaps giving further evidence or argument in support.
- Disagree completely, and explain why.

- Acknowledge that there could be some truth in what has been said, but question some aspects of it.
- Ask the speaker to explain some aspect of what they have said.
- Point out that the speaker may have overlooked something – 'What about…?'
- Say that you think the speaker may be misunderstanding something.
- Even if you disagree completely, do so respectfully. You might, for example, say:
  - 'I can see where you're coming from, but…'
  - 'You have a right to that opinion, but…'

Moving the discussion on

Many of the best discussions are an exploration of ideas rather than a sort of boxing ring in which speakers try to browbeat their opponents. It may be necessary to move the discussion on because the exploration has gradually come to a halt, or even because there is so little agreement.

A good way to do this is to extend an idea that has been voiced, with a 'What if…?' For example:

> 'OK, so you you're not prepared to sacrifice anything to slow down global warming at the moment, but what if Africa became so hot that there were widespread famines?'

Referring back to points made but not fully explored earlier can also be helpful. So can asking for the views of people who have not yet said very much.

Leading a discussion

If you are leading (**chairing**) a discussion, your main **responsibilities** are:
- Getting things going by introducing a few of the issues, or possible opposing views, to focus people on the topic.
- Trying to involve everyone, even the reluctant speakers.
- Making sure that the discussion is not dominated by one or two speakers.

- Putting open-ended questions (ones that cannot be answered yes or no) to the group or to individuals to move the discussion on.
- Summing up views from time to time, especially if the subject is becoming confused.
- Drawing out what ideas or views speakers have in common.
- Keeping people focused and interested; in a school discussion this is particularly important.

> Think of a controversial issue, such as what you should study at school. Write down three or four views on this, on pieces of paper. Shuffle them and pick one. Speak a line expressing this view. Then pick another one. Find a way to express this viewpoint, linking it to the first.

Progress Check

1. What is the likely difference in impact of 'I think that…' and 'It might be that…'?
2. If you express complete disagreement, how should you attempt to express it?
3. How might the question 'What if…' be useful in a discussion?

10.6 Writing and rehearsing a playscript

Writing a play

You may be asked to write an individual play, or to devise a group play, or to turn part of a novel into a play. If you are making up the play yourself or with others, these tips should help:

There must be conflict, tension and resolution, even in a comedy.

Every line spoken should serve a purpose – either revealing character or developing the plot, even if you want the play to be naturalistic (seeming like real life).

It should be clear to the audience what is going on, unless you are holding information back for dramatic effect.

Write out the play in proper script form, with any stage directions required.

Devising a play

This is when a group of people get together and make up the play by suggesting and discussing ideas. So, for example, you might begin with a situation that has conflict and tension built into it, such as a teenager being 'grounded' but desperately wanting to go to an event. The group would then think of what might happen next, and then how that might develop towards a conclusion.

It is helpful if the group considers all ideas put forward, perhaps inviting the proposer to suggest how an idea might develop. It is unhelpful to be dismissive.

A devised play still needs to be scripted. You could divide up the work of writing it down.

Rehearsing

To begin with, you can rehearse with scripts. Concentrate first on **blocking**, which is working out where all the actors should be at all points in the play, including entrances and exits. Then focus on **delivery**: how people speak their lines, and how the other characters respond. Remember, you should be acting in character whenever you are on stage, whether or not you have lines to say.

Ask yourself what a character wants (their **motivation**), and what they are thinking, at the point when they say a line. For example, are they saying the line to get sympathy, or to threaten someone?

Even in rehearsals, try to take the play seriously. Remember, when you perform, you will need the audience to believe in you as a character.

For more on scripts, see Topic 3.9. For Shakespeare, see Topic 1.6

Learning lines

How well do you need to know your lines? Should you practise till you can get them right? No. You should practise **until you cannot get them wrong**! Then you can concentrate on putting the right feeling into them, and relating to the other characters, not just on what you have to say next.

Practise a short speech, with blocking and gestures. Try to learn at least a few lines off by heart that you can then practise.

Practise by uncovering a line at a time and trying to remember what comes next. Then do this with whole speeches. Put some feeling into them, even at this stage: it will help you to remember them.

Also learn your **cues** – the other characters' lines that tell you when to come onstage or speak.

Progress Check

1. What three elements should all plays have, even a comedy?
2. What is *blocking*?
3. What is a *cue*?
4. How much should you practise your lines?

Worked questions

1. **Improve the following speech:**

> Dogs are loads better than cats. That's why they're called 'man's best friend'. Ever since the earliest caveman trained the first wild dog puppy to fetch a stick, they have been helping us to hunt, guard our homes, and stuff like that. Their role in human life constantly expands: finding earthquake victims under debris, sniffing out drugs, etc. Intelligent and loyal, they easily earn the dosh it takes to feed them.
>
> Cats, on the other hand, are total rubbish. Throw a stick for a cat and it will look the other way. Ask it to strap on a keg of brandy and help you look for someone buried in an avalanche, and it will slink off behind the sofa. True, there is some evidence to suggest that stroking a cat helps nervy types to stay calm, but it's not as if the cat wants to help: it just likes being stroked. Similarly, they'll catch mice, but only for a laugh. They even bring live mice into the house and let them escape.
>
> Added to this, cats leave manky messes on your lawn and kill thousands of little tweety-birds every year. Dogs, conversely, can be trained to behave proper. They can understand and respond to a wide range of commands. A well-trained dog can do many jobs more efficiently than a human helper. Cats are just furry parasites who go wherever the food is. Dogs are lovable and will stick by you come what may. Tell your dog to sit and it will still be sat there hours later.

a) Make the register consistently suitable for a debate. *(6 marks)*

b) Put it all into Standard English. *(6 marks)*

c) Add some rhetorical devices: triples, alliteration and parallelism. *(8 marks)*

Dogs are <u>in every way superior to</u>[1] cats. That's why they're called 'man's best friend'. Ever since the earliest caveman trained the <u>earliest</u>[2] wild dog puppy to fetch a stick, they have been helping us to hunt, guard our homes, and <u>round up our sheep</u>.[3] Their role in human life constantly expands: <u>finding earthquake victims under debris, sniffing out drugs, and guiding the blind</u>.[4] <u>Intelligent, loyal and quick to learn</u>,[5] they easily earn <u>their keep</u>.[6]

Cats, on the other hand, are untrainable. <u>Throw a stick for a dog and it will bound after it. Throw a stick for a cat and it will look the other way.</u>[7] Ask a cat to strap on a keg of brandy and help you look for someone buried in an avalanche, and it will slink off behind the sofa. True, there is some evidence to suggest that stroking a cat helps <u>the anxiety-prone</u>[8] to stay calm, but it's not as if the cat wants to help: it just likes being stroked. Similarly, they'll catch mice, but only <u>to amuse themselves</u>.[9] They even bring live mice into the house and let them escape.

1. Register
2. Parallelism
3. Register, and a triple
4. Triple
5. Triple, with alliteration
6. Standard English
7. Parallelism
8. Register
9. Register

Added to this, cats leave <u>malodorous</u>[10] messes on your lawn, kill thousands of <u>songbirds</u>[11] every year, and leave hairs all over the sofa. Dogs, conversely, can be trained to behave <u>in a civilised manner</u>.[12] They can understand and respond to a wide range of commands. <u>A well-trained dog can do many jobs more efficiently than a human helper. A well-trained cat can just about manage to use a litter tray</u>.[13] Cats are just furry parasites who go wherever the food is. Dogs are lovable and will stick by you come what may. Tell your dog to sit and it will still be <u>sitting</u>[14] there hours later.

2. Rewrite the following in a more formal register suitable for a debate.

a) The speaker for the proposal banged on for ages about school uniform. *(2 marks)*

The speaker for the proposal spoke at length about school uniform.

b) Kids are going to nick stuff so long as they're not shown what's what. *(2 marks)*

Children will steal so long as they are not taught moral values.

c) I reckon it's the mums and dads who're to blame. *(2 marks)*

In my view it's the parents who are to blame.

d) The council's plans for a new skate park are well dodgy. *(2 marks)*

The council's plans for a new skate park are ill-advised.

e) You've got the wrong end of the stick. *(2 marks)*

You have misunderstood.

f) If we rip off farmers in poor countries they'll never stand on their own two feet *(2 marks)*

If we exploit farmers in poor countries they will never become self-sufficient.

Practice questions

1. **Rewrite the following in Standard English.** *(10 marks)*

> Me and Rosa was just having a bit of a giggle down the park, by the swings, one day. We was laughing at this little kid who'd been stuffing her face with this box of chocs and had chocolate all over herself. She was in a right state. Her mum come over and gave her what for. Turned out the chocs wasn't even meant to be for the kiddy. She'd nicked them out of her mum's bag. They was meant to be for her gran or something. Well, if I'd done that at her age, my mum would've gone up the wall. We didn't have much dosh to spend on stuff like that.
>
> After a bit, me and Rosa got bored. After all, we wasn't little kids no more, playing on swings and that. And we'd been sat there for an hour or more. So I says to Rosa, 'Why don't we go round yours and do our homework?'
>
> She looks at me like I was mental and says, 'We done it already! Don't you remember?'
>
> Tell you the truth, I'd forgot.

2. **What rhetorical devices are used in the following?**

   a) Forward into the future! *(1 mark)*

   b) Many are called; few are chosen. *(1 mark)*

   c) This government is wallowing in a swamp of broken promises. *(1 mark)*

   d) It must be tough having to heat a home with that many rooms. *(1 mark)*

   e) Parents, children, grandparents, rich and poor, young and old, black and white – they all love us! *(1 mark)*

   f) If we cannot swim in the tide of change, we will go under. *(1 mark)*

   g) The fizz, pop and whoosh of fireworks will once again be heard in the land. *(1 mark)*

   h) The prime minister spoke with icy passion. *(1 mark)*

   i) The family that plays together is the family that stays together. *(1 mark)*

   j) Time marches on and waits for no man. *(1 mark)*

   k) People like you voted for me, and it is people like you that I will serve. *(1 mark)*

   l) Does this government think that we're going to fall for that old trick? *(1 mark)*

   m) Her reputation was in tatters – like a silk scarf caught in the shredder. *(1 mark)*

   n) He's mad, bad and dangerous. *(1 mark)*

Answers to progress check questions

1.1 Skimming, scanning and close reading
1. Reading quickly for an overview.
2. Names and numerals.
3. Linking words such as 'although' and 'but'.

1.2 Inferring meaning
1. To deduce (work out) meaning that is not obvious.
2. To suggest meaning without stating it openly.
3. Yes.

1.3 Reading critically
1. It is a way to judge how successful an author has been.
2. Standards, or measures of success.
3. No: it is often more effective to imply meaning.

1.4 Reading to compare texts
1. How the author addresses the reader.
2. Tones.
3. You should write about each aspect in turn, for each text: Text 1 content, Text 2 content, etc.

1.5 Understanding pre-20th-century texts
1. They are often longer, with more sub-clauses.
2. Their meaning may have changed.
3. From their context.

1.6 Appreciating Shakespeare
1. It is unrhymed.
2. Five.
3. The shipwreck image; Capulet's fury at Juliet disobeying him; the planned church wedding; Capulet saying that God 'lent' them Juliet, and the idea that she is a 'curse'.

2.1 How purpose and context influence style
1. For example, inform, explain, persuade, advise, warn, review, describe.
2. Writing contexts (or text types).
3. It aims to inform and explain, so the language is clear, straightforward and in Standard English.

2.2 Identifying the audience
1. Content and style (including level of formality).
2. It will assume knowledge of, and interest in, the subject; it may use technical terms.
3. A youth audience.

2.3 What is register?
1. Serious subjects require formality.
2. It is more formal.
3. A less formal one.

2.4 What is tone?
1. False.
2. Adjectives.
3. Verbs.

2.5 Commenting on language
1. They create meaning.
2. Point, Evidence, Explanation.
3. False.
4. Embedded.

2.6 Reading texts which inform or explain
1. What, Who, Where, When, How.
2. Why.
3. To tell the reader what it was like.

2.7 Reading persuasive texts
1. Logical argument.
2. Emotive language.
3. Use of language techniques for impact.
4. A list of three.

2.8 Reading texts which advise or warn
1. False.
2. Imperative.
3. Sympathetic but firm.

2.9 Reading reviews
1. False.
2. Information, evaluation, entertainment.
3. True.

2.10 Reading descriptive writing
1. No – it should select.
2. Making readers imagine what something looks, sounds, feels, smells, or tastes like.
3. Extract A, by choosing words expressing feeling; e.g. 'hideous'.
4. By selling his goods.

3.1 Setting and atmosphere
1. Place, time, weather.
2. Setting creates an appropriate atmosphere for events to unfold.
3. By choosing to describe different details, and choosing different language.

3.2 Characterisation and themes
1. By what they do, say and think, and how others speak about or respond to them.
2. Revenge, conflict, gangs/tribes, violence (and reconciliation?).
3. His family were killed by the Yusulu and he has been a rebel soldier.

3.3 How dialogue reveals character
1. Speech marks (quote marks).
2. There is a new paragraph for a change of speaker.
3. It reveals character and relationships.
4. 'Hastily' (he is anxious not to get in trouble) and 'gratefully' (naively thinks he is being offered a drink).

3.4 Plot and structure
1. Conflict or a problem.
2. The hero/heroine: the character we are encouraged to identify with most.
3. Crisis (plural *crises*).
4. During the falling action.

3.5 Narrative viewpoint and tense
1. First person, past tense.
2. Third person, present tense.
3. Third person, from character's point of view.
4. The narrator can only describe events that he or she is involved in or hears about.

3.6 Style and imagery
1. Simile.
2. It is more compressed, speaking of a thing as if it actually *is* the thing to which it is compared.
3. The character and likely style of speech of the narrator.

3.7 Using evidence to comment on a text
1. Themes; style and imagery.
2. False.
3. A quote.
4. Be selective and focus closely on what you select.

3.8 Comparing texts
1. It highlights their main characteristics.
2. A change of direction or idea from the sentence before.
3. Comparison or difference.
4. The start of a paragraph.

3.9 Dialogue and stage directions in a play
1. From what they say and do.
2. Stage directions.
3. So the audience wants to know what will happen.

4.1 What is a poem?
1. The sound of a poem, including its rhythm, contributes to its meaning.
2. All the elements of a poem: sound, imagery, the literal meaning of the words; and there is not usually a single straightforward meaning that everyone would agree on.
3. Three: the poet ('I met…'); the traveller reporting what he saw; Ozymandias himself, in the words he must have ordered to be carved on his statue.
4. Evidence

4.2 Rhythm, metre and poetic form
1. Five.
2. Any set structure that its rhythm makes.
3. 'Ozymandias' is a sonnet.

4.3 Similes and metaphors
1. Like, as, than.
2. It is condensed: it speaks of one thing as if it actually *is* another thing.
3. Winter, dusk, a dying fire.

4.4 Personification
1. Metaphor.
2. Describing abstract things as if they were people, gods or animals.
3. Wordsworth describes war as a dog owner.

4.5 Rhyme
1. Similarity and difference.
2. A repeated pattern of rhyme; it can be shown with a new letter for each new rhyme.
3. A pair of rhyming lines. It gives a sense of completion.
4. When two words almost rhyme, as in Brontë's use of 'above' and 'move', which creates a sense of unease or uncertainty.

4.6 Alliteration and assonance
1. Consonant (non-vowel) sounds.
2. Assonance. (Hear the 'oo' sounds.)
3. They create a sense of heavy, dull drowsiness.
4. It creates a sense of harmony.

4.7 The poem's 'voice'
1. The tone in which the poet speaks (e.g. angry); a fictional persona.
2. He uses the simple language of working-class speech, with slang and colloquialisms.
3. The working-class poor on either side of a war have no real reason to kill each other, other than self-defence. They are similar.

5.1 What is a sentence?
1. What the sentence is about.
2. The part of the sentence that says something about the subject, including a verb.
3. An exclamation mark!
4. A word taking the place of a noun: 'it', 'he', 'she', etc.

5.2 Using simple sentences
1. A subject and a predicate.
2. It will make the writing jerky.
3. It can create tension or give the impression of a character's fleeting thoughts.

5.3 Using coordinated sentences
1. A conjunction.
2. It shows a relationship between the halves; *or* indicates an alternative.
3. Yet.

5.4 Using subordinated sentences
1. A subject and a predicate containing a verb.
2. Background information.
3. True.
4. No: that would make it a coordinated sentence.

5.5 Varying sentence lengths for impact
1. To create variety (prevent the reader from becoming bored) and to create rhythm.
2. They quicken the pace and create tension.
3. Short.
4. Their length can gradually be increased.
5. For example: I've never liked you. You're self-centred and you use people. But I could accept that, were it not for the fact that you persist in believing that you're a model of selfless generosity.

5.6 Ordering information in a sentence
1. Just one.
2. The beginning and the end.
3. The middle.
4. A subordinated sentence.

5.7 Active and passive sentences
1. Passive.
2. The car.
3. Using the passive form. For example, 'The baby was left on the doorstep.'
4. The active form.

5.8 Cumulative sentences
1. It *accumulates* information.
2. It makes complete sense on its own.
3. It can include an unexpected or contradictory detail at the end, perhaps with a repeated phrase preceding it.

5.9 Paragraphing
1. They break text up into manageable sections.
2. When there is a change of speaker.
3. When there is a change of topic.
4. They create suspense by giving added importance to each line.

5.10 Using tenses correctly and effectively
1. Past, present, future.
2. Past continuous.
3. Past or present.
4. For example, I *had been* to Florida before.

5.11 Subject–verb agreement
1. 'We were joking.'
2. 'We are tired.'
3. Standard.
4. Use a singular verb form with a collective noun.

5.12 Using pronouns
1. 'He looked at his car. It was new and he was proud of it.'
2. Possessive pronouns.
3. A subordinated sentence.
4. 'I know the girl whose sister wrote this song.'

6.1 Ending and beginning sentences
1. A full stop, question mark or exclamation mark.
2. An exclamation mark.
3. It is a 'comma splice'. It should be divided into two sentences.

6.2 Commas and dashes
1. 'I love Canada, which has cold winters and hot summers, most of all.'
2. The 'and' is usually regarded as replacing a comma.
3. 'My cousin who lives in Ely…'.
4. A break in the flow of a sentence.

6.3 Colons and semicolons
1. A colon.
2. A semicolon.
3. When one or more listed items uses a comma.

6.4 Quotation marks
1. When Lady Macbeth dies, Macbeth calls life 'a tale told by an idiot'.
2. He told me not to tell anyone. 'If you do,' he said, 'you'll regret it.'
3. The speaker does not think that the show is at all entertaining.

6.5 Apostrophes for possession and omission
1. My sister's hamsters' cage needs cleaning.
2. Should I put my country's needs before both my parents' happiness?
3. I can't read who they're addressed to. Does that say O'Connor or O'Brien?

7.1 Where English comes from
1. 'English' comes from 'Angles'.
2. Ordinary, everyday words, in frequent use.
3. The Vikings.
4. 'Friend' is Anglo-Saxon and more informal; 'companion' is Norman and more formal.

7.2 Making word choices
1. Choosing words carefully to say exactly what you mean.
2. I was astounded….
3. 'He whispered'.
4. Tautology.

7.3 Learning and using new words
1. Read widely, and try to work out the meaning of unfamiliar words.
2. This will help you to see how they fit into a sentence grammatically, and therefore what other words could replace them.
3. Make a note of them, and use them in speech or writing as soon as possible.

7.4 Using a dictionary or thesaurus
1. Its origin – where it comes from.
2. Aardvark, absolutely, absolve, abstain, accessory, ace, acute.
3. Synonyms mean the same as another word (e.g. 'scared' and 'frightened'); antonyms are opposites (e.g. 'big' and 'small').
4. A thesaurus will give synonyms, and words that are only broadly similar in meaning.

7.5 Prefixes
1. Anti: against; pre: before; semi: partly.
2. For example, submarine, sub-tropical.
3. Ungrateful, ingratitude.
4. Deactivate.

7.6 Suffixes
1. Enjoyable, flexible, edible, regrettable.
2. Unforgiving, unresolved, impolite, illegible.
3. Joyless, fearful, careful.
4. Dissatisfaction, dematerialise, discontented.

7.7 Nouns and noun phrases
1. They are all *proper nouns*.
2. It is a noun which is not a proper noun.
3. A phrase which takes the place of a noun in a sentence.
4. As a singular.

7.8 Adjectives
1. In introductory descriptions of people or places.
2. Yellow, narrow, golden.
3. Three.
4. By describing what a character does and says.

7.9 Verbs and adverbs
1. They bring writing to life and give a sense of action.
2. No – it is acceptable to use some ordinary words.
3. Verbs and (sometimes) adjectives.
4. You can often achieve more impact with a well-chosen verb.

7.10 Improving your spelling
1. *Ghoti* spells *Fish*.
2. Look, say, cover, spell.
3. Are you rough and tough enough?

7.11 Spelling rules
1. It lengthens the vowel sound.
2. I before E except after C.
3. Birches.
4. Poppies.

7.12 Homophones
1. *Homo* (same) and *phone* (sound).
2. Principal.
3. Stationery.
4. The two girls didn't know where their practice room was.

8.1 Writing in a consistent register and tone
1. Formal.
2. Imitating speech, and a colloquial expression.
3. Audience, purpose, form.
4. Positive.

8.2 Writing to explain
1. Thinking of what they are likely to know, and need to know.
2. To number steps.
3. Language that cannot be taken in more than one way.
4. Finding buried treasure.

8.3 Recounting events
1. The purpose and audience of the writing.
2. The information needs to be of interest to the reader; small details such as exact timing, which might be important in a witness statement, are unlikely to be worth including. However, how you felt at the time could be of great interest.
3. Both types of writing involve selecting information and presenting it in an interesting way, setting the scene, sometimes withholding information for dramatic effect, and revealing character – fictional or your own.

8.4 Describing a place
1. Be selective.
2. It is boring and gives no idea what *makes* it lovely.
3. It appeals to the senses.
4. It is a boring description and gives no examples.

8.5 Describing a person
1. Link their appearance to their character.
2. Make them express character or lifestyle.
3. That they were nervous and impatient.

8.6 Writing letters
1. A formal register.
2. Two – yours and the recipient's.
3. The 'Dear Sir', etc.
4. When you have used 'Dear Sir or Madam' because you do not know the person's name.

8.7 Writing a story
1. Yes, as in Jack London's 'To Build a Fire'.
2. Setting creates atmosphere.
3. The perspective from which the story is told: first or third person.
4. Tension, conflict, suspense.

8.8 Writing a poem
1. First person.
2. Put the person in an unfamiliar setting.
3. A stanza is like a paragraph in a poem.

8.9 Arguing your case
1. Logical argument.
2. Emotional appeal; choose words for their emotional impact on the reader.
3. In a logical order so that each flows on from the previous one.

8.10 Writing a review
1. To decide whether to read the book, etc., and to compare the reviewer's opinion with their own.
2. Information and evaluation.
3. Present tense.
4. Past tense.

8.11 Summarising
1. Make a bullet list.
2. Short, expressed in few words, and without unnecessary information.
3. The subordinated sentence.

9.1 Improving your first draft
1. Link words like 'However' improve the flow of writing, linking ideas and helping the reader to see how they connect.
2. Consistency of information.
3. If it is not always clear who is speaking.

9.2 Editing your sentences for impact
1. You might turn them into coordinated or subordinated sentences to improve the flow of ideas.
2. To make them more interesting, accurate or concise.
3. Punctuation.

9.3 Proofreading
1. Proofreading is the final stage.
2. By making the meaning unclear, for example by inaccurately indicating a clause.
3. Saying the same thing twice.

10.1 Spoken and written English
1. Speech is helped by body language, facial expression and tone of voice.
2. A listener cannot 'rewind' a live speech.
3. It is non-standard grammar.

10.2 Using rhetorical devices in a speech
1. A language technique, especially used to argue or persuade.
2. A list of three things (nouns, adjectives, verbs, adverbs).
3. 'It's the answer…'.

10.3 Speaking from notes or using a PowerPoint
1. Speaking directly to the audience is more engaging and less likely to be boring.
2. Visual methods such as mind maps or spidergrams can be used for planning, then numbered for ordering and used for the talk. They enable you to see the whole talk at a glance.
3. Towards the audience, not the screen.

10.4 Preparing for a debate
1. Two.
2. The idea put forward and argued by the proposing team.
3. It involves cooperative planning, and overall knowledge of possible counter-arguments to your own arguments.

10.5 Contributing to a discussion
1. 'I think that…' is more assertive and leaves less room for modifying your view later, or for others to put forward an alternative view without confronting you.
2. Respectfully, acknowledging the other person's right to that viewpoint.
3. This could move a discussion on.

10.6 Writing and rehearsing a playscript
1. Conflict, tension, resolution.
2. How actors move about the stage.
3. The indication (usually a line) that an actor should enter or speak.
4. Until you cannot get them wrong!

Answers to practice questions

Chapter 1

1. ⟲ 6–10

  a) The fire made everywhere as 'light as day for 10 miles around'. **(1 mark)**

  b) A strong wind **(1 mark)** and the fact that there had been a period of unusually warm, dry weather. **(1 mark)**

  c) The fire was so widespread.

  d) He is surprised because, owing to their astonishment, despair or sense of resignation, 'they hardly stirred to quench it' **(1 mark)**: they made very little effort to put out the fire or even to save their belongings, instead running about ineffectually as if too upset to focus on the task ('like distracted creatures'). **(1 mark)**

  e) He says that even at night it is like daylight for 10 miles around.

  f) Prodigious means amazing, extraordinary.

  g) 'Devoured'.

2. ⟲ 13–17

  a) He is bitterly negative about life. **(1 mark)** He thinks life is short and meaningless, and that time drags on in an equally pointless way. **(1 mark)**

  b) They could mean (a) that Lady Macbeth should have lived longer and died naturally in old age, at an appropriate time, **(1 mark)** or (b) she would have died eventually, so her dying now makes no difference. **(1 mark)**

  c) It breaks the steady flow of the iambic pentameter, forcing us to speak it in a dragging, drawn out way: 'To*mor*row…' **(1 mark)**; an extra syllable adds to the effect. He sees the future as dragging tediously on. **(1 mark)**

  d) Time is seen 'creeping' like a slow person, **(1 mark)** and our 'yesterdays' have 'lighted fools', like someone carrying a candle to see someone (the 'fools') to their bed. **(1 mark)**

  e) Macbeth portrays life as insubstantial, a 'shadow', **(1 mark)** and like a bad actor who overacts, shouting and overdoing his gestures ('struts and frets'), as if what he had to say were meaningful, when in fact it is not. **(1 mark)** When he is gone, he is never heard of again. **(1 mark)** Life seems to matter at the time because of its 'sound and fury', but actually it is stupid and pointless ('a tale told by an idiot'). **(1 mark)**

Chapter 2

1. ⟲ 21–31, 36–37

  a) The main purpose of the page is to advise newcomers to surfing on how to surf safely, and to inform them about what they need in order to do this. The register is fairly formal so that it will seem authoritative, especially in the opening paragraph. The phrase 'accredited training centres' is more formal than 'clued-up surf outfits' would be. On the other hand, some phrases are slightly more informal, so as not to put people off by seeming too serious so that they will just discard the leaflet. The phrases 'starting out' and 'catch waves' are less formal than 'embarking on this sport' and 'gain access to waves'. The tone is fairly relaxed, but sensible, with only the occasional hint that your life could depend on taking the advice, as in 'vital…strong currents'. **(2 marks)**

    The target audience is young people who are not yet experienced surfers. If they were, they would not need to be told about the equipment. The slightly informal touches, as in 'kit' and 'catch waves' (which is a surfing phrase) would appeal to a young audience. **(2 marks)**

    The fact that this is a leaflet means that the information has to be presented briefly, and concisely, and without putting readers off with scare-stories. **(2 marks)**

  b) People will only read this voluntarily. Hence the design acknowledges that readers want fun. **(1 mark)** The picture is of someone enjoying surfing, not drowning. **(1 mark)** The angled, spotted typeface of the heading reflects this. **(1 mark)** The images help to get the reader's attention and also suggest fun, being apparently taped onto the page like holiday snaps. **(1 mark)**

2. ⟲ 21, 26–29, 30–31

  a) He wants to entertain us by sharing (and exaggerating) his own fears about camping. Phrases like 'lying in the dark alone in a little tent' deliberately create this effect by dramatising what he imagines. **(1 mark)** Part of the technique is to paint a vivid picture of what he imagines, especially in phrases appealing to our senses, such as 'quiet grunts and mysterious snufflings'. We can enjoy his fear without having to be there. **(1 mark)**

  b) He seems anxious about bears. **(1 mark)** Hence the 'the unutterable relief of realizing that the bear has withdrawn to the other side of the camp'. **(1 mark)** He knows that most of his readers will never have been in a situation in which they might encounter bears. **(1 mark)** They will need sensory help to imagine this, as in 'the sudden rough bump of its snout', but they will probably share some of his attitude once they do. **(1 mark)**

  c) The register and tone are those of a piece of writing intended to entertain. Of course, bears really do prowl around people's tents in the American woods, and Bryson is partly informing us of this, so he exaggerates just enough to entertain without making the experience seem unbelievable. He invites us to laugh at his own fearful imagination, as well as his limited knowledge of bears, and the woods as a whole. **(4 marks)**

    nothing but a few microns of trembling nylon – this emphasises just how little there is to protect the camper.

    mysterious snufflings – faintly ironic; 'snufflings' sounds quite playful, and 'mysterious' suggests someone rather stupidly wondering what the noise could be.

    that unwelcome tingling – understatement!

    alarming wild wobble – more understatement, made more funny by the 'w' alliteration.

    Bears adore Snickers bars, you've heard – funny because of the use of 'you', and the word 'adore', as if the bears were human.

    wait, shhhhh…yes! – This almost puts us right there in the tent with him.

    I tell you right now. I couldn't stand it – an endearingly frank confession. **(4 marks)**

Chapter 3

1. ⟲ 48–51, 58–59

  a) The word 'declared' shows Donna's self-confidence, and the fact that she assumes that she will be obeyed; **(1 mark)** 'sidled' suggests that Marcia is acting furtively, not letting passers-by know what is going on. **(1 mark)**

b) They are in a joking mood, enjoying their position of power. Feeling relaxed because they know they are in control, they laugh at the idea that Sade can evade them by saying 'Excuse me'. **(1 mark)** Marcia's playing with her hair shows that she is relaxed, perhaps even exaggerating this mood to taunt Sade. However, the phrase 'you'll still have to do it, you know' is more threatening. **(1 mark)**

c) Donna calls Sade 'her', as if she were not present. 'Top speed' shows that Donna feels she can compel Sade. Her disrespectful playing with Sade's name ('Sha-day-aday') adds to this. **(1 mark)** The word 'propelled', with the passive form, shows Sade as a victim. Then she is 'being marched', the passive form and word choice again showing her powerlessness. **(1 mark)** She is 'towed', like a something on a rope. This comes to a climax in the 'rag doll' simile, as if she is the other girls' toy. **(1 mark)**

d) She tries to resist, with the politely assertive 'I don't want to see anything. Excuse me.' **(1 mark)** She makes herself 'go rigid' in resistance. She is then incredulous as she begins to think that the girls can compel her, despite this being in public. **(1 mark)** The word 'mumbled' suggests that she has given in. **(1 mark)**

Chapter 4

1. ⊃ 70–72, 77–80

Various answers are possible. Most likely suggestions include – Kipling creates a strong sense of an abandoned place. The atmosphere is mysterious and melancholic. We wonder why the road was shut, and who the anonymous 'They' refers to. The repeated phrases 'the woods', 'road through the woods' and 'There was once a road through the woods' create a haunting sense that although the road has been shut and is now overgrown, it still somehow continues.

The lines from 'You will hear the beat of a horse's feet' to 'The misty solitudes' suggest that the old road is haunted by a woman who once rode along it. The internal rhyme of 'beat…feet' create the rhythm of a horse's hooves, the alliteration and onomatopoeia in 'swish of a skirt' brings the woman back to life by appealing to our senses. The phrase 'misty solitudes' is eerie.

The description of animals now secretively inhabiting the woods adds to a sense of abandonment, and yet of life continuing. By the time we reach the end of the poem, the final line seems like a complete contradiction, because the apparently non-existent road has become so real. **(8 marks)**

2. ⊃ 70–72, 79–80

Various answers are possible. Most likely suggestions include – The title emphasises the fact that Hardy imagines he can hear this woman that he once loved and still misses so much. The alliteration in 'Woman much missed' and 'first… fair' and the repetition of 'call to me' create a sense of loss and longing, as if the memories come back to him repeatedly, echoed in repeated sounds. The rhythm, consisting of one stressed syllable followed by two unstressed, adds to a sense of sadness. It is like an old man limping.

His question in the second stanza suggests a forlorn hope, mixed with uncertainty. He gives himself up to the memory, painting a vivid picture of her in her 'air-blue gown'. The whole of the third stanza is also a question, in which he accepts that perhaps he is just hearing the breeze. Its dull 'listlessness' and the idea of it 'travelling' across the wet field, rather than blowing in a more lively way, add to a sense of loss.

The rhythm changes completely in the final stanza as Hardy shifts the focus from the woman to himself. It echoes the way that, as an old man, broken by sadness, he is

'faltering forward'. The alliteration adds to the limping effect. The penultimate line suggests extreme lack of comfort. A 'thorn' offers no comfort, and the cold north wind 'oozes' through it. The poems ends with the inescapable fact of his loss: 'the woman calling'. **(8 marks)**

3. ⊃ 70–72, 75, 79–80

Various answers are possible. Most likely suggestions include – The fluid, positive-sounding rhythm suggests the elation that most people involved in the war must have felt at its end. No one person is identified, and the fact that each stanza begins with 'Everyone', and repeats it in the second stanza, gives the poem a sense of this being a universal feeling. The second stanza seems like a confirmation of the first, as they partly mirror each other. Both opening lines say the same thing in slightly different form – both including 'Everyone' and 'suddenly'; both second lines begin with 'And'; and both end with a sense of something that will carry on into distant space and time.

The language is mostly very positive. Singing itself suggests joy, and the word 'lifted' applied to it adds to the sense of joy, as if the weight of war has been 'lifted' from the singers. This sense of relief is also found in the extended image of birds released from captivity, enjoying their freedom to fly wherever they want. The alliteration of 'Winging wildly … white' emphasises this, perhaps even simulating their wingbeats. The land over which they fly is a spring landscape, with orchards in blossom and the fields lushly green, both suggesting hope and growth.

It seems odd, however, that beauty then comes 'like the setting sun', which is normally associated with endings rather than beginnings. However, it could be argued that this simile hints at the lives lost in the war. Indeed, Sassoon refers to 'tears' and 'horror' in this stanza, and the horror 'drifts' away rather than evaporating in an instant. In '… O, but' he seems to have to drag himself away from these feelings to reassert the sense of joy and freedom. **(8 marks)**

Chapter 5

1. ⊃ 104–105

I was feeling pretty pleased with myself. I had just got my first Saturday job, in a greengrocer's, and already I had been congratulated on my hard work and positive attitude. Then, however, a rather grumpy-looking customer entered the shop, an elderly lady with her hair in a bun.

'Young lady,' she said, 'I want two pounds of potatoes, a bunch of asparagus, and a quarter of mushrooms. And make it snappy.'

'Certainly,' I said, trying hard to be polite. After all, wasn't the customer always right?

I gave her the veg, took her £10 note and gave her the change.

'I gave you a £20 note,' she said.

My positive mood was fading fast. This woman was a shop assistant's nightmare. She looked at me steely-eyed, like my old head teacher in primary school. Her hand was held out. I knew for sure that she had only given me £10. I wondered if I should call for the manager.

Instead I decided to stick to my guns. 'It was a ten,' I said, quietly but firmly. **(1 mark for each)**

2. ⊃ 107–108

The two boys were strolling through the park kicking cans, wondering how to spend the rest of their day. When they came to the boating lake, they were surprised to see an empty boat, with its oars pulled just out of the water. It was just sitting there. The taller boy smiled.

'Terry,' he said, 'do you fancy a boat trip?'

Terry grinned. <u>He</u> had never had the money to go on a boat trip. This was <u>his</u> big chance.

'Give us a hand, Lee,' Terry said as <u>he</u> clambered in.

<u>They</u> were in the middle of the lake when <u>they</u> realised that there was a problem with the boat. <u>It</u> was filling up with water. **(1 mark for each)**

3. ⊃ 104–105

<u>In the early 21ˢᵗ century</u>, most people <u>lived</u> in centrally heated and well-insulated houses. They <u>could</u> shop once a week if <u>they wanted</u>, and put food in the fridge or freezer. <u>They had</u> sophisticated ovens and, <u>if they were</u> really lazy, <u>they could</u> pop ready-meals in the microwave and have them on the table in a few minutes. Then <u>they could</u> eat them in front of the TV or DVD, or listening to music on <u>their</u> MP3 players, or even while playing games on <u>their</u> Xbox or texting a friend. <u>Their</u> opportunities for technology use and media consumption <u>were</u> endless.

The pace of change <u>has constantly increased. Life now</u> is even easier, with developments in technology that <u>our ancestors could barely imagine</u>. We control our devices by thought power, and even communicate by telepathy. Instead of watching flat TV screens, <u>we enjoy</u> lifelike 3-D hologrammatic presentations, with sound effects. <u>We even</u> hook up to simulators that make us feel immersed in the illusion of other 'realities'. Travel, too, <u>is</u> very different. <u>It is</u> solar-powered and we <u>have abandoned</u> the wheel: flying saucers <u>have become</u> everyday items. **(1 mark for each)**

4. ⊃ 104–105

Various answers are possible. One suggestion is – On the other hand, global warming will continue. Climate change will raise sea levels, flooding low-lying countries and making farming impossible in most of Africa, leading to starvation and mass migration. There is still just about time for us to avoid this. But will we make the necessary sacrifices to save the planet for future generations?

Chapter 6

1. ⊃ 114
   a) All things considered, it's a good result, I think.
   b) Unlike Scotland, which has North Sea oil, Wales has few mineral resources now.
   c) I have the people's respect, which is more than can be said for my opponent, the labour candidate.
   d) The soldiers, seeing themselves outnumbered, beat a hasty retreat.
   (1 mark for each)

2. ⊃ 116
   a) There's no need to speak: I know everything.
   b) There's only one reason we're not dead: they need us alive.
   c) To lose one parent may be regarded as a misfortune; to lose both looks like carelessness.
   d) Moses only saw the Promised Land; Aaron entered it.
   e) We need to take the following: a two-man tent, with tent pegs; our sleeping bags, and maybe pillows; a cooking stove, with spare gas cylinders and matches; and a torch.
   (1 mark for each)

3. ⊃ 117–118
   a) Dickens, through his narrator, Pip, calls Miss Havisham 'the strangest lady I have ever seen, or shall ever see'.
   b) Martin Luther King's famous 'I have a dream' speech is a masterpiece of rhetorical language.
   c) Sir Andrew Aguecheek in *Twelfth Night* says, 'I was adored once too.'
   d) She looked at the sky. 'I think', she said, 'I might come inside after all.'
   e) 'I don't think I'll get the job,' he said sadly. 'They called me "a talentless idiot with no ideas". That can't be good, can it?'
   (1 mark for each)

4. ⊃ 119–120
   a) It's time we gave the school its due. They've done all they can to improve Kevin's concentration.
   b) Karen's a star. She doesn't know how to sing in tune, but her cakes can't be faulted. Hers are the only ones I don't wish I hadn't eaten.
   c) 'Can't you see, I'll make you famous. You'll be on every TV set in the land!'
   d) 'My little darlin', there's nuffin' I wouldn't do for you.'
   e) There is a big audience out there, thanks to the boss's hard work and my two brothers' publicity. But they're here because we're Britain's finest.
   (1 mark for each)

Chapter 7

1. ⊃ 127
   a) He <u>sprinted</u> for the bus.
   b) She <u>denied</u> it.
   c) He was campaigning for Scotland's <u>independence</u>.
   d) He is a <u>hypocrite</u>.
   e) I want to get a job in <u>industry</u>.
   (1 mark for each)

2. ⊃ 126–127

Ewan was feeling rather <u>resentful</u> about having to clean the car. His father had practically <u>ordered</u> him to do it. It was so <u>unjust</u>. After all, it was not his car, and he only ever needed to be given lifts in it because his parents <u>insisted</u> on living so far away from the town – in a <u>remote</u> farmhouse. His parents treated him like their <u>slave</u>! He <u>trudged</u> to the tap to fetch another bucket of water, but then he remembered that there was a hose in the garden shed. He found it and <u>attached</u> it to the tap. This made the job considerably easier. He was spraying the car and listening to his i-Pod when the church band came <u>marching</u> up the road.

(1 mark for each)

3. ⊃ 127

I paced around my cell. If I did not find a way to escape, I would soon be facing a <u>firing squad</u>. I did not think of myself as <u>a coward</u>, but it was hard not to feel a sense of <u>despair</u> in the present circumstances.

To calm my mind, I thought about how I had got to this point. True, I had joined the <u>revolution</u>, but I had done this for the best possible reasons. I was a man of <u>honour</u>; I was not a <u>traitor</u>. All I wanted was <u>equality</u>.

In my <u>excitement</u>, I found that I was beating my fist on the cell wall. Imagine my <u>surprise</u> when I found that one of the stones was loose. I got my fingers round it and tugged. It came out. With some effort, I prised out the stone next to it. Had I found a way to gain my <u>liberty</u>?

(1 mark for each)

4. ⊃ 145–150

I had promised to do the supermarket shopping as Mum was <u>too</u> tired after work. <u>Unfortunately</u> I had only left myself about half an <u>hour</u>. Would it be <u>enough</u>? Perhaps if I really hurried. First I had to get breakfast <u>cereal</u> – I <u>knew</u> that much. The trouble is, <u>there's too</u> much choice. Also, I hadn't had a lot of <u>practice</u>. <u>Where</u> are the cornflakes, I thought. An assistant pointed to an <u>aisle</u>, but when I got <u>there</u> it was full of <u>stationery</u> and <u>diaries</u>.

After about ten <u>minutes</u> I was doing better. I had almost filled the basket. Still, the time was rushing <u>past</u>, and I still had to find some iced <u>lollies</u>, <u>potatoes</u> and <u>tomatoes</u>. And I mustn't <u>forget</u> to ask for a <u>receipt</u>, Mum said. Just then, as I looked down past the <u>queue</u> of customers at the till, I noticed someone acting <u>strangely</u>. He was <u>quietly</u> tucking a bottle of wine up his sweatshirt. What should I do? I was in a hurry. It would be a <u>relief</u> to discover that it was just a <u>mistake</u>. Oh no! Now I recognised him: it was our next-door <u>neighbour</u>!

5. Shannon sat <u>hunched over, biting her nails distractedly and sniffing back the tears,</u> *[body language shows anxiety and distress]* outside the Head Teacher's office. The other girl sitting next to her, Becky Davitt, had been to blame but the teacher had resolved to punish them both.

    The door opened and the Head appeared. He looked at Becky Davitt and <u>sighed with weary resignation.</u> *[shows lack of surprise and that he sees her as a problem]*

    '<u>Becky Davitt,</u>' he began, <u>glaring at her.</u> *[reported speech turned into dialogue, with vivid verb expressing his negative view]* 'You're always in trouble. I'm sick of having to deal with your bad behaviour.'

    <u>Davitt continued to stare out of the window, alms folded. She screwed up her mouth as if chewing, half-closed her eyes and glanced at her watch.</u> *[her body language shows exaggerated disrespect and indifference]*

    When the Head recognised Shannon <u>his eyebrows raised</u> *[shows surprise]* and he took a deep breath.

    'Well, Shannon. I wasn't expecting to see you here, I must say. Can you explain?'

    Shannon opened her mouth to speak. 'Sir, I tried to tell Miss Peace, but ...'. <u>She broke off as she caught sight of Becky</u> *[shows her fear]* looking hard at her and, without the Head noticing, drawing her finger slowly across her throat like a knife.

    'Well, Shannon ...' The Head shook his head and looked away, then back. '<u>I'm afraid you give me no choice.</u>' *[shows reluctance to punish her]*

Chapter 8

1. Answers will vary. **(1 mark for each bullet point and 5 for the whole summary)**
2. Answers will vary. **(1 mark for each bullet point and 5 for the whole summary)**
3. ⟳ 177
    Various answers possible. Here is one suggestion.
    - Tintern Abbey is an exciting sight from the river.
    - The river is tidal to Bigsweir.
    - The tide is a problem but has advantages.
    - If you check tide times you can ride the tide upstream and back.
    - You can ride the outgoing tide to get to Tintern, avoiding rapids.

    Tintern Abbey is exciting viewed from the river, which is tidal as far as Bigsweir. The tide can be a problem, but it does have its advantages. If you check the tide times online you can ride the tide upstream and back with little effort. You can also ride the outgoing tide to Tintern, thus avoiding the rapids at Coed Ithel Weir. (62 words) **(10 marks for a summary of fewer than 70 words)**

Chapter 9

1. ⟳ 181–184
    Various answers possible. Here is one suggestion.
    Travel to Mars
    Ever since the USA and USSR began the space race in the 1960s, with the Russian Yuri Gagarin being the first man in space, nations have wanted to assert their status by showing that they can take part in this race. Even India, a country in which thousands of people live in poverty, homeless and starving, has recently sent a space rocket to Mars. Surely this is just misguided international rivalry.

    At this point in human history, the whole of planet Earth is threatened. Pollution is causing global warming at an accelerating pace, which is melting the polar ice caps, and the Amazon is being destroyed. We should be putting all the resources we can spare into saving our own planet, not sending rockets to other planets.

People say that going to Mars fulfils the key human instinct to explore, but we can explore in different ways. For example, we can find out more about how our fragile ecosystems on Earth work, we can study wildlife, and we can explore the depths of the ocean. **(12 marks)**

2. ⟳ 185
    <u>My girlfriend and I</u> went out for a meal in a new <u>restaurant</u> called <u>Edmundo's</u> last night. <u>The</u> food was over-priced and not really worth it. <u>There</u> was a <u>fountain</u> in the middle of the <u>floor, which</u> was <u>stone-tiled</u>, so the <u>place</u> echoed <u>quite</u> a lot and it <u>wasn't</u> always easy to <u>hear</u> a conversation. The food was tasty but barely <u>adequate</u>: I only had <u>two potatoes</u> with my beef. <u>Still,</u> <u>walking</u> around the <u>place,</u> <u>I noticed that</u> the other <u>diners</u> seemed to be enjoying <u>themselves.</u> **(1 mark for each)**

3. ⟳ 185
    <u>Strangely</u> enough, one of my <u>favourite places</u> is the local supermarket car <u>park. This</u> is because I go <u>skateboarding</u> <u>there</u> with my <u>friends</u>. A <u>manager</u> at the supermarket used to complain sometimes and tell us to go <u>somewhere</u> else <u>because</u> we <u>were</u> scaring <u>off</u> the customers and <u>losing</u> the supermarket <u>money, but</u> this was <u>rubbish. I</u> talked to some of the customers and they used to like watching us. <u>Anyway,</u> we <u>were</u> always careful to keep out of the way of cars. <u>Another</u> point is that the <u>council is</u> meant to be making us a skate park and <u>they've</u> never got round to it. Using the car park keeps us <u>off</u> the streets. It also has some nice, gentle <u>slopes,</u> and sheltered spots to just hang out and chat. **(1 mark for each)**

Chapter 10

1. ⟳ 188–189
    Various alternatives are possible. Here is one example.

    Rosa and I were just amusing ourselves in the park, by the swings, one day. We were laughing at a little girl who had been eating a box of chocolates and had chocolate all over herself. She was in a terrible mess. Her mother came over and told her off. It turned out that the chocolates weren't even meant to be for the little girl. She'd stolen them from her mother's bag. They were meant to be for her grandmother, or something like that. Well, if I had done that at her age, my mother would have lost her temper. We didn't have much money to spend on things like that.

    After a while, Rosa and I got bored. After all, we weren't little children anymore, playing on swings and that sort of thing. And we'd been sitting there for an hour or more. So I said to Rosa, 'Why don't we go to your house and do our homework?'

    She looked at me as if I were mad and said, 'We did it already! Don't you remember?'

    To tell you the truth, I'd forgotten.

2. ⟳ 190–191
    (1 mark for each correctly identified device)
    a) Alliteration
    b) Antithesis
    c) Exaggeration (and metaphor)
    d) Irony
    e) List
    f) Metaphor
    g) Onomatopoeia
    h) Oxymoron
    i) Parallelism
    j) Personification
    k) Repetition
    l) Rhetorical question
    m) Simile
    n) Triple (triad, tricolon)

Mixed test-style paper

1. **Shakespeare paper**

Imagine you are going to direct a performance of these scenes from Shakespeare's *Macbeth*. How should the actors show their relationship in the first scene, and how it has changed in the second?

Support your ideas by referring to both extracts in your answer. Spend 15 minutes carefully reading the two extracts. Then try to complete the task in a further 45 minutes.

Extract 1: Act 1, Scene 7, lines 35–82

Macbeth tells Lady Macbeth that he has decided *not* to carry out their plan to murder King Duncan in order to become king himself. Lady Macbeth is disappointed in him.   *(18 marks)*

LADY MACBETH	Was the hope drunk Wherein you dressed yourself? Hath it slept since? And wakes it now, to look so green and pale At what it did so freely? From this time Such I account thy love. Art thou afeard To be the same in thine own act and valour As thou art in desire? Wouldst thou have that Which thou esteem'st the ornament of life, And live a coward in thine own esteem, Letting 'I dare not' wait upon 'I would,' Like the poor cat i' the adage?
MACBETH	Prithee, peace: I dare do all that may become a man; Who dares do more is none.
LADY MACBETH	What beast was't, then, That made you break this enterprise to me? When you durst do it, then you were a man; And, to be more than what you were, you would Be so much more the man. Nor time nor place Did then adhere, and yet you would make both: They have made themselves, and that their fitness now Does unmake you. I have given suck, and know How tender 'tis to love the babe that milks me: I would, while it was smiling in my face, Have plucked my nipple from his boneless gums, And dashed the brains out, had I so sworn as you Have done to this.
MACBETH	If we should fail?
LADY MACBETH	We fail! But screw your courage to the sticking-place,

And we'll not fail. When Duncan is asleep –
Whereto the rather shall his day's hard journey
Soundly invite him – his two chamberlains
Will I with wine and wassail so convince
That memory, the warder of the brain,
Shall be a fume, and the receipt of reason
A limbeck* only: when in swinish sleep
Their drenched natures lie as in a death,
What cannot you and I perform upon
The unguarded Duncan? What not put upon
His spongy officers, who shall bear the guilt
Of our great quell?

MACBETH   Bring forth men-children only;
For thy undaunted mettle should compose
Nothing but males. Will it not be received,
When we have marked with blood those sleepy two
Of his own chamber and used their very daggers,
That they have done't?

LADY MACBETH   Who dares receive it other,
As we shall make our griefs and clamour roar
Upon his death?

MACBETH   I am settled, and bend up
Each corporal agent* to this terrible feat.
Away, and mock the time* with fairest show:
False face must hide what the false heart doth know.

limbeck vessel for distilling liquids
Each corporal agent each part of my body
mock the time deceive the world

Extract 2: Act 3, Scene 2, lines 27–46

Macbeth has murdered Duncan and become king, but he is afraid that his old friend Banquo
will reveal his secret and ruin him, and that Banquo's son Fleance may become king.
Macbeth and Lady Macbeth are planning a banquet. Macbeth hints at his plan to have
Banquo murdered before he reaches the palace.

LADY MACBETH   Come on;
Gentle my lord, sleek o'er your rugged looks;
Be bright and jovial among your guests tonight.

MACBETH   So shall I, love; and so, I pray, be you:
Let your remembrance apply to Banquo;
Present him eminence,* both with eye and tongue:
Unsafe the while, that we
Must lave* our honours in these flattering streams,
And make our faces vizards* to our hearts,
Disguising what they are.

LADY MACBETH	You must leave this.
MACBETH	O, full of scorpions is my mind, dear wife! Thou know'st that Banquo, and his Fleance, lives.
LADY MACBETH	But in them nature's copy's not eterne.
MACBETH	There's comfort yet; they are assailable; Then be thou jocund: ere the bat hath flown His cloistered flight, ere to black Hecate's* summons The shard-borne beetle with his drowsy hums Hath rung night's yawning peal, there shall be done A deed of dreadful note.
LADY MACBETH	What's to be done?
MACBETH	Be innocent of the knowledge, dearest chuck, Till thou applaud the deed.

present him eminence praise him
lave wash
vizards masks
Hecate goddess of witches

2. **Reading paper**

Spend 15 minutes carefully reading the two extracts. Then try to answer the questions in a further 45 minutes.

Extract 1: Stephen Crane, 'The Open Boat': a story based on a real event (1897)

None of them knew the colour of the sky. Their eyes glanced level, and were fastened upon the waves that swept toward them. These waves were of the hue of slate, save for the tops, which were of foaming white, and all of the men knew the colours of the sea. The horizon narrowed and widened, and dipped and rose, and at all times its edge was jagged with waves that seemed to thrust up in points like rocks. Many a man ought to have a bath-tub larger than the boat which here rode upon the sea. These waves were most wrongfully and barbarously abrupt and tall, and each froth-top was a problem in small-boat navigation.

The cook squatted in the bottom and looked with both eyes at the six inches of gunwale which separated him from the ocean. His sleeves were rolled over his fat forearms, and the two flaps of his unbuttoned vest dangled as he bent to bail out the boat. Often he said: 'Gawd! That was a narrow clip.' As he remarked it he invariably gazed eastward over the broken sea.

The oiler, steering with one of the two oars in the boat, sometimes raised himself suddenly to keep clear of water that swirled in over the stern. It was a thin little oar and it seemed often ready to snap.

The correspondent, pulling at the other oar, watched the waves and wondered why he was there.

The injured captain, lying in the bow, was at this time buried in that profound dejection and indifference which comes, temporarily at least, to even the bravest and most enduring when, willy-nilly, the firm fails, the army loses, the ship goes down. The mind of the master of a vessel is rooted deep in the timbers of her, though he commanded for a day or a decade, and this captain had on him the stern impression of a scene in the greys of dawn of seven turned faces, and later a stump of a top-mast with a white ball on it that slashed to and fro at the waves, went low and lower, and down. Thereafter there was something strange in his voice. Although steady, it was deep with mourning, and of a quality beyond oration or tears.

'Keep 'er a little more south, Billie,' said he.
'A little more south, sir,' said the oiler in the stern.

A seat in this boat was not unlike a seat upon a bucking bronco, and by the same token, a bronco is not much smaller. The craft pranced and reared, and plunged like an animal. As each wave came, and she rose for it, she seemed like a horse making at a fence outrageously high. The manner of her scramble over these walls of water is a mystic thing, and, moreover, at the top of them were ordinarily these problems in white water, the foam racing down from the summit of each wave, requiring a new leap, and a leap from the air. Then, after scornfully bumping a crest, she would slide, and race, and splash down a long incline, and arrive bobbing and nodding in front of the next menace.

A singular disadvantage of the sea lies in the fact that after successfully surmounting one wave you discover that there is another behind it just as important and just as nervously anxious to do something effective in the way of swamping boats.

a) Identify two words or phrases in paragraph 1 that indicate the movement of
the boat. *(2 marks)*

....

b) Explain how, in paragraphs 1–3, the author makes the reader aware of how vulnerable the men are, and the size of their boat in relation to the size of the waves.

Support your comments by quoting two or three phrases from this section. *(3 marks)*

....

....

....

c) What impression of the captain's character and current frame of mind do we get, and how is this created? You might, for example, say what 'scene in the greys of dawn' he is remembering, and how it has affected him.

Support your comments with quotations from this section. *(4 marks)*

....

....

....

....

....

....

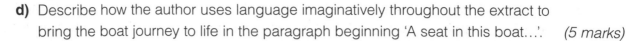

d) Describe how the author uses language imaginatively throughout the extract to bring the boat journey to life in the paragraph beginning 'A seat in this boat…'. *(5 marks)*

....

....

....

....

....

....

....

....

e) Write about the tone of Stephen Crane's description – what his attitude towards the story seems to be. (He is the 'correspondent' in paragraph 4.)

Support your answer with examples of Crane's word choices. *(6 marks)*

....

....

....

....

....

....

....

....

....

....

Extract 2: Antarctic explorer Ernest Shackleton describes a 16-day boat journey to fetch help for his expedition (1912)

Cramped in our narrow quarters and continually wet by the spray, we suffered severely from cold throughout the journey. We fought the seas and the winds and at the same time had a daily struggle to keep ourselves alive. At times we were in dire peril. Generally we were upheld by the knowledge that we were making progress towards the land where we would be, but there were days and nights when we lay hove to,* drifting across the storm-whitened seas and watching, with eyes interested rather than apprehensive, the uprearing masses of water, flung to and fro by Nature in the pride of her strength.

Deep seemed the valleys when we lay between the reeling seas. High were the hills when we perched momentarily on the tops of giant combers. Nearly always there were gales. So small was our boat and so great were the seas that often our sail flapped idly in the calm between the crests of two waves. Then we would climb the next slope and catch the full fury of the gale where the wool-like whiteness of the breaking water surged around us.

We had our moments of laughter – rare, it is true, but hearty enough. Even when cracked lips and swollen mouths checked the outward and visible signs of amusement we could see a joke of the most primitive kind. Man's sense of humour is always most easily stirred by the petty misfortunes of his neighbours, and I shall never forget Worsley's efforts on one occasion to place the hot aluminium stand on top of the Primus stove after it had fallen off in an extra-heavy roll. With his frostbitten fingers he picked it up, dropped it, picked it up again, and toyed with it gingerly as though it were some fragile article of lady's wear. We laughed, or rather gurgled with laughter.

hove to with the sails rigged so that they do not need to steer

f) From the information in paragraph 1, explain in your own words in what ways the men were uncomfortable. *(2 marks)*

....

....

g) Explain how, in paragraph 1, Shackleton makes the reader aware of the danger of the men's situation and their response to it.

Support your comments by quoting two or three phrases from this section. *(3 marks)*

....

....

....

....

h) Explain how Shackleton uses word choices and sentence structures to bring vividly to life what the journey was like.

Support your comments with quotations from this paragraph. *(4 marks)*

....

....

....

....

....

....

i) Referring to the final paragraph, explain the role played by humour in this journey. *(5 marks)*

....

....

....

....

....

....

j) Explain how Shackleton uses metaphor, simile, personification and visual details throughout the extract.

Support your answer with examples of Shackleton's language. *(6 marks)*

....

....

....

....

....

....

....

....

3. Writing paper

This paper is 1 hour and 15 minutes long. Spend: 45 minutes on Section (a), the longer task; 30 minutes on Section (b), the shorter task. Spend the first 15 minutes planning your Section (a) answer.

Section (a) has 30 marks. Section (b) has 20 marks, including 4 for spelling.

a) Longer writing task

Write a magazine article entitled 'An experience that changed my life'. In the article, describe the experience and explain in what ways it was life-changing. *(30 marks)*

b) Shorter writing task

Write a letter to Baz Luhrmann, director of the film *Romeo + Juliet*, describing a book you have read, why you think he should make it into a film, and what things he should particularly focus on.

You do not need to include any addresses. *(20 marks)*

1. ⟲ 9–17, 32–33, 52, 58–63

In the first extract, it is obvious that Lady Macbeth is a strong, assertive woman, ambitious for her husband and prepared to use all her persuasive powers to make him change his mind about murdering Duncan. The actor playing her should speak with strength and passion.

However, she is also manipulative, playing on her husband's weaknesses. She asks him if his former ambition ('hope') was just drunkenness. The word 'dressed' suggests that he was not really ambitious, but was just 'dressing up'. This could be spoken insultingly.

She could speak the words 'green and pale' with mock sympathy: she does not really feel sorry for him. When she says, 'Such I account thy love,' she could make a dismissive gesture, and perhaps turn away as if rejecting him, which might make him feel insecure. She could then turn back to renew her argument. She assumes that he must kill Duncan to be king, and that he should be prepared to commit murder. She therefore argues that not doing so is just cowardice.

Macbeth defends himself, saying that to kill Duncan would make him less than a man, but his self-defence is feeble compared with his wife's attack. He should seem weak at this point, perhaps guilty, or perhaps trying to win her round, but aware of his lack of argument.

When she says, 'What beast was it…' she is twisting his words for her own purposes, at the same time as reminding him of his intention. It is interesting that Macbeth does not argue the case for not killing Duncan. The actor could play the role as if he is not entirely convinced himself, which would make it more believable when he is persuaded.

Lady Macbeth's most powerful argument is her most manipulative: she calls him a coward: 'When you durst do it, then you were a man': he is not even a man if he will not kill Duncan. She backs this up with a chilling declaration: that she would dash out her own baby's brains if she had sworn, as she claims he has, to do so.

By the end of the scene, Macbeth has been convinced and admires his wife's courage: her 'undaunted mettle'. They are once again united in their murderous plan.

In the next scene, however, the relationship has changed dramatically. Lady Macbeth is no longer able to dominate Macbeth. She tries to tell him how to behave at the banquet, to smooth over his 'rugged looks' and be 'jovial', and he agrees, but immediately directs her to flatter Banquo – despite knowing that in fact he has arranged for him to be murdered. In other words, he is now deceiving her, as well as everyone else.

In fact he seems almost too committed to deception. He might sound bitter and even slightly mad when he says their faces must be masks to their hearts. When she says, 'You must leave this,' she seems to be worrying about his mental health, and this should show in the actor's manner – unlike that in the earlier scene.

Most of all, when Macbeth refers to his plan to have Banquo murdered, he only mentions 'A deed of dreadful note', and says no more. When she asks what it is, he will not share it with her. He tells her to be 'innocent of the knowledge' till she can 'applaud' what has been done, but his calling her 'dearest chuck' seems unconvincing, as if he is being ironic. After all, affection would seem out of place when planning to kill his friend.

The two scenes show how much the pair have grown apart, and that Macbeth is becoming his own man, independent of his wife.

This model answer would earn a very high mark because it addresses all parts of the task:
- *It shows what the characters' relationship is in the first extract.*
- *It shows what the characters' relationship is in the second extract.*
- *It provides evidence and analysis for each scene.*
- *It shows how the relationship has changed.*
- *It suggests ways in which a stage production could highlight these changes.*

The answer brings out Lady Macbeth's strength and assertiveness, coupled with her ability to manipulate Macbeth. At times, it analyses key words, such as 'dressed', showing how Shakespeare uses language. The answer also analyses Macbeth's character, with appropriate suggestions for how the actor playing him could show it: 'The actor could play the role as if …'. The response also evaluates Lady Macbeth's arguments: 'Lady Macbeth's most powerful argument is her most manipulative'.

The response goes on to show how the relationship changes, focusing on the fact that Macbeth is now deceiving his wife and on her growing concern for his mental state. It offers interpretations of key phrases, such as 'dearest chuck', showing an awareness of the fact that different interpretations are possible.

The response finishes with a short but effective paragraph summarising the key changes.

2. ⟲ 5–12, 28–33, 40–41, 48–49, 56–59, 73–78

a) 'swept', 'narrowed and widened, and dipped and rose', 'rode upon the sea'. **(1 mark each for any two of these)**

b) The waves are large: 'jagged with waves that seemed thrust up in points like rocks'. The word 'thrust' makes them threatening, as does their being compared to rocks. Crane humorously compares the size of the boat with that of a 'bath-tub'. The cook is separated from the sea by only 'six inches of gunwale' (the edge of the boat). The oiler has only 'a thin little oar and it seemed often ready to snap'. The use of both 'thin' and 'little' makes the oar seem pathetic. **(1 mark each for explaining any three of these four points)**

c) The scene that the captain is remembering is the shipwreck that has led to the men being in this tiny boat. **(1 mark)** The captain, being 'rooted' in his ship, is very downcast by the loss. The ship, like a commander's army, or a businessman's firm, was the most important thing in his life. **(1 mark)** He is now in a state of 'profound dejection and indifference', as if past caring what happens. His voice reflects this, being 'deep with mourning', a sadness beyond even tears. **(1 mark)** In addition to this, he is 'injured', though as Crane makes no further mention of his injury, it cannot be severe.

d) Crane describes the journey as being like riding a bucking bronco (an unbroken horse in a rodeo). He extends this simile by saying that the boat 'pranced and reared, and plunged like an animal'. **(1 mark)** The boat is like a horse trying to jump a fence that is 'outrageously high', as if too much is being asked of it. It sounds as if Crane is not really a seaman, so that the way the boat manages to ride the waves is to him a mystery – a 'mystic thing'. **(1 mark)** The boat is slightly personified in the way that she 'scornfully' bumps the crest of the wave, as if refusing to go right into it. **(1 mark)** Crane uses a lot of active verbs to describe the lively movement of the boat: 'slide, and race, and splash', 'bobbing and nodding'. **(1 mark)** The repeated 'and' emphasises the amount of motion going on. **(1 mark)**

e) Crane seems to be almost amused by the boat journey, while at the same time making it clear that the boat is small and the waves are big and threaten to swamp it. **(1 mark)** A number of his word choices and phrases suggest this. Comparing the boat to a 'bath-tub' makes the journey seem unheroic, almost comical. **(1 mark)** The phrase 'wrongfully and barbarously' is comic in that there is no point in calling the sea's behaviour wrong or barbaric: it cannot be civilised. **(1 mark)** The correspondent wondering why he is even in the boat suggests that he is dismissive of the whole experience, as if he does not belong on the sea at all. **(1 mark)** The image of the bucking bronco is, again, mildly humorous. **(1 mark)** Finally, the phrase 'singular disadvantage of the sea' is an example of dry ironic humour, as to speak in this way suggests that there are options, which there were not: the men are stuck in the boat. **(1 mark)**

f) They have too little room in the small boat **(1 mark)**, and are constantly drenched by the sea, and cold **(1 mark)**.

g) They had to 'fight' the sea, as if it was an enemy, and they have 'a daily struggle' to survive. **(1 mark)** The short dramatic sentence 'At times we were in dire peril' states the truth of their danger. **(1 mark)** They had become resigned to the danger and to their fate, so that they were 'interested rather than apprehensive' as they watched the huge waves, as if saying, 'I wonder if I'm about to die.' **(1 mark)**

h) We see 'the storm-whitened seas', the 'wool-like whiteness' and the 'uprearing masses of water'. **(1 mark)** The huge size of the 'combers' (waves) is emphasised by the sentence structure in the second paragraph. Shackleton uses parallelism in 'Deep seemed the valleys…' and 'High were the hills…' to contrast these 'hills' and 'valleys', that were in fact not land at all. Placing the adjectives at the start of the sentences emphasises their contrast. **(1 mark)** He uses a similar parallelism in 'So small was our boat and so great were the seas' **(1 mark)**. The image of the sail flapping in the 'valley' between waves, before they catch the 'full fury of the gale' again creates a powerful contrast **(1 mark)**.

i) The men do get some relief in the form of humour. Shackleton says these moments are 'rare…but hearty enough': although coming seldom, they are heart-felt. **(1 mark)** Their 'cracked lips and swollen mouths' make it difficult to laugh – they can only 'gurgle' **(1 mark)**, but they still appreciate at least 'primitive' (unsophisticated) jokes **(1 mark)**. Shackleton observes that human beings are most easily amused by the misfortunes of others, **(1 mark)** and he describes an example of this: Worsley's efforts to replace a hot stand on top of a cooker, with his frostbitten fingers **(6 marks)**.

j) Shackleton uses personification effectively in the first paragraph when he speaks of 'Nature in the pride of her strength'. **(1 mark)** Perhaps seeing the wild sea in these terms made it more manageable: there is a sense of respect in his tone, but perhaps it also helped to personify the sea into an opponent. **(1 mark)** There is also personification in the 'fury' of the gale, which makes it easier for readers to understand. **(1 mark)** The most striking metaphor is in the second paragraph, when Shackleton compares the 'hills' of the huge waves with the 'valleys' of the troughs between them. This makes the sea seem like a landscape. We also see the boat 'climb the next slope', as if climbing an actual hill. **(1 mark)**

Shackleton uses an amusing simile, saying that it is as if Worsley were cautiously handling 'some fragile article of lady's wear', which is the more amusing because it suggests that Worsley would be equally uncomfortable handling this. **(1 mark)**

We also get an impression of the wildness of the sea, stirred into foam, with its 'wool-like whiteness', an interesting visual simile, since they are far from any sheep. **(1 mark)**

3. **a)** Answers will vary. However, see Topic 8.3 for guidance.
  b) Answers will vary. See Topic 8.6 for guidance on writing letters.

Key word dictionary and index

abstract noun *12, 138*
Word for an idea or concept that is not part of the physical world (e.g. love)

active sentence *98*
One in which the **subject** acts; *see also* **passive sentence**

adjectival phrase *29*
Phrase performing the action of an adjective (e.g. 'sad little' or 'mildly amusing')

adjective *29, 126, 128, 140, 144*
A describing word: it provides information about a **noun** or **noun phrase**

adverb *127, 128, 144*
Word which adds information to a verb or, less often, an adjective

advice writing *36*
Writing used, for example, in safety leaflets or 'agony' columns

alliteration *31, 79, 190*
Repetition of **consonant** (non-vowel) sounds, especially at the beginnings of words

alphabetisation *131*
Ordering according to the alphabet

ambiguity *185*
Possibility of being interpreted in more than one way (can be deliberate or accidental); adjective form: ambiguous

Anglo-Saxon *123*
Old English; language spoken in England especially before 1066

antagonist *52*
Enemy of protagonist in a story

antithesis *190*
Opposites or contrasts

antonym *132, 133*
The opposite of a word

apostrophe *108, 119*
Punctuation mark used to show omission (as in 'didn't') or ownership (as in 'Will's pen')

argumentative writing *174*
Writing which attempts to persuade by putting forward a logical argument

assonance *80*
Repetition of **vowel** sounds, especially in the middle of words

atmosphere *47*
Mood, especially created by description of setting, evoking emotional expectation

audience *23, 159*
The group of people who will read a text, see a film, etc.

ballad *72*
Traditional verse form, usually with four lines in each stanza

blank verse *16*
Unrhymed **iambic pentameter**, used especially by Shakespeare

blocking *198*
Working out where actors should be at all points in a play, including entrances and exits

burying information *97*
Hiding information through sentence form, as in 'Mistakes have been made' (does not say by whom)

chairing *196*
Leading a discussion or meeting

characterisation *48*
Techniques by which characters are presented in a novel, story or play

class, word *128*
Grammatical group, especially noun, verb, adjective, adverb, pronoun

class divisions *15*
Social groupings based on family background, wealth and education

clause *90, 113*
Phrase containing a **subject** (what it is about) and a **predicate** (a statement about the subject)

climax *53*
Moment of greatest danger and suspense (may also be main **crisis**)

close reading *6*
Reading in detail, as you would read a passage in an exam

collective noun *106*
Noun for a group of the same thing (e.g. 'flock')

colloquial *156, 188*
In popular informal use (noun form: colloquialism)

Key word dictionary and index

proofreading *185*
Checking for relatively small errors, especially in spelling, punctuation and grammar

proper noun *138*
A name: for example, for a person, country or ship

protagonist *52*
Hero or heroine in a story

recount events *159*
Give an account of things that happened

redrafting *185*
Process of improving on what you have written

refrain *78*
Repeated line in verse, especially at the end of a stanza

register *26, 155, 181*
Range of language used, especially relating to level of formality

relative pronoun *108*
Used in a subordinated sentence, in a clause referring to the main clause (e.g. 'which', 'who'); *see also* **pronoun**

repetition *12, 185, 190*
Using a word or phrase more than once

reported speech *117*
Speech referred to without quoting actual words spoken

resolution *53*
Stage in story when events come to a close, with sense of completion (happy or tragic)

review *176*
An evaluation of a text or production, consisting of information about the text and the reviewer's assessment of how successful it is

rhetoric *35, 174, 190*
Art of using words persuasively

rhetorical device *34, 190*
Language technique, especially used in persuasion, such as alliteration and imagery

rhetorical question *190*
One which expects no answer (may express anger or criticism)

rhyme *77*
An appealing combination of similarity and difference in sound when two words are heard close together

rhyme scheme *77*
A repeated pattern of rhyme

rhyming couplet *16, 78*
Pair of rhyming lines, especially at the end of a poem, or a Shakespeare scene, giving a sense of completion

rhythm *16*
A quality of timing and repeated emphasis, or beats. In poetry, the rhythm is created by the stressed and unstressed syllables

rising action *53*
Stage in a plot when events gradually intensify, with crises leading to a main crisis

scanning *6*
Searching text for specific information

semicolon *116*
(;) Punctuation mark used to break up items in a list where commas are needed within one or more items, or as a slightly stronger mark than the comma, but where there is a special connection between two statements

sentence *9, 86, 183*
A statement giving (or requesting) a piece of information that makes sense in itself; it consists of a subject (what it is about) and a predicate (what is said about the subject)

sequence *162*
To place in order (e.g. paragraphs)

setting *46*
Where the action of at least part of a novel, story or play takes place; time of day; weather **signposting words** *see* **linking words**

simile *13, 56, 191*
Image which compares two things using **like**, **as** or **than**. It makes us see a thing, or a character, or something the character does, more vividly

simple sentence *86, 183*
Sentence which consists of a **subject** and a **predicate**

skimming *5*
Reading a text quickly for an overview

slang *27, 156*
Popular, informal vocabulary used informally by particular social groups

sonnet *69*
Poem with fourteen lines of **iambic pentameter** in which the first eight lines (the octave) establish an idea, and then the final six lines (the sestet) comment on it, or develop it in a different direction

spidergram *193*
Visual method for generating ideas or planning

stage directions *55*
Notes indicating how an actor should behave or speak lines

Key word dictionary and index